# CATHOLIC LOYALISM IN ELIZABETHAN ENGLAND

# Catholic Loyalism
# in Elizabethan England

*by*
*Arnold Pritchard*

THE UNIVERSITY OF NORTH CAROLINA PRESS

CHAPEL HILL

© *1979 The University of North Carolina Press*
*All rights reserved*
*Manufactured in the United States of America*
*ISBN 0-8078-1345-1*
*Library of Congress Catalog Card Number 78-10208*

Pritchard, Arnold, 1949–
Catholic Loyalism in Elizabethan England.

Bibliography: p.
Includes index.
1. Catholics—England.   2. Archpriest controversy,
1598–1602.   3. Church and state in England—History.
I. Title.                                                    *Qp 23 79*
BX1492.P78              261.7'0942              78-10208
ISBN 0-8078-1345-1

# Contents

*To my mother and father*

# *Preface*

I had been interested in sixteenth-century England for several years before the idea of doing any serious work on Elizabethan Catholicism entered my head. As I suspect is the case with many historians, I had the impression that English Catholics were a small band of exiles, martyrs, and political plotters, pushed around by the great religious and political currents of their day, but with little history of their own worth bothering about. My interest was aroused when I found that Elizabethan Catholicism had an internal history of its own and that the English Catholics wrestled not only with the practical difficulties of an oppressed minority compelled to operate in secret, but with moral and political problems every bit as agonizing as those that faced many better-known religious traditions. The greatest internal division through which the Elizabethan Catholics passed came in the last decade of Elizabeth's reign, when the community was torn by a series of dissensions about the organization of the mission and about its relationship to the English political and social order. These disputes culminated in the "archpriest controversy" of 1598–1602, during which a group of priests who became known as "Appellants" twice appealed to Rome against the ecclesiastical regime that the papacy had set up in England.

The clash between the Appellants and their opponents was the longest and noisiest controversy within the Elizabethan Catholic body, but it was not an isolated episode. The Appellants were the most voluble opponents of what might be called the militant view within English Catholicism. The most immediately controversial aspect of the militant program was support for the efforts of foreign Catholic powers to overthrow Elizabeth; the most controversial aspect of the Appellant (or loyalist) view was loyalty to the queen.

The primary purpose of this book is to analyze the mentality of the loyalist Catholics and to compare it with that of their better-known militant coreligionists. Most people aware of the problem know that the differences between militant and loyalist Catholics covered many issues besides that of allegiance to the crown, and this book deals with several of those issues. But I still believe that the most serious issue facing the Elizabethan Catholics was, in the broad sense of the term, political. Almost all of the peculiar problems that they confronted were caused by the hostility between the Catholic church and the English political order. No matter how apolitical a particular Catholic may have been by inclination, if he was seriously concerned with the problems of English Catholicism he would sooner or later be forced to confront the problem of his religious community's relationship to the wider community of England, whose symbol of unity was the monarchy.

I hope that I have contributed something to the understanding of the differences between the loyalist and militant Catholics. I know that the subject is worth trying to understand. The controversies were important for the history of Catholicism in England. I suspect (although I do not have the learning to say) that they provide a clue to the conflicting beliefs that divided European Catholics in their attitudes toward the political aspects of the Counter-Reformation. But perhaps most important, the conflicts within English Catholicism show persons who were, in many cases, of relatively ordinary talents struggling with the particular way in which issues of universal moral importance were presented to them. Most of the specific issues that faced Elizabethan Catholics are long dead. The questions of the rights and obligations of authority and conscience, however, are eternal, and so is the interest of people trying to deal with these questions in the special situations with which history confronts them.

Readers who are already relatively familiar with the history of Elizabethan Catholicism may wish to read the appendix first; for them it can function as a prologue to set some of the issues in historiographical perspective.

One of the salutary things about writing this book has been that I have been made aware of how much even such a modest effort of historical inquiry rests on the efforts of others—of historians, archivists, editors, spread through several countries and generations. I can render only some inadequate thanks for the most obvious debts.

This work began as a Ph.D. dissertation at Yale University, and I have to thank my dissertation adviser, J. H. Hexter, for constant encouragement and advice. Steven Ozment and Robert Harding, the other readers on my committee, were also very helpful critics. T. H. Clancy of Loyola University, New Orleans, and John Bossy of the Queen's University of Belfast have been generous with helpful advice, as has a reader of the University of North Carolina Press whom (since the press's policy in such matters is anonymity) I am unable to identify. Mr. Bossy and Peter Holmes have kindly allowed me to refer to their unpublished dissertations.

For permission to refer to unpublished documents in their custody, I wish to thank His Grace the Archbishop of Canterbury and the Trustees of the Lambeth Palace Library; the Cardinal Archbishop of Westminster; Father F. J. Turner, librarian of Stonyhurst College; and the authorities of the Public Record Office. The staff at each of these institutions, as well as at the Jesuit Library on Mount Street in London, was very helpful and kind in many ways; I should particularly mention Miss Elizabeth Poyser of the Westminster Diocesan Archives and Father Francis Edwards and Father Geoffrey Holt of the Jesuit Library. I am also grateful to the libraries of the universities of Cambridge and of London for allowing me to read unpublished dissertations in their possession, to the Connecticut State Library for last-minute reference help, and to the staff of the Yale University Library for many large and small assistances. Yale gave me fellowship support for most of my time in graduate school, and a grant from the Yale Concilium for International and Area Studies enabled me to spend several months working in England. I am also grateful to The University of North Carolina Press for undertaking publication, particularly to Executive Editor Lewis Bateman and Managing Editor Gwen Duffey for their help along the way. Needless to say, no one besides myself bears responsibility for any errors or inadequacies that remain. I once thought that this traditional disclaimer was a pious platitude; now I know how true it is.

Many friends in New Haven and elsewhere have helped me in many ways to get through the various traumas to which graduate students and aspiring authors are subject. There are really more than I can mention, but among those who helped most directly with the progress of the book itself (sometimes in rather unusual ways) were

Bill Tighe, Betsy Gilliam, Mike Root, Kathy Staudt, and Barbara Newman. My wife Gretchen deserves special mention, for translating some passages from Italian, for some eleventh-hour typing, for listening patiently to wearying harangues about English Catholicism, and for constant sympathetic support at a time when her own work was occupying a great deal of her attention.

# CATHOLIC LOYALISM IN ELIZABETHAN ENGLAND

# CHAPTER I

# Introductory: The Situation of the Elizabethan Catholics

The first parliament of the reign of Elizabeth I in 1559 made illegal the celebration of the Mass, the denial of the royal supremacy over the church, and various other essentials of the Catholic religion. It also required all subjects to attend the services of the established church on Sundays and holy days, on penalty of a fine of twelve-pence for every absence. The parliament of 1562–63 added penalties for upholding the pope's authority; a first such offense was made subject to the penalties of praemunire, while a second offense was made treason. This parliament also extended the Oath of Supremacy as a test of religious loyalty to a wide range of laymen and clerics.

In spite of this legislation, the first decade of Elizabeth's reign saw comparatively little active persecution of Catholics; later during her rule some Catholic writers looked back on the period with nostalgia as a time of general live-and-let-live.[1] Enforcement of the anti-Catholic laws was slack; the Oath of Supremacy was widely evaded, and the fine for nonattendance at church was apparently often left uncollected. The level of active hostility between Protestants and Catholics in the 1560s was comparatively low largely because the dividing line between the two religious camps was not as clear as it later became. A study of Yorkshire has found evidence of widespread vaguely conservative religious sentiment early in Elizabeth's reign, manifested mainly by the continuation of traditional practices such as using holy water, images, and other religious objects or praying with Latin primers.[2] Apparently, however, there was comparatively little actual recusancy (i.e., refusal to attend Anglican services) before the

1570s. Although the Catholic church did formally forbid attendance at Protestant services,[3] little was done to make the decision known in England. Most people of Catholic sympathies, and even some Catholic priests, apparently saw no harm in complying with the minimum legal requirement of being present at Anglican worship, although many disassociated themselves from actual participation by not receiving communion or by ostentatious lack of attention to the proceedings.[4]

Ironically enough, it was almost certainly during this period of relatively little active persecution that the Catholic church lost most of its hold on the English people. A. O. Meyer has pointed out some convincing reasons for this diminishing influence: the physical and moral isolation of Englishmen of Catholic sympathies from the international church and the positive attractions of a vernacular liturgy and Bible.[5] But, in a sense, to ask why most Englishmen left Catholicism so quickly is to ask the wrong question. To a Catholic theologian, the community in communion with Rome that has existed in England since Elizabeth's reign may be the continuation of the church to which virtually all Englishmen belonged before the Reformation. The ordinary subject, however, may have seen as much of the continuation of the church to which he had always belonged in the Anglican church as in the Catholic. The Anglican church kept the buildings and the hierarchical structure of the pre-Reformation church; it retained the close integration with the political and social hierarchy; the parish church remained the center of much of the social and political as well as the religious life of the local community. To leave the established church for a small sect that retained the Latin mass, a celibate clergy, and the supremacy of a faraway pope might have seemed even to conservative people a greater break with the past than did acceptance of the changes of 1559. The Catholic community in England from Elizabeth's reign on drew on many of the loyalties and traditions of the pre-Reformation church, but historically speaking it was a new creation.[6]

This creation might not have taken place without the transformation of the political and religious situation between 1568 and 1574. Several factors increased tension between England and international Catholicism—the imprisonment in England of Mary Queen of Scots; the northern rebellion of 1569; the Ridolfi plot; increasing rivalry with Spain; and most of all, the papal bull *Regnans in Excelsis* (1570), which excommunicated Elizabeth and declared her subjects absolved of their obligation of obedience to her. All these events made the government much less indulgent toward signs of Catholic sympathies among the queen's subjects. But perhaps the most important cause of long-term change in the nature of English Catholicism and of the government's attitude toward it was the result not of high-level politics, but of the initiative of a few English exiles.

Some English Catholics had been going abroad since 1559. As might be expected, most of the exiles were gentlemen and clerics, the latter including a substantial number of academics, particularly from Oxford.[7] At first, the academics generally settled into their traditional role of writing apologetics. Even the seminary for English students founded at Douai in the Spanish Netherlands in 1568 was not at first conceived as a base for missionary work in England. But the idea of the mission soon took hold. In 1574 the first missionary priests were sent to England, and in 1577 Cuthbert Mayne, their first martyr, was executed. Under its founder and first president, William Allen, Douai (which operated at Rheims from 1578 to 1593) played the preeminent role in the training of priests in the mission's early days. It was soon joined by the seminary founded at Rome in 1578 and by seminaries founded at Seville and Valladolid after the defeat of the Spanish Armada. By the 1580s there were several hundred priests in England. In 1580, in response to Allen's requests, the first Jesuit missionaries were sent on the English mission; a very small but very important Jesuit mission continued to work in England throughout Elizabeth's reign.

The idea of a missionary movement operating in secret to evade a persecuting government was a radical departure from the previous methods of the Catholic church in England—or indeed, in Europe as a whole.[8] In many ways the mission was very successful, providing by far the most concrete link between Catholics in England and the rest of the church and making it possible for a much larger number of people in England to live as Catholics. Perhaps most crucially, the missionaries helped make English Catholics more self-conscious and more conscious of the differences between themselves and the Protestant majority. Apparently due primarily to the missionary priests, the practice of attending Anglican services to comply with the minimum requirements of the law seems to have been reduced.

Without the missionary priests, the Catholic community in England would probably never have come into existence, but the nature of the community that they helped create was to a great degree determined by elements beyond their control. Given the mounting persecution that met the expansion of the mission, the missionaries could hope to work with some degree of security only where they had either some popular sympathy or the protection of influential persons in the area—usually members of the gentry and aristocracy. The geographical and social makeup of the Catholic community was varied, but it tended to be very heavily influenced by the distribution of the Catholic gentry and nobility. Many Catholic landowners attempted to protect their fellow Catholics as well as they could, and some had a conscious policy (whether out of benevolence or concern for security) of preferring Catholic tenants and servants.[9] The importance of the support that the Catholic nobility and gentry gave to the mission can be seen from the frequent strong correlations between the geographical distribution of recusancy and the estates and influence of Catholic landowners. In Cornwall, for example, recusants were most numerous in those parishes where the Arundells, the county's most prominent Catholic family, had their estates, while the survival of a comparatively large Catholic community in Sussex was due largely to the influence of the first Viscount Montague and, after his death in 1592, his widow and grandson.[10]

Catholics were most numerous in the North of England and in parts of the Welsh border; the two strongest Catholic counties were Lancashire and Monmouthshire. It was in parts of the remote highlands of the north that Catholicism came closest to being a "popular" religion, not so limited as elsewhere to some gentry families and their immediate dependents. In most of southern England there were fewer Catholics, and Catholicism seems to have been much more a form of "nonconformism of the gentry"[11] than in the north. There were relatively large numbers of Catholic magnates in west Sussex and in Hampshire, the only area of lowland England where the presence of Catholic aristocrats seems to have had much influence on the general religious tone of an area. Significant numbers of Catholic gentry lived also in the west Midlands, parts of the Thames valley, and, rather surprisingly, in the most strongly Protestant region of the country, East Anglia.[12]

Virtually all of the Catholic gentry seem to have had little desire to take up active opposition to the crown and considered themselves loyal subjects of the queen. But the government was naturally cautious in taking Catholic protestations of loyalty at face value. English relations with the papacy, Spain, and the other forces of the militant Counter-Reformation grew increasingly strained up to the outbreak of war with Spain in 1585. Before the crises of 1568–72, it was possible to believe that the problem of religious conservatism did not require strong action. Before the arrival of the missionary priests, Catholicism in England seemed likely to wither away if left to itself. After the mid-1570s, neither of these beliefs seemed justified. Instead of the widespread but vague and shallow religious conservatism of the 1560s, the government was faced with a small (though they might not have realized how small) but more highly committed Catholic community, increasingly marked off from the Protestant majority and showing no sign of disappearing of its own accord. Naturally, the government feared the English Catholics as a potential fifth column in the war with Spain. The political propaganda and other activities of some prominent Catholic exiles, as well as the occasional plots against Elizabeth's life in which some more marginal characters engaged, gave considerable plausibility to this view. It is not surprising that the government responded by increasing the severity of both the laws against Catholics and their enforcement.[13] In 1571 it was made treason to bring into the country, publish, or put into effect any bull, writing, or instrument from Rome. In 1581 it was made treason to reconcile others to the Catholic church, to be reconciled oneself, to seek to withdraw others from their allegiance to the queen, or to seek to withdraw them from the established church to Rome. The fine for recusancy was raised to twenty pounds for each four-week period, a sum absolutely prohibitive for all but the wealthiest Catholics. In 1585 it was made treason for any subject of the queen ordained priest in the Catholic church since 1559 to be in England at all, and it was made a capital offense knowingly to give a priest aid or comfort. It was also made subject to the penalties of praemunire to send money overseas to the aid of Jesuits, seminary priests, or their colleges. In 1593, Catholic recusants were forbidden to travel more than five miles from home without special license.[14]

The enforcement of the laws was always erratic, but the persecution was severe enough to make adherence to Catholicism a very costly choice for many of those who made it. The government, which had a good idea of where its enemies' strength lay, generally struck hardest at the wealth of the Catholic laity and at the lives and liberty of the Catholic clergy. The laity was harassed with fines, spells of imprisonment, and occasionally execution; 63 Catholic lay men and women of Elizabeth's reign have been recognized as martyrs.[15] Death for the cause was, however, rare for the laity, and the large majority probably never were imprisoned or fined. For the priests, prison was a more likely fate than not, and death was common. The biographical dictionary of the seminary priests[16] lists 803 priests trained at the English seminaries on the Continent during Elizabeth's reign. Of these, 649 were apparently sent to England, although in some cases there is no definite evidence that they actually arrived in the country. At least 377 of the priests were imprisoned, in some cases more than once. And 133 of the missionary priests, or slightly more than 1 in 5, were executed.

The longest-standing debate about the English Catholic mission and the government's reaction to it has been whether the missionary movement was "religious" or "political" and whether the missionaries who were executed died as martyrs or as traitors.[17] This dispute is partly the result of the different needs of propagandists on both sides of the issue. Even in the sixteenth century it was more widely considered proper to kill a person for treason than for Catholicism, and the distinction has become more pronounced since then. But various interpretations may also rest on genuine differences in perception of an ambivalent enterprise.

The English government always claimed that Catholics were executed as traitors, and in spite of the manifold injustices that it inflicted, the government's general attitude is perfectly comprehensible. The Catholic missionaries were trained at institutions under papal patronage and financed partly by the pope and Spain, and their most prominent leaders, William Allen and Robert Parsons, were open advocates of a foreign invasion of England. Once in England, they persuaded the queen's subjects to disobey her ecclesiastical laws out of obedience to the pope. No sixteenth-century politician could have regarded such activity as a purely spiritual enterprise. Whatever the motives of the missionary priests, if they had succeeded in winning over a large number of Englishmen to Rome, their success would have constituted a grave political threat to Elizabeth's government. The persecution of Catholics was evil, but it was not the result of any particular wickedness on the part of the rulers of England. Given analogous circumstances, it is doubtful that any government in Europe, of any religion, would have been less severe than that of England; many would have been worse.

Nevertheless, Catholic writers, in their many works praising and defending their martyrs, constantly denied that the missionary priests had any political purpose, and in almost all cases their claims seem to have been correct. The actual operation of the missionary movement seems to have been kept separate from political activities —even though some of the most prominent exile leaders were involved in both. No political tests were imposed on students at the English seminaries on the Continent. Political discussion among the students at Douai was forbidden, and the crucial question of the pope's right to depose temporal rulers was not discussed in Douai classrooms.[18] The faculties of priests sent into England normally forbade them to discuss matters of state.

The majority of priests seem to have followed the policy of the exile leaders in maintaining that the mission had nothing to do with politics; the fact that most of them were executed under the statute that defined a priest's mere presence in England as treason certainly indicates that the government could find nothing more incriminating against them than the exercise of their priesthood.[19] The refusal of most captured priests to answer when the authorities asked the "bloody question" about which side they would take in the event of a papally sponsored invasion of England was frequently regarded by Protestants as evidence of their disloyalty, but their refusal may in many cases have represented a sincere belief that the question was irrelevant to their work in England.

The persecution fell on many people who took little active interest in politics, but the Catholic community was persecuted because the government saw it as a factor in politics. In fact, for the leaders of the missionary movement political questions were very difficult to avoid. By necessity, the schools and bases that the Catholic exiles used to support the mission were located in territory controlled by powers hostile to the Elizabethan regime. It was therefore necessary that those responsible for setting the policy of the mission at least acquiesce in attempts to overthrow Elizabeth, and it is not surprising that many of them went a good deal further than passive acquiescence and supported such efforts vigorously and actively.[20] Sir Francis Englefield, a privy councillor under Queen Mary, entered the service of Philip II and urged on him the necessity of restoring Catholicism in England by force of arms.[21] Even more important, the most prominent leaders of the seminary priests, William Allen and Robert Parsons, were deeply involved in efforts to overthrow Elizabeth and establish a Catholic regime in England. Especially after Parsons returned from the English mission in 1581, the two men used every opportunity to urge the pope, Spain, the Guise faction in France, and whoever else would listen to use their political and military power against Protestant England. Their entreaties were frequently coupled with assertions that the sympathies of the English people were still predominantly Catholic and that many would side with a Catholic invader. To the powers of Catholic Europe, Englefield, Allen, and Parsons all portrayed the English missionaries as potential helpers for a Catholic invasion, either by the effect they had on their flock's sympathies or as actual organizers of English Catholic assistance to the invader.[22]

In addition to acting as leaders of the exile movement, Allen and Parsons played a major role as writers and propagandists.[23] As a recent writer has pointed out, Allen, Parsons, and their party were not as consistently militant in print as they were in action.[24] But at least after about 1580, Allen's and Parsons's occasional loyal-sounding noises seem to be of very little importance. They seem never to have been taken seriously by the English government and virtually always seem dictated by some immediate goal—usually that of making Catholics appear completely innocent, so as to be able to denounce the persecution with convincing fervor. They sometimes used what one might call the "Brutus-is-an-honorable-man" trick; that is, combining reiterated general expressions of respect for a person (in this case, Elizabeth) with an argument intended to damn that person and her cause in the eyes of one's audience.[25]

But the most compelling reason for taking Allen's and Parsons's occasional ostensibly loyal utterances with a large dose of salt is that these statements are utterly inconsistent with both their actual political conduct and the great bulk of their writings on politics. In their most directly political works, Allen and Parsons clearly set forth a strong moral justification of the attack on the English government by the forces of both the international Counter-Reformation and English Catholics who joined in that effort. The politically militant wing of English Catholicism is not the main subject of this book, but the way in which Allen and Parsons formulated a long-standing tradition on the relations of the church and temporal rulers set the terms of their later debate with their Catholic opponents, and this development must be understood before considering the ideas of those opponents.

# CHAPTER II

# Allen and Parsons: The Political Theory of Militant Catholicism

Pius, Bishop, servant of the servants of God, in lasting memory of the matter.

He that reigneth on high, to whom is given all power in heaven and earth, has committed one holy Catholic and apostolic church, outside of which there is no salvation, to one alone upon earth, namely to Peter, the first of the apostles, and to Peter's successor, the pope of Rome, to be by him governed in fullness of power. Him alone he has made ruler over all peoples and kingdoms, to pull up, destroy, scatter, disperse, plant and build, so that he may preserve His faithful people . . . in the unity of the Spirit and present them safe and spotless to their Saviour. . . .

[after a recital of Elizabeth's offenses]

. . . Therefore, resting upon the authority of Him whose pleasure it was to place us . . . upon this supreme justice-seat, we do out of the fullness of our apostolic power declare the aforesaid Elizabeth to be a heretic and favourer of heretics, and her adherents in the matters aforesaid to have incurred the sentence of excommunication and to be cut off from the unity of the body of Christ.

And moreover [we declare] her to be deprived of her pretended title to the aforesaid crown. . . .

. . . We charge and command . . . the nobles, subjects, peoples and others aforesaid that they do not dare obey her orders, mandates and laws.[1]

When Pius V declared Elizabeth to be deposed from her throne, he was acting in accordance with a tradition of papal authority over temporal rulers that stretched back to the eleventh century.[2] His claim of the right to judge and depose secular rulers would not have seemed strange to Gregory VII, to Innocent III, or to Boniface VIII. Pius's successors also claimed the right to judge Elizabeth, and one of them, Sixtus V, applied the same principle in his attempt to keep Henry of Navarre from the throne of France.

The principle of the pope's right to political supremacy over secular rulers had, of course, its ups and downs, both in practice and in theory. The Reformation naturally denied the pope's power over temporal rulers as a by-product of its denial of his spiritual supremacy, while the conciliar movement within the Catholic church had also challenged the position as head of the church on which the pope's supremacy over temporal rulers depended. Temporal rulers naturally had rarely been willing to recognize the pope as their political superior in any real sense, and they had rarely lacked churchmen and writers to defend their independence—the most notable of whom was Marsilius of Padua. But the circumstances of the religious wars were almost bound to lead to a reassertion of the principles of papal supremacy. The two most prominent leaders of the militant wing of English Catholicism joined enthusiastically in this reassertion, and in the process of doing so they revealed a great deal about their ideas of the relationship between religion and politics—and indeed, between religion and life.

Perhaps the most nearly classic exposition of the ideology of the politically aggressive party within English Catholicism was given by the party's leading member, William Allen, in four works published during the peak of his political activity, between 1581 and 1588. Characteristically, Allen wrote each of the works to serve a practical purpose and in response to a particular situation. *An Apology and True Declaration of the Institution and Endeavors of the Two English Colleges* (1581) was intended to answer Protestant charges that the missioners being trained at the English colleges at Douai and Rome were primarily political conspirators. *A True, Sincere, and Modest Defence of English Catholics* (1584) was a reply to Lord Burghley's *The Execution of Justice in England*, which defended Elizabeth's policy toward Catholics as a necessary protection against political sedition. *The Copy of a Letter . . . Concerning the Yielding Up of the City of Daventry* (1587) defended the action of Sir William Stanley, a colonel in the English army in the Netherlands, who had been moved by his Catholic convictions to surrender the town of Deventer to the Spaniards and enter the Spanish service. *An Admonition to the Nobility and People of England and Ireland* (1588) exhorted Elizabeth's subjects to rise in aid of the Spanish Armada, whose landing in England Allen believed to be imminent. But Allen, like many sixteenth-century writers, usually based even his occasional political writings on first principles, and in these works a logical and consistent view of the nature and relations of the authority of the church, the authority of the state, and the obligations of individuals emerges as a basis for his views on the issues facing English Catholics.

The starting point for Allen's political ideas is his conception of the nature and role of the Catholic church. In replying to Protestant pretensions to be guided to salvation by Scripture alone, Allen asserts the position of the church, guaranteed by Christ's promise of the guidance of the Holy Spirit, as the true interpreter of the Scriptures.[3] He quotes the long tradition of church fathers and councils in support of the primacy of the church as the rightful judge of Christian belief.[4] He asserts that the Catholics have won every fair debate with their opponents and that if only Elizabeth would allow a fair debate in England, they would have no trouble proving their case again.[5] Although Allen clearly believes that manifest reason as well as tradition (indeed for him, the two are largely the same) is on the side of the authority of the Catholic church, he spends little time actually arguing in its defense. The weight of the authorities to whom he appeals is, to him, so overwhelming as to make that unnecessary.

In fact, Allen believes that the Catholic church is so clearly the only bearer of salvation to mankind that he finds it impossible to imagine the possibility of reasonable and principled people holding other views. The present position of Catholicism in England is due to

the prejudice and partiality of the present condition and sway of time, which by authority, force and fear of laws, favor of the prince, domestical education, plausible preaching and persuasion of profit, peace and pleasure, doth sometimes alter and infect the very judgment and reason of the inward man, and much oftener doth bias and pervert the external actions of many worldlings, even against their own natural inclination, knowledge, and conscience . . . who because they be wise, can not be Protestants 23 years, that is to say, any long time together, but yet because they are also worldly, can not or will not confess their former fall to their disadvantage in this life, which they prefer before eternal glory.[6]

Elsewhere, Allen refers to "times of heretical regiment, where Politiques [to him, politically inspired hypocrites] have all the government," which they use to defend their temporal good at the cost of their spiritual welfare. Those who accept death in the cause of heresy are not hypocrites, but they earn no respect from Allen, for they, "shedding their blood obstinately in testimony of falsehood . . . are known malefactors, and can be no martyrs, but damnable murderers of themselves."[8]

The late sixteenth century is frequently and properly described as an age dominated by conflicts between religions. But Allen, as many of his contemporaries on both sides of the great religious divide, sees no real conflict between religions. He sees only a conflict between the one obviously true religion and various mixtures of hypocrisy, worldliness, and willful obstinacy.

The main end for which the one true church exists is the honor of God and the salvation of souls. When one considers the importance of these aims and the fact that Allen believes that the laws for achieving them can be known with considerable certainty, it is not surprising that he judges temporal rulers according to how well they serve these goals. Christian rulers, he believes, ought to regard crimes against God more seriously than mere temporal crimes, however serious. Allen approves the example of Queen Mary, who, he claims, had ample evidence to execute Thomas Cranmer and others for treason and conspiracy, but chose instead to burn them for heresy, "as for their more heinous crime, and which a Christian prince ought to regard far more, than any thing committed against his regality."[9]

Clearly, God cannot be honored and souls cannot be saved by governments separated from the communion of the one true church, and Allen's denunciations of the Elizabethan government are more eloquent on this point than on any other. He denounces the idea that princes have no spiritual superiors except God. "If princes have souls, they must needs be under the account and charge of prelates."[10] The English statute making the monarch head of the church "can have no excuse, . . . making indeed a king and a priest all one: no difference betwixt the state of the church and a temporal common wealth: giving no less right to heathen princes to be governors of the church in causes spiritual, than to a Christian king: it maketh one part of the church in different territories to be independent and several from another, according to the distinction of realms and kingdoms in the world."[11] In effect, Allen says, the principle of royal headship of the church denies the unity of the universal church and makes the prince into a sort of national god.[12] Naturally, all sorts of material and moral disasters can be expected from this situation, and Allen catalogs them in great detail.[13]

To prevent these disasters from taking place, Allen invokes the time-honored principle of the authority of the pope over princes, up to and including the right to depose them, when questions involving the salvation of souls are at stake. Allen probably devotes more time to the defense of the papal deposing power than to any other point. Allen regards the pope as the political superior of all Christian rulers; he is "our chiefest magistrate and master on earth."[14] This does not mean that the pope is or should be involved in the day-to-day administration of temporal kingdoms; "so long as the temporal state is no hindrance to eternal felicity, & the glory of Christ's kingdom, the other [the church] inter-meddleth not with her actions." But Allen gives a great deal of biblical evidence to prove that when the actions of the state hinder the goals of the church, "though their spiritual power immediately and directly concerneth not our temporal affairs; yet indirectly (and as by accident) it doth not only concern our souls but our bodies and goods, so far as is requisite to our souls' health, & expedient for the good regiment therefore, and the church's utility, being subject to their spiritual governors."[15] In themselves, then, the laws of the temporal state and the commands of the temporal magistrate have no claim to ultimate moral authority. On any issue involving the church or the salvation of souls, the decisions, and indeed the continued existence, of temporal authorities are subject to the judgment of the church, and particularly its supreme pastor. To Allen, the positive law of the institutional church is, for all practical purposes, infallibly based on the divine and natural law that is the foundation of all valid morality. It is reasonable, then, that merely human laws and commands must be judged by its standards. It is also predictable that the laws of England and the conduct of its ruler are judged and found wanting.

But if the papal authority were to be made effective against disobedient rulers, subjects would have to disobey their temporal rulers; they would have to be persuaded that their allegiance to the church and the pope took precedence over their allegiance to their temporal ruler. The clearest discussion of the obligations of the individual under Allen's system of political morality is in his defense of the conduct of Sir William Stanley in surrendering Deventer to the Spaniards and joining the Spanish army. Allen has no doubt that Stanley made the right, and indeed the morally necessary decision, for "the rendering up of such towns, and places of the low countries as be in any English men's custody, is not only lawful, but necessary to be done, under pain of mortal sin, and damnation." This is because Elizabeth is waging an obviously unjust war in the Low Countries, and anyone who serves in an unjust war is in mortal sin and morally bound to make restitution to those whom he injures. The war is unjust for several reasons that Allen thinks ought to be obvious even to non-Catholics. Elizabeth is violating the rights of Philip II to his ancient patrimony, attacking him without just cause, and supporting rebels against their lawful sovereign. This last, Allen holds, has been an unfortunate general feature of Elizabeth's foreign policy since her accession to the throne. Nor can one excuse one's participation in an unjust war by pleading the prince's command, "for injustice done by public pretended authority, is more shameful, than that which is done by private offenders. St. Augustine affirming, that 'whole kingdoms, when they agree upon open iniquity, are nothing else, but a great laronage,' that is, a brotherhood of thieves."[16]

But although Allen believes that these arguments are sufficient to absolve Elizabeth's subjects of allegiance to her, they are not the most compelling reasons for disobeying her. Elizabeth's war is wrong "principally, for that it is waged, for defence of heresy, and heretics, and for the eversion of the Catholic faith: that is to say, directly against God, and his holy church."[17] By fighting in such a cause, a Catholic cuts himself off from the church, places the commandments of men ahead of those of God, and insures his own damnation if he is killed. No human authority has the authority to command against God, and in any case, Elizabeth, being excommunicate, has lost whatever right to the throne she had, and therefore has no more right to command anybody to do anything.[18] Rebellion against her is not wrong, since "to revolt, is of itself, lawful or unlawful . . . according to the justice, or injustice, of the cause, or difference of the person, from or to whom, the revolt is made." In a war when religion is at stake, Allen makes clear, it is entirely up to the pope, whose authority and wisdom are derived from Christ, to command Catholics to what extent to obey their temporal rulers.[19]

Allen may never have used the term *Res Publica Christiana* in the works discussed here. Nevertheless, the center of his political thought is the concept of a Christendom united on the basis of the divine law of which the church is the divinely authorized interpreter. He believes that in order for the moral unity of Christendom to be real and secure, it must be institutionally visible as well. Allen's strong support of the power of the pope over temporal rulers and his strong opposition to the principle of state control of the church are both motivated by his conviction that political and institutional unity is necessary for enforcing the moral unity of Christendom.

The primary political obligation of the individual in Allen's system is to maintain the universal moral law of Christendom and the political framework that supports it. Elizabeth may legitimately be resisted because she has systematically violated the universal moral law, primarily by rejecting the pope, but in a host of other ways as well. When a ruler fails so blatantly to carry out her responsibilities, the good Catholic is obliged to do what he can, under the direction of the highest authority, to bring the lawbreaker to justice. Allen justifies the conscientious disobedience of Sir William Stanley and urges rebellion against Elizabeth on strongly conservative and authoritarian grounds—in order to bring a lawless subordinate to justice in the name of a higher ruler who represents a higher principle. It is by this conservative principle that Allen can be consistent in defending both persecution of heretics and conscientious disobedience to immoral rulers, which to the modern mind seem diametrically opposed to each other. The heretic and the wicked ruler both set themselves up in opposition to the general good of the Christian community: the one by obstinately clinging to his private ideas of Truth in the face of manifest reason and the traditional authority of the church; the other by pursuing his temporal advantage, whatever damage he does to his own country or to Christendom in general. The heretic begins by attacking the doctrinal basis of the Christian community; the wicked ruler, by attacking its political structure. But the doctrinal basis and institutional forms of Christendom are so closely linked that an assault on one will inevitably become an assault on the other. The suppression of both the heretic and the wicked ruler is therefore equally necessary for the public good, and who except Peter's successor has the right to judge when the public good is sufficiently threatened to justify such action?

Allen's propaganda tracts provide a good summary of the political ethics that supported the efforts of the Allen-Parsons party to bring about a Catholic conquest of England. But although after Allen's death the Appellants assailed the main ideas set forth in his political works, they always downplayed Allen's own role as a political militant. The reluctance of the Appellants to attack the greatest and most widely respected leader of the Catholic exiles may partly account for the savagery of their attack on the man whom they considered their main opponent, Robert Parsons. Any of Allen's words or actions that the Appellants could not reconcile with their own principles were ascribed to Parsons's malignant influence,[20] and Parsons's own works were attacked repeatedly with great vigor and at great length. The greatest Appellant anger was directed against two works, *A Conference About the Next Succession to the Crown of England* and the *Memorial for the Reformation of England.* These works would be worth attention, if only because they were major objects of Appellant fury. But they are also significant because, taken together, they set forth both a more solid philosophical basis for the Allen-Parsons party's political activities and a more detailed account of its ultimate objectives than Allen provides in his tracts.

The *Conference About the Next Succession* was published in 1594, under the pseudonym of R. Doleman. Parsons's opponents attributed the work to him, but Parsons never admitted sole authorship, and it seems at least possible that several persons besides Parsons contributed to the *Conference.*[21] But Parsons's role in the production of the book was a prominent one, and it can certainly be taken as a statement of the party of which, after Allen's death in 1594, Parsons was the most prominent member.

The *Conference* is formally a dialogue in two parts among a group of Englishmen and Irishmen, set in Amsterdam in the spring of 1593. Almost the whole work, however, is occupied by two long speeches. Part 2 consists mainly of a discourse by a common lawyer, explaining the basis of the various candidates' claims to the English throne. The common lawyer claims to be impartial, and some modern scholars seem to have taken his protestation at face value;[22] but many contemporaries took Part 2 as a brief for the succession to the English throne of the Infanta of Spain, who like her father Philip II was descended from Edward III through the Lancastrian line.

Part 1, however, sheds more light on the theoretical basis of the political activities of the politically militant English Catholics. In this section, a civil lawyer speaks on the principles by which succession to thrones should be determined.[23] The civil lawyer aims at refuting the claims of absolute divine-right monarchy, particularly as set forth by the French Politique Pierre du Belloy. Doleman sums up Belloy's central principles in a few propositions: that all families that rule kingdoms were placed in their positions by God and God alone may depose them; that a prince's children or next of kin must automatically succeed him on the throne; that no prince may be limited in his powers by human law; and that no prince, however mad, wicked, or otherwise unfit to govern, may be denied the throne or resisted by his subjects.[24]

Doleman's attack on divine-right absolutism is based on a largely classical definition of the origin and nature of the commonwealth. References from Aristotle, Cicero, Plato, and other ancient authors, as well as the universal practice of the human race, demonstrate that man is intended by nature (and therefore by God) to live in society.[25] Man cannot live in society without magistrates to enforce physical and moral order. "Wheresoever a multitude is gathered together, if there be not some to repress the insolent, to assist the impotent, reward the virtuous, chasten the outrageous and minister some kind of justice and equality unto the inhabitants, their living together would be far more hurtful than their living asunder, for that one would consume and devour the other, and so we see, that upon living together followeth of necessity some kind of jurisdiction in magistrates."[26]

But although the existence of the commonwealth and the necessity of the magistrate's authority are ordained by God and nature, particular forms of government are not. It is "left unto every nation and country to choose that form of government, which they shall like best, and think most fit for the nature and conditions of their people."[27] On the whole, Doleman thinks that hereditary monarchy is the best form of government, but he does not attribute to it any divine sanction that other forms of government lack.[28] Indeed, even this best form of government has its drawbacks, "for that a king or prince is a man as others be, and thereby not only subject to errors in judgment, but also, to passionate affections in his will: for this cause, it was necessary that the commonwealth, as it gave him this great power over them, so it should assign him also the best helps that might be, for directing and rectifying both his will and judgment."

The first means by which Doleman's commonwealth keeps its ruler on the right path is by laws, which Doleman says are usually made upon due and wise consideration for the good of the commonwealth. The law also is inflexible and impartial, "but telleth the same tale to every man." In these qualities laws resemble the perfection of God, "so that a prince ruling by law is more than a man, or a man deified, and a prince ruling by affections, is less than a man, or a man brutified."[29]

The second method by which commonwealths help their princes rule is by the assistance of "councils and councillors," which turns out to mean what an American constitutional theorist might call a system of checks and balances. As examples, Doleman cites "the parlements of England and France, the Cortes in Spain and diets in Germany, without which no matter of great moment can be concluded."[30] He also mentions the king's privy councillors, whom he "is bound to hear." These admixtures of "Aristocratia" and "Democratia," Doleman holds, prevent the state from falling into tyranny, which is the frequent result of unrestrained rule by a single person.

But Doleman believes that hedging the king around with laws and institutions that restrict his power may sometimes not be enough, and that it is often necessary and right to deny the crown to the person who is next in line by "propinquity of blood" or to remove a ruler from the throne. Doleman holds that the idea that a king must be obeyed whatever he does or commands destroys the end of the commonwealth, "which was to live together in justice and order . . . but if they [kings] be bound to no justice at all, but must be born and obeyed be they never so wicked, then is this end and butte of the commonwealth, & of all royal authority, utterly frustrate: then may we set up public murderers ravishers thieves and spoilers to devour us instead of kings and governors to defend us, for such indeed are kings that follow no law, but passion and sensuality, and do commit injustice, by their public authority."[31]

Doleman holds that it is permissible, by divine and human law, for the commonwealth, which conferred authority on the prince for the good of the commonwealth, to revoke that authority when it is used in a way inimical to the ends for which it was instituted.[32] A king who rules in opposition to justice, equity, and law is simply a tyrant; and a tyrant is "the worst and most hurtful creature under heaven," for his goal is to destroy his commonwealth. A subject may justly disregard any oaths of obedience that he has sworn to such a ruler, for no oath is binding when its fulfillment would injure the public good.[33]

Doleman further supports his ideas on the mutual obligations of rulers and subjects with arguments that look back to medieval political ideas and forward to the social contract. He holds that since princes were originally admitted to rule by the choice of the people, it is "not likely . . . that any people would ever yield to put their lives, goods and liberties in the hands of another, without some promise and assurance of justice and equity."[34] The king's power is "not absolute, but *potestas vicaria or delegata*" or, one might say, the power of an agent. This power "is given with such restrictions cautels and conditions, yea, with such plain exceptions, promises and oaths of both parties . . . as if the same be not kept, . . . on either part, then is the other not bound to observe his promise neither . . . for that in all bargains, agreements and contracts, where one part is bound mutually and reciprocally to the other . . . if one side go from his promise, the other standeth not obliged to perform his."[35]

The logical structure of Doleman's critique of divine-right absolutism thus rests on two related points. First, the commonwealth and its ruler are instituted by an agreement of people and ruler, to meet the people's material and moral needs. Second, if the ruler breaks his side of the agreement and rules in a manner destructive of the aims of the commonwealth, the people are justified in deposing him. Doleman supports these views not merely by abstract argument, but by very extensive use of examples drawn from history and from actual practice. He recounts dozens of cases in which bad kings have been removed from their thrones and unfit heirs barred from the succession in spite of their having the strongest genealogical claims. His examples are drawn from the histories of Israel, classical antiquity, and many European states, and the particular circumstances vary widely. But Doleman draws similar conclusions from the great majority of cases; one example can illustrate his major lessons.

Doleman tells how Charles of Lorraine, uncle and lineal successor of King Louis V of France, was denied the throne and Hugh Capet crowned instead, "by election and approbation of the commonwealth." Doleman quotes at length from the speech made by the representative of "the states of France" to the deposed Charles on that occasion. The representative admits that by the "ordinary laws and rights" of France, the crown would belong to Charles. However, he continues, the same laws that give Charles his claim to the succession also judge him unworthy of it, for he has not lived "according to the use and custom of your country of France" but has allied himself with the Germans and adopted "their vile and base manners." Since Charles has "abandoned the ancient virtue sweetness and amity of the French,"

we have also abandoned and left you, and chosen Hugh Capet for our king . . . and this without any scruple or prejudice of our consciences at all, esteeming it far better and more just to live under Hugh Capet the present possessor of the crown, with enjoying the ancient use of our laws, customs privileges and liberties, than under you the inheritor by nearness of blood, in oppression, strange customs and cruelty. For even as those which are to make a voyage in a ship upon a dangerous sea, do not so much respect, whether the pilot which is to guide the stern, be the owner of the ship or no, but rather whether he be skillful, valiant, and like to bring them in safety to their way's end . . . so our principal care is, that we have a good prince to lead and guide us happily in this way of civil and politic life, which is the end why princes were appointed.[36]

This speech could serve as a summary of most of Doleman's points and an application of them to the case at hand. Princes are instituted to help their subjects lead a "civil and politic life," and if there is good reason to believe that a prince's rule has been or will be inimical to that end, the commonwealth may justly replace him with one more likely to achieve it.

But the most important argument that this example (and most of the others that he uses) adds to Doleman's abstract argument is drawn from the consequences of Charles's deposition. The French, Doleman points out, felt no qualms of conscience for the overthrow of Charles, "which God hath also since seemed to confirm, with the succession and happy success of so many noble and most Christian kings as have issued out of this line of Hugo Capetus unto this day."[37] Almost every one of Doleman's accounts of the overthrow of a bad king includes a similar description of the success enjoyed by the new ruler and of the commonwealth's prosperity under his rule. Doleman asserts that the frequent success and beneficial effects of attempts to overthrow wicked rulers prove that God favors them. This was no trivial argument in an age when many saw political and military success or failure as manifestations of divine favor or disfavor. Doleman probably devoted so much attention to the problem because he realized the importance of showing that his principles held good not only in abstract theory but also in man's concrete experience of God's action.

Doleman's discussions of particular rebellions illustrate his views on the occasional rightness and necessity of rebellion. His belief that a king rules only upon conditions imposed as part of an agreement with his subjects is illustrated by a long chapter on coronations and the oaths that usually accompany them. Doleman examines the actual coronation ceremonies of several European nations and finds that in all of them princes take some kind of oath to rule justly and to uphold the rights of their subjects. He holds that the coronation ceremony makes clear and explicit the agreement that must exist between a prince and his subjects.[38] The terms of the agreement, he believes, are especially clear in countries enlightened by Christianity or in which succession to the crown is orderly and peaceful. The "agreement, bargain and contract" that are sealed by coronation oaths are as binding as any contract can be, and Doleman vigorously attacks Belloy's assertion that the people's consent to that agreement is merely a matter of external ceremony, adding nothing to a king's intrinsically absolute power.[39]

Perhaps the most important aspect of Doleman's discussion of coronation ceremonies is implied rather than expressed. He never explicitly says that a king must satisfy a particular religious test in order to be a legitimate ruler, but the coronation ceremonies that he describes are always religious ceremonies. Bishops and archbishops, usually the primates of the nation involved, preside over the ceremonies, and the king's promise to remain faithful to the church and to uphold its rights is always a prominent part of the agreement under which he is crowned. The word "Catholic" is sometimes used in these promises and sometimes not. But even when that word is not used, the reader can get the message. The whole picture of imposing ecclesiastical ceremony and of promises given by kings to the hierarchy of a church whose independent rights they must respect presupposes a Catholic world. Even though Doleman never explicitly defines the spheres of clerical and lay authority, the reader is not surprised to find him quoting with approval Thomas Becket's reminders to Henry II of the oaths that he had sworn to defend the church and quoting as a valid precedent the pope's excommunication of three English prelates who had consecrated Henry's son without Becket's permission.[40]

But although the ecclesiastical aura surrounding the coronation ceremonies implies the importance of religion as part of the compact between ruler and people, Doleman does not systematically discuss the relationship between religion and politics until the last chapter of part 1 of the *Conference*. At the beginning of that chapter, a listener asks the civil lawyer how one may judge when there is sufficient cause to justify a change in the normal line of succession. The lawyer answers that the commonwealth has the right to revoke the authority that it has granted and that the commonwealth must decide what is a sufficient cause for doing so.[41]

The civil lawyer opens up a potential ethical mare's nest when at the end of this speech he says that even a private man may resist if the commonwealth chooses a ruler such as "a Turk or Moor . . . or some other notorious wicked man, or tyrant," for the rule of such a person would threaten "God's glory, and the public wealth." The audience, however, does not seize this apparent opportunity to inquire into the limits of the commonwealth's authority over the conscience of its members. Instead, the civil lawyer is asked to conclude his discourse by discussing "what were the true causes and principal points, which ought to be chiefly regarded, as well by the commonwealth as by every particular man, in this great action of furthering or hindering any prince towards a crown."[42]

The civil lawyer answers that the commonwealth should choose those most likely to achieve the ends for which princes were instituted. The prince has "three things committed to his charge, first religion, then justice, then manhood and chivalry, for the defence of the realm." The civil lawyer says that he has already covered the last two points, which guarantee the subject's temporal welfare and that he will limit himself to the question of religion, by which subjects "do attain unto their end spiritual and supernatural, which is the salvation of their souls."[43]

Doleman leaves no doubt that he considers a prince's religious policy the most important consideration in evaluating his rule. Even the heathen, enlightened solely by the light of nature, realized that the highest good of the soul could be achieved only by union with God in the hereafter and that consequently all human actions and institutions must be evaluated above all with this end in mind.[44] Doleman assumes that the quest for salvation is a communal concern. The light of nature taught the heathens that the highest honor that man could do to God in this life was "the honor of sacrifice and oblations," which, in the form of the Mass, is the highest communal act in the Catholic church. Although the religion of the heathen has often been perverted by the devil, even they realize "that by God & nature, the highest and chiefest end of the common wealth, is *Cultus Dei* the service of God, and religion, and consequently that the principal care & charge of a prince and magistrate even by nature itself, is to look thereunto."[45]

Doleman thus sees the maintenance of religion, and particularly the public worship of God, as the highest and most necessary aim of the commonwealth. He pours scorn on "Christians in name" who see no higher goal for government than "bodily wealth, and a certain temporal king, [*sic*, perhaps a misprint for "kind"] of peace and justice among their subjects." Even the more sociable animals, Doleman claims, rise that far.[46] The chief end of the commonwealth is "to assist their subjects to the attaining of their supernatural end, by honoring and serving God in this life, and by living virtuously, for that otherwise God should draw no other fruit or commodity out of human commonwealths, than of an assembly of brutish creatures, maintained only for to eat drink and live in peace." A community that does not recognize its relationship to God and fulfill the obligations of that relationship is preventing its subjects from fulfilling the ends of their human natures and is therefore not, properly speaking, a human community at all. It is merely an association for satisfying men's purely animal needs. Doleman therefore regards any prince who does not pay proper attention to his subjects' religious needs as a traitor to God and thinks that no cause can so well justify a commonwealth in refusing to accept a prince "as if they judge him faulty in this point, which is the head of all the rest, and which all the rest do serve."[47]

But, Doleman's narrator says, there are some who will assert that only "an infidel or heathen" should be barred from the throne of a Christian commonwealth and that one should not resist "a Christian prince though he be somewhat different from me in religion." In reply, Doleman insists that both reason and the Athanasian Creed teach us that "there is but one only religion that can be true among Christians." Furthermore, "seeing that to me there can be no other faith or religion available for my salvation than that only which I my self do believe, for that my own conscience must testify for me, or against me: certain it is, that unto me and my conscience he which in any point believeth otherwise than I do . ̀ . is an infidel, for that he believeth not that which in my faith or conscience, is the only and sole truth, whereby he must be saved." Once Doleman has decided that precise doctrinal certainty is necessary for salvation, the conclusion that follows is "so long as I have this opinion of him [a prince with whom one disagrees on religion] albeit his religion were never so true, yet so long . . . as I have this contrary persuasion of him, I shall do against my conscience and sin damnably in the sight of God, to prefer him to a charge where he may draw many other to his own error and perdition."[48]

If followed to its conclusion, Doleman's combination of the necessity of correct belief for salvation and the obligations imposed on an individual even by an erring conscience makes it possible for a person holding erroneous views to be condemned to eternal damnation either for resisting the true doctrine or for violating his conscience by a failure to resist it. The problem could of course be solved by a ringing statement of the obvious truth of the Catholic religion and its claims on the individual conscience; in a later work, in fact, Parsons said that the purpose of the *Conference* was to make Catholics aware of their political obligations.[49] But to make such a statement in the *Conference* itself would have meant abandoning the pretense that the book was an impartial examination of the question of the English succession. However, the ecclesiastical trappings and religious oaths of the coronation ceremonies make it fairly clear that the book is intended for Catholics; and whether or not part 2 of the *Conference* is intended as a brief for the Infanta, no non-Catholic would have written a book that took her claim to the English throne at all seriously. Since Doleman could not have expected to influence any but Catholic readers, he could be virtually sure that anyone whom he persuaded of the conscientious necessity of opposing to the utmost a prince of a contrary religion would already have a Catholic conscience. Given his desire to appear impartial in order to achieve maximum propaganda effect, this was probably the best Doleman could do.

Doleman does not hesitate to apply his principles to the English situation. Anyone, he says, who consents to the accession to the English throne of a ruler who can be expected to promote a religion contrary to his own sins against his conscience and is morally responsible for all the temporal and spiritual calamities that may follow.[50]

If the reader's ethical sense and fear of the hereafter are not enough to dissuade him from supporting a prince of a contrary religion, Doleman points out that such a course of action would be very foolish "if we consider reason of state also, and worldly policy." One may make agreements with and extract promises from a potential ruler, but "seeing the prince once made and settled, must needs proceed according to the principles of his own religion, it followeth also that he must come quickly to break with the other party, though before he loved him never so well (which yet perhaps is very hard if not impossible for two of different religions to love sincerely)." Even if the prince's own intentions are benevolent, those of a religion contrary to the government's will inevitably be widely regarded with suspicion and dislike. They will be excluded from preferments and honors and "subject to a thousand molestations and injuries, which are incident to the condition and state of him, that is not current with the course of his prince and realm in matters of religion." Like it or not, he will be regarded as an enemy to the state and will ultimately have to choose between damning his soul by outward conformity to what he holds to be false and the loss of "all the temporal commodities of this life."[51]

Doleman may have intended this description as an appeal to the experience of English Catholics, for what he describes as a hypothetical threat was for them a very present reality. Doleman wants his Catholic readers to realize that their troubles stem from the fact that people of differing religions are natural enemies. Since no real trust can exist between men of different religions, each religious group must, for its own self-preservation, attempt to render the others powerless—and, of course, the surest way of rendering a group powerless is to destroy it. Like it or not, Doleman implies, the Catholics are engaged in a life-and-death struggle, and it would, of course, be the sheerest idiocy voluntarily to permit a member of the other side to become ruler of England.

But Doleman could not really complain about the existence of an inevitable struggle between religious groups, for it follows directly from his own ethical principles. He assumes that there is only one true form of Christianity and that only through that form can God be truly honored and souls saved. Clearly, he concludes, the establishment and maintenance of the true form of Christianity is the highest obligation of both the state and its subjects. When one adds this principle to Doleman's belief in the right and duty of the commonwealth to overthrow evil rulers and to the Allen-Parsons party's belief in the obvious truth of the Catholic faith, one has a complete justification for the Catholic exiles' crusade against the Elizabethan regime in favor of a Catholic succession. In Doleman's world the only possible alternatives, as well as the only morally acceptable ones, are total victory and total defeat.

The political theory of the *Conference About the Next Succession* is complemented by Parsons's *Memorial for the Reformation of England*. In the *Memorial* Parsons gives a detailed outline of how England should be governed after å Catholic ruler has been placed on the throne. The work was apparently completed around 1596, although Parsons says that it was based on ideas that he had been writing down for seventeen or eighteen years.[52] It was not published until 1690, when Edward Gee, a Church of England clergyman and prolific anti-Catholic writer, edited an edition with an introduction and notes designed to blacken Parsons's character and to point out the horrible fate that England had recently escaped by the Glorious Revolution. During Parsons's lifetime, the *Memorial* circulated only in manuscript form. Several Appellant writers attacked it vigorously, but with inaccurate ideas of its contents.[53] An examination of the work, however, leads one to believe that a complete and careful reading would not have reduced the vigor of the Appellant attack. The title of the book is indicative of its aim; England is to have not merely a change of government but a "Reformation," a change that affects the basic structure and spirit of the nation.

In the first three chapters of the *Memorial*, Parsons demonstrates the thoroughness that he wishes to bring to the task of restoring Catholicism in England. He explains that England will have both a unique opportunity and a unique obligation to establish a rightly reformed Catholic church.[54] He urges that the reform of the English church be guided by the example of the primitive church and not be limited to the decrees of the Council of Trent, which were moderated to accommodate the general corruption of Christendom.[55] Parsons thinks that Mary Tudor was not rigorous enough to reestablish Catholicism on a sound basis. England's reconciliation to Rome in 1554 was "huddled up . . . by a certain general absolution only, without due search and consideration of what had been committed, or what satisfaction was to be made to God and man." Mary was in general too easily satisfied by formal professions of Catholicism, without any evidence of real commitment to the faith or any satisfaction for past offenses against it. Priests who had married were allowed to say mass without confessing, those who had preached against Catholics under Edward VI were allowed to preach for them under Mary, commissioners against Catholics became commissioners against Protestants, and in general "the matter went as a stage-play, where men do change their persons and parts, without changing their minds or affections."[56] It is no wonder that such a policy brought so little benefit to Catholicism and that heresy quickly returned. Next time, reconciliation to Rome must be a sign of heartfelt repentance for the great national sin,[57] and the nation's commitment to the Catholic church must go deeper than a superficial acceptance of Catholic formulas and structures.

The changing of the nation's heart must begin with changing its power structure. Parsons holds the common sixteenth-century view that "the prince in every commonwealth is the head and heart from whence all life and vigour principally cometh unto the same."[58] It is, therefore, crucial for England's next Catholic ruler to insure that his whole regime be thoroughly Catholic in spirit as well as in appearance. The prince must give an example of a pious life himself and must encourage all who would advance the Catholic faith.[59] Catholics who have been constant under persecution must be appointed to all principal offices, in preference to the supple timeservers who Parsons thinks often won favor under Mary.[60] The prince must exclude from his council not only heretics, but also "cold and doubtful professors of Catholic religion."[61]

But although it is vital to fill all existing offices with zealous Catholics, Parsons does not think that will be enough. He proposes the establishment of a "Council of Reformation" (the word "Inquisition," he thinks, had better be avoided)[62] to be appointed by prince, pope, and Parliament and to include several bishops and other men fit for the work. For a limited term (Parsons suggests four to six years), this body is to be given sweeping powers over the church and the religious life of England.[63] The council is to control much of the revenue of the church, to control appointments to benefices, to examine all priests who come into the realm and to decide which ones should be allowed to stay, to appoint censors to regulate the people's morals,[64] to visit and reform the universities and the Inns of Court, and to perform a host of other functions. This council probably attracted more anger among Parsons's Catholic critics than did anything else in the *Memorial*, and with good reason. It is obvious that such a council could not exercise its powers in the way that Parsons would want them exercised without offending a host of vested interests. Its appointment and sweeping powers are a very clear sign that when Parsons talked of reforming England, he meant business.

The first task of the Catholic regime that Parsons considers is the extirpation of heresy and the reestablishment of loyalty to Catholicism among the population. In some respects, Parsons's prescriptions for accomplishing this task do not seem particularly severe. Although he wishes to forbid heretical preaching, worship, and proselytizing, Parsons thinks that it might be best, for the first few years, not to press people's consciences in religious matters but to allow them to express their doubts freely. Parsons does not make this suggestion out of any belief in the principle of liberty of religion, which he denounces as the worst thing in the world.[65] He suggests a temporary toleration only because he thinks that in the long run it will help form stronger allegiances to Catholicism. Such an approach will disarm the slander that the Catholic church persecutes before she instructs,[66] and will allow every man "more boldly and confidently [to] utter his wounds, and so be cured thereof, which otherwise he would cover, deny or dissemble to his greater hurt, and more dangerous corruption of the whole body."[67]

The point of toleration, then, is to enable heretics and doubters to come into the Catholic church from sincere conviction rather than from fear. This purpose can be achieved only by vigorous Catholic educational activity during the period of toleration. Parsons gives a detailed plan for such activity; he uses much space drawing up rules for disputations and for public lectures comparing Catholic and heretical authors.[68] He shows great confidence in the efficacy of such activities for advancing Catholicism; the Protestants, he says, have always denied Catholic requests for a fair disputation, since they know that their cause would be discredited.[69] Once the people have a chance to see Catholicism and Protestantism openly and fairly compared, all those who "are of a good nature . . . and do hold a desire to know the truth, and follow the same" will see the truth and gladly come into the one true church. After this, the policy of toleration will be unnecessary, for the only ones left outside the church will be "willful apostates, or malicious persecutors, or obstinate perverters of others." Parsons says that it is not for a man of his vocation to suggest how to deal with such people. He contents himself with reminding the prince that his government should approach as nearly as possible that of God, and that although God has "a sweet hand to cherish the well-affected," he also has a "strong arm, to bind the boisterous, stubborn and rebellious."[70]

Parsons's plan for winning the English people back to Catholicism is thus characterized by a sort of enlightened ruthlessness. He is as determined as Mary Tudor was to restore Catholicism as the one faith of England, but he is willing to sacrifice some speed in establishing external uniformity in order ultimately to establish Catholicism on a solid basis of popular agreement. Although Parsons expects this agreement to be reached largely by individuals' acceptance of the obvious truth of Catholicism, the establishment of the purified Catholicism that he desires requires more than the acceptance of the faith by individuals. The establishment of a true Catholic commonwealth will require many changes in English habits, customs, and institutions. Parsons devotes most of the *Memorial* to a discussion of these changes; a few examples may illustrate his major concerns.

The success of heresy in England, Parsons thinks, was due largely to dissension between the clergy and the laity.[71] Both sides are to blame for this: the laity for their envy of the clergy, which led them to accept the idea of the priesthood of all believers,[72] and the clergy because many of them did not live up to the obligations of their high calling.[73] Both of these faults must be overcome in the reformed Catholic England that Parsons desires. He repeatedly urges the absolute necessity of a virtuous and able clergy.[74] The laity, in turn, must recognize that the vocation of the priest, who holds the keys to eternal life, is much higher and more important than that of even the highest layman. Laymen must therefore submit to the clergy in everything that pertains to their salvation.[75]

Parsons gives extensive advice on how the church may be established and maintained in virtue. Bishops should give an example of piety, frugality, and other virtues; they should have a competent maintenance without living in pomp and should attend diligently to their pastoral responsibilities.[76] Bishops can help to insure a plentiful supply of virtuous and able priests by establishing seminaries where men's fitness may be tested, while priests must be kept busy enough at works of piety and edification that no one who is unfit for the work will wish to be ordained.[77] Each bishop should keep an up-to-date record of the abilities and moral character of all priests in his diocese, so that clerical appointments can be made on merit rather than by favoritism or influence.[78] The prince should keep a similar list for the whole country.

The idea of these lists hints at measures more likely to be controversial than the proposition that bishops and clergy should lead godly and sober lives. The bishops' keeping lists of worthy priests could have only a limited effect as long as much ecclesiastical patronage was in the hands of wealthy laymen. Parsons does not hesitate to urge the measures necessary to allow his plans for training a virtuous clergy to have their full effect. The providing of priests for benefices ought to be in the hands of the bishops; the patrons, Parsons says vaguely, "should be recompensed with some other privilege or honour to be done to them in their parishes." Perhaps, if this system is impossible, patrons should be allowed to present "some three or four able men together, both for learning and manners," from whom the bishop could make the final choice. Even this possibility of compromise loses much of its importance in view of Parsons's assumption that the church should regain the patronage that fell into lay hands as a result of the dissolution of the monasteries and subsequent plun-derings of the clergy—that is, most lay-controlled church patronage in England.[79]

Parsons does not consider explicitly the possible reactions of the nobility and gentry of England to being stripped of their control of church patronage; he assumes that since it must be done to achieve his purposes, it will be done. This assumption is quite typical of Parsons's attitude toward vested interests that stand in the way of the church's obtaining the independence and resources to do its job effec-tively. Indeed, from the point of view of the typical nobleman or gentleman, the replacement of the existing ecclesiastical patronage network by a strict merit system under the control of an austere and dedicated church hierarchy probably would not have been the worst of Parsons's proposals. Parsons says that one of the main reasons that God did not bless the attempted restoration of Catholicism under Mary with success was the failure to make any adequate satisfaction for the theft of the monastery lands.[80] Perhaps because he knows of Parliament's concern to prevent Mary Tudor from returning the lands that had been taken from the church under Henry VIII, Parsons realizes that it would be inexpedient to demand a "rigorous and exact satisfaction," but he holds that no Christian conscience could be se-cure without some satisfaction.[81] He suggests that the old rents of Assize (which he estimates will usually come to between one-third and one-half of the annual income from the land) be returned to the church and that the present possessors be assured of the rest of the income. Notorious opponents of the church, however, are not to be let off so easily; Parsons sees no reason why their ill-gotten gains should not be entirely restored to the church.[82] It is difficult to guess whether the landowning class would be more distressed at paying, in effect, a very heavy tax on their land or at the idea that the clergy whom they were accustomed to bully and exploit would collect money from them and decide whether they could keep their lands.

Parsons's willingness to attack lay vested interests to make the church strong and independent of lay control is matched by his will-ingness to reform the church internally in order to make it more fit for its work. Parsons does not think that it would be in England's best interests simply to return to their original possessors the rents, lands, and ecclesiastical livings recovered from the despoliation of the monasteries. Most of the old houses belonged to the Benedictines, an order that by 1596 included very few Englishmen. In any case,

England's greatest need is not for the erection of a great number of houses of contemplatives seeking primarily their own spiritual good.[83] Parsons thinks that the recovered rents, lands, and livings should be put into a common treasury, under the control of the Council of Reformation. The council should use the money primarily for "colleges, universities, seminaries, schools, for increasing of our clergy, as also of divers houses of other orders, that do deal more in preaching and helping of souls, and for that respect will be more necessary to the clergy of England, in this great work at the beginning, and for many years after." Such a policy will mean fewer monasteries than before, but "more perfection of reformation, edification, and help of the gaining of souls than before."[84] The church in a re-Catholicized England cannot be content with resuming the tranquil and inward-looking round of contemplation and ritual. It must prepare itself for spiritual battle—for teaching, pastoral care, and a vigorous life among the people. If the Benedictine order is not a fit instrument for the task, it must make way for those who are.

These points give a good idea of Parsons's view on the nature and role of the church in a re-Catholicized England. The church must be active, outward-looking, disciplined, and freed from the limitations imposed by undue lay influence—an altogether fit instrument for making the Catholic faith the predominant force in English life. The goal of raising Catholicism above all other interests governs Parsons's approach to other English institutions as well. All members of Parliament must be sworn to defend Catholicism, and it must be made treason to propose any change in the faith.[85] Some representatives of the religious orders must be admitted to the House of Lords in place of the old abbots, and some members of the clergy ought to be chosen to sit in the House of Commons.[86] Perhaps bishops should be given a veto power over the election of knights of the shire within their dioceses.[87] In order to establish the right moral tone at the universities, all headships of houses, fellowships, scholarships, and other offices of the universities may have to be made vacant, so that fitting men may be appointed everywhere. The Council of Reformation is to gather the revenues of the colleges into a common purse, to be used for the general improvement of the universities. The revenues of the heads of colleges are to be drastically reduced, their terms of office limited to three years, and the colleges subject to frequent visitations.[88]

The list could be longer, but these examples should suffice.

Parsons wants radical changes in the whole English structure of power and influence, not because he is a political or social radical on principle, but because of his desire to subordinate all institutions to his religious purpose. Parsons does occasionally make traditionalist noises; for example, he says that the prince will have to restore to the nobility and gentry all the privileges that heretical oppression has taken away.[89] But such professions are usually very general. Whenever he discusses a particular issue, Parsons shows little concern for the concrete vested interests that support political and social traditionalism. On every particular issue, the interests of classes or institutions must give way to the interests of truth. Since Elizabethan England, like most societies, was not very well arranged for the purpose of subordinating itself to a religious ideal, it is natural that in Parsons's work these interests are compelled to give way rather frequently.

But it is perhaps not primarily his lack of concern for particular vested interests that makes Parsons such a radical critic of the English establishment. If he is essentially indifferent to the establishment's particular interests, Parsons despises its methods of doing business. He insists on nothing so much as the necessity of advancement in church and state depending on virtue and ability, as judged by strictly impartial authority. Nothing seems to irritate him more than preferment depending on bribery, favoritism, influence peddling, and friends or relations in the right places.[90] The interests of religion and of the nation can be served well only if each man is appointed to office according to his "known zeal, ability, and talent for the same, and according to the measure of his suffering for God's cause," rather than "if for particular favours, kindred, bribes, interest, any be preferred, or such as are not known to have any zeal in God's affairs."[91]

It is, of course, a commonplace that "favours, kindred, bribes, interest" were basic means of conducting Elizabethan politics and administration. All governments tend to some degree to become instruments for serving the interests of those within them and those powerful enough to influence them; the Elizabethan regime was, in this respect, not conspicuously better than the average. This tendency had been repeatedly attacked in Tudor times, although more frequently during the reigns of Elizabeth's father and half-brother than in her own; Thomas More's *Utopia* is the best-known example. But Parsons's attack on the corruptions of the English establishment was much more frightening to defenders of political and social stability than More's, and for good reason. More indicted English society in the name of abstract principles of justice and morality. Parsons's justice and morality were part of a religious orthodoxy that was embodied in a concrete institution, a church that might well appreciate the chance of sitting in judgment on the arrangements of the English power elite and changing them if they did not suit the church's purposes. More was also a servant of the English monarchy and was not part of any organized movement for radical change. His attempts to fight the corruption of English society were limited to literary efforts and to the relatively innocuous method of trying to regulate his own conduct according to his principles. Parsons was using his considerable talents in the service of a movement of English Catholics whose schools and seminaries were spread across Catholic Europe, which had sent hundreds of priests into England, and which had extensive links both with people in England of dubious loyalty to the crown and with the massive power of the international Counter-Reformation. Parsons did not imagine the constitution of an imaginary island; he proposed concrete changes in particular aspects of English life in the interests of a particular religious and political movement.

Parsons is often aware that his program would threaten some established interests. He claims, however, that the chances of carrying out a sound Catholic reformation in England are very good, because the English Catholics have been tried in the fire of persecution and will be full of zeal for the task of reformation.[92] Parsons had some reason for believing this; any Englishman who was still a Catholic in 1596 was more likely than most people to attach great importance to particular religious beliefs. But even if one accepts Parsons's almost certainly false belief that the sympathies of the English people in 1596 were still predominantly Catholic, history could not have provided him with much hope that his program would be willingly accepted. European Catholics had long been playing the game of patronage and influence as well as Protestants had ever played it, and they would continue to do so. Even in a period when religion was of great social importance, many men in any large religious group would be reluctant to place their worldly concerns at the disposal of a man of Parsons's stamp. Even a Catholic who had demonstrated great loyalty to his faith could have his doubts about the demands made by Allen and Parsons for the subordination of all other loyalties to the conquest of England by the militant forces of the Counter-Reformation. Even a devout Catholic might have loyalties other than the Catholic church, and he might have ideas about the nature of the Catholic faith itself very different from those of Allen and Parsons. In fact, for many reasons, the great majority of the English Catholics showed little apparent enthusiasm for the Allen-Parsons program. To understand this lack of zeal, one must consider the conditions under which English Catholics lived and the ways in which some of them justified their position.

# CHAPTER III

# Loyalist Sentiment before 1595

Allen and Parsons were politicians and political writers by necessity, not by choice. They used political means because they thought such tactics were necessary to achieve a religious purpose. In reality, their greatest contribution to the survival of Catholicism in England was not their political activity but the organization of the seminaries that supplied the English Catholics with their priests. Most missionary priests appear to have avoided politics as much as possible, concentrating instead on their job of preserving the Catholic faith in England through religious instruction, pastoral counsel, the administration of the sacraments, and, when possible, through the conversion of Protestants or of those not firmly committed to either religion. This task required faith and courage of a very high order, but it did not require the acceptance of all the assumptions that underlay the political or military activities of Spain, the pope, or the leaders of the English Catholic exiles. Most of the missionaries accepted the views of Allen and Parsons on the necessity for Catholics to avoid participation in the established church; indeed, the survival of Catholicism in England is due largely to the missionaries' winning many of the English Catholics to this view.[1] But many of the missionaries saw no need to take a position on either the question of the legitimacy of the use of force to overthrow the queen and reestablish Catholicism or the right of the pope to depose secular rulers.

There were several very good reasons to insulate the activities of the missionaries from politics as much as possible. Most obvious was the very large moral advantage that it gave them. The English

Catholic missionaries demonstrated as effectively as anyone of their age that the blood of the martyrs is the seed of the church; they could not possibly have had such an effect on public opinion if they had been perceived by all as political agents. Probably the most common theme of Catholic propaganda during Elizabeth's reign was that the Catholic martyrs suffered for religion and conscience and were innocent of anything that could reasonably be called treason. Their labors were rarely if ever publicly connected with the political and military operations of the Catholic powers against England, even by writers who were involved in both.

The second reason for avoiding direct political involvement by the missionaries was the attitude of the Catholic laity, upon whose goodwill the clergy depended even more than in countries where the Catholic church was established. The missionaries had to depend on the Catholic nobility and gentry not only for their livelihoods but often for their lives. Naturally enough, the attitudes of the Catholic landowning class and the situation that they faced during Elizabeth's reign had a great effect on the nature of the mission as well as on its success.

It is a truism that the majority of the Catholic landowners considered themselves loyal subjects of the queen. There were many possible reasons for this. One would expect men of the Catholic magnates' social position to be natural conservatives, reluctant to challenge the monarchy's position as keystone of the hierarchical structure of society. The nature of the religion practiced in the households of Catholic magnates is also related to their political attitudes. "Seigneurial" Catholicism has been described as "a complex of social practices rather than a religion of internal conviction" and "a Catholicism less concerned with doctrinal affirmation or dramas of conscience than with a set of ingrained observances which defined and gave meaning to the cycle of the week and the seasons of the year, to birth, marriage and death."[2] Such a religion, heavily based on customary communal observances, could show very strong resistance to external pressure but was unlikely to become the sort of activist, moralistic, and strongly doctrinal religion that aggressively challenged European governments in the sixteenth and seventeenth centuries. The missionary priests reduced many forms of compromise with the establishment, the most important of which was the practice of occasional attendance at Anglican services to satisfy the law. But they did not put an end to the tendency to try to accommodate oneself to the demands of the government as far as one's conscience would allow, especially in matters touching directly on one's political loyalty. It seems likely that most of the missionary priests did not try very hard to influence the laity's position. The clergy's attitude is perhaps most strongly illustrated by the reaction to the Jacobean oath of allegiance when the government demanded, under the penalties of praemunire, a declaration of loyalty in terms bound to be theologically offensive. The clergy, while almost all finding the oath unacceptable, seem rarely to have imposed any major spiritual sanctions on the many laymen who took it.[3]

The Catholic laity's adoption of an essentially passive political attitude was made easier by their almost complete isolation from the international Catholic church in the early years of Elizabeth's reign. Largely because of the influence of the Hapsburgs, who were anxious to stay on good terms with Elizabeth, the papacy did not excommunicate Elizabeth until 1570.[4] While the Inquisition and the Council of Trent did forbid participation in heretical services,[5] little was done to make this decision effective. Hardly any priests were dispatched to England until the 1570s; Douai, the first English seminary in exile, was founded only in 1568, on the private initiative of William Allen and a few other English exiles. The English Catholics, helped by those Marian clergy who either were deprived by Elizabeth or lived double lives as open Anglicans and secret Catholics, were left to face the government's demands with little outside support, either moral or material. It is not surprising that they found moral expedients for complying with those demands as far as was necessary for survival.

The nature of the persecution that the Elizabethan Catholics faced may also have influenced their attitudes. It is important here not to be deceived by special pleading. There are those who write as though all Elizabethan Catholics faced an efficient, ruthless persecution based purely on religious bigotry, which made no distinctions between one Catholic and another. Others, much taken with Elizabeth's alleged desire not to open windows into men's souls, write as if Elizabeth's government was entirely uninterested in the religious beliefs of her subjects unless they became active traitors. For once, the truth really does lie somewhere in the middle. The persecution was very real, and its long-range goal was the suppression of Catholicism per se, regardless of the apparent political loyalty of any particular Catholic. Of the sixteen Catholics whose payments accounted for most of the revenue from recusancy fines in the few years after 1587, none was ever accused of any kind of treasonous political activity; they seem to have been singled out because of their prominence as bulwarks of recusancy in their counties.[6]

But the level of suffering that government persecution inflicted on many Catholics varied very considerably in severity over space, over time, and from individual to individual. Significant numbers of Catholics managed to retain offices in local government well into Elizabeth's reign,[7] while the provisions for imprisoning and fining Catholics quite likely never touched the majority even of stubborn recusants.[8] This uneven treatment was due partly to the complex, inefficient, and frequently corrupt array of administrative and judicial agencies by which the government tried to deal with the problem.[9] The inefficiency of the repressive machinery helped many Catholics to protect their interests by the usual Elizabethan political methods based on local factions. Even when Catholics had been effectively purged from the commissions of the peace and other local government offices, local officials were often unenthusiastic persecutors of Catholics. Apart from any genuine repugnance that they may have felt for the task, many influential men in the counties were bound to their Catholic neighbors by ties of kinship and economic and political interest.[10]

The degree to which Catholics succeeded in defending their interests within the normal political framework varied widely. Almost all recusants eventually were excluded from office holding and other fruits of royal favor. The severity with which fines and confiscation of property were imposed was more erratic and could be affected by the government's attitude, the attitude and effectiveness of local officials, the recusant's connections, his political and legal ingenuity, and a host of other considerations. But the attitude of any Catholic facing the government's repressive measures was bound to be affected by the nature of the persecution. The fact that the persecution developed slowly (its most severe phase was not reached until the 1580s) and was erratic in its effectiveness meant that the Catholics never faced the sort of crisis of survival that might have been caused by a determined, efficient effort to wipe out Catholicism. The Catholic community was never confronted with an obvious choice between violent resistance to the government and oblivion. At each stage of the persecution, accommodation and evasion appeared a more plausible choice than violent resistance.

The means by which this evasion was carried on were also vital to the formation of Catholic attitudes. It has been observed that politics based on ties of kinship, economic interest, and political faction can operate most effectively when untroubled by issues that arouse strong feelings. Obviously, the most promising approach for Catholics was to play down the political relevance of their Catholicism as far as possible, and the easiest way to do this was to stress their loyalty to the crown.

The Catholics' downplaying of the political relevance of their religious convictions was important in order to avoid the hostility of their fellow nobles and gentry, with whom they played the game of local politics. It was probably even more important in moderating the hostility of the crown, for although the government regarded Catholicism as intrinsically undesirable, it did make distinctions among Catholics based partly on their political behavior. A Catholic could be very heavily punished without engaging in any activity that appeared to be politically disloyal, but Catholicism alone rarely made his situation as bad as it could be; the available evidence tends to indicate that although Catholicism was often a major economic and political handicap, few families were ruined entirely by the financial consequences of recusancy.[11] Catholicism combined with any hint of active political disaffection, however, was usually disastrous; it was in these cases that Elizabeth's government most often cut through all the barriers to government action to impose a swift and terrible retribution. The kind of salutary lesson that Catholics might take from the government's differing treatment of obviously loyal Catholics and those who gave some grounds for suspicion may be seen in the careers of two of the country's most prominent Catholics: Philip Howard, Earl of Arundel, and Anthony Browne, Viscount Montague.

Philip Howard, born in 1557, was the scion of the most prominent noble family in England, a family that, as he was painfully aware,[12] had a rather unfortunate history under the Tudors. The most recent and perhaps most spectacular of the family's misfortunes was the beheading in 1572 of Howard's father, the Duke of Norfolk, for his role in the Ridolfi plot. The family history does not, however, seem to have affected Howard's early career very much. After receiving a degree from Cambridge, he appears to have plunged into the court whirl much as other young men of his class did; he was apparently concerned with pleasing the queen with presents and the like, cutting a fine figure, and having a good time.[13] He conformed to the established church, and so far as one can tell gave little sign of a particularly religious disposition.

Around 1581 or 1582, the Earl of Arundel (he inherited the title from his maternal grandfather in 1580) seems to have lost whatever degree of royal favor he had, and he withdrew from court. About the same time, he began to show Catholic sympathies.[14] Sir Francis Walsingham regarded him as "fallen away in religion" by January of 1584, and he probably came under suspicion a good deal earlier; the French ambassador, Mauvissière de Castelnau, later dated his conversion at 1582 or 1583.[15] In late 1583 Arundel came under suspicion for possible involvement in the Throckmorton plot; although nothing could be proved, he suffered several months' imprisonment.[16] In September 1584 he was formally received into the Catholic church.

In April 1585 Arundel, worried by the government's suspicious attitude toward him, attempted to flee the country in secret; he left behind a letter to the queen in which he tried to justify his action. He was apparently betrayed to the government; his ship was captured soon after leaving port, and Arundel was imprisoned in the Tower. In his letter to the queen he repeatedly claims that he has done nothing to offend the queen and says that he is sure that her "gracious disposition" will understand his decision to leave England. He emphasizes that his chief reason for flight is the fact that a Catholic cannot live in England without constant danger to his material and spiritual welfare.[17] But one might expect the crown to be skeptical about the claims of innocent intentions made by a wealthy and prominent recent convert to Catholicism fleeing to the Continent in 1585, and some passages of Arundel's letter made it very easy to believe that his behavior was not caused entirely by his concern for his tender conscience. He denounced his enemies at court, whose malicious poisoning of the queen's mind he held responsible for his loss of favor, and went on to say that he had seen Elizabeth "countenance mine adversaries in mine own sight of purpose to disgrace me" and that because of her "open disgrace" and "bitter speeches," he "was generally accounted, nay . . . I was in manner pointed at, as one whom your majesty did least favour and most dis-grace, and as a person whom you did deeply suspect, and especially mislike."[18]

At his interrogation shortly after his capture, Arundel admitted to having corresponded with William Allen and apparently said that after fleeing overseas he "would have served any place that Doctor Allen had judged fit for him, so it had been for the Catholic cause."[19] He said that this offer of service would not include doing anything against the queen or the state, but again, the queen and her councillors may be excused for their skepticism. Arundel may indeed have been simply a sincere convert to Catholicism, seeking freedom to practice his religion and taking the opportunity to vent his spleen against those who had used him ill. But the government was faced with a wealthy and prominent courtier who had lost out in the scramble for influence at court and who had soon afterward adopted a proscribed religion, railed about the injustice with which the queen and those around her had treated him, and attempted to flee the country with the intention of offering his services to a man whom the government regarded as a notorious traitor. Arundel's conversion to Catholicism must have appeared to the government as merely part of a dangerous pattern of disaffection which had to be dealt with severely.

Indeed, the English government was not alone in its doubts about Arundel's motives and in its suspicion that he was politically dangerous. The French ambassador wrote to Henry III shortly after Arundel's capture that "this young lord the Earl of Arundel took some new discontentment, either from seeing himself very little respected here, or from being in his heart of the Catholic religion."[20] The next year the conspirator Anthony Babington, although he denied any contact with Arundel, said that "he presumed that the Earl of Arundel would have been a fit man to have been sounded in respect of his earnest affection and zeal to the Catholic religion."[21]

In view of all these considerations, it is not surprising that Arundel was brought to trial in the Star Chamber, and sentenced to pay a ten-thousand-pound fine and to be imprisoned during the queen's pleasure. His troubles did not end there. In 1588 he was accused of urging a priest imprisoned with him in the Tower to say a mass for the success of the Spanish Armada. Arundel's denial of these accusations was very likely true; the case against him rested on the testimony of two very frightened fellow prisoners, who said what the government wanted to hear. Nevertheless, he again made it very easy for the government to see him as disaffected. He asserted his loyalty to the queen but refused to answer the question of where his allegiance would lie in the event of a papal invasion of England.[22] And although he denied praying for the success of the Armada, he apparently had prayed for "the Catholic cause."[23] To a Protestant councillor, the distinction may have seemed academic. Arundel's subsequent condemnation for high treason was scarcely a triumph for civil liberties, and the fortitude with which he bore the barbarous cruelty of his imprisonment (in spite of his conviction he was not executed; he died in the Tower in 1595) won him great admiration and has recently resulted in his canonization. But although there is no conclusive evidence that Arundel ever committed any specific act of political disloyalty, his words and actions gave considerable cause for suspicion that his religion was not sufficiently divorced from his politics to make him a reliable subject. His treatment was harsh, and perhaps unmerited, but in the political world of the religious wars, it was probably inevitable.

The career of Anthony Browne, first Viscount Montague, offers a sharp contrast to that of Philip Howard. Born around 1528, Montague was the son of a Henrician courtier and diplomat who, among other achievements, acquired large holdings of monastery lands. Browne himself suffered a brief imprisonment in the Fleet Prison in 1551 for hearing Mass, but he did not suffer severely under Edward VI. Under Mary, he enjoyed quite a distinguished career; created Viscount Montague in 1554, he was steward of Hampton Court and of numerous other lordships and manors, served as ambassador to Rome and Venice in 1555, and as lieutenant general of the English forces in Picardy in 1557. In April 1557 he became a privy councillor, and in March 1558, lord lieutenant of Sussex.[24] Clearly, Montague was a coming man, rapidly working his way to national prominence in the service of the monarchy.

One might have expected the accession of Elizabeth in 1558 to confront Montague with a clear choice between his Catholic convictions and his public career. Whatever results he may have expected, it quickly became obvious that Montague was not about to abandon his beliefs. In 1559 he was the only temporal peer to speak against the Act of Supremacy in the House of Lords,[25] and in 1562 he spoke against the act compelling certain officeholders to swear to the royal supremacy. But Montague's political influence and public career were not ended by his opposition to the crown's religious policy. He served as an ambassador to Spain in 1560 and to Flanders in 1565 and 1566. Between 1569 and 1585 he shared the lord lieutenancy of Sussex with the Protestant Lord Buckhurst, to whom he was allied by friendship and by the marriage of his grandson to Buckhurst's daughter;[26] between them, Buckhurst and Montague seem largely to have dominated county politics. In 1585 Montague was removed from the lieutenancy, but he seems to have retained some influence in Sussex patronage.[27] He was one of the commissioners who tried Mary Queen of Scots in October 1586. According to an account written by Burghley and published under the name of a missionary priest who had recently been executed, Montague appeared before the queen at Tilbury in 1588 at the head of a troop of almost two hundred horsemen, including his sons and grandsons, vowing to hazard all he had in token of his loyalty.[28] It has been remarked that "the story may or may not have been true. Certainly, Burghley knew that it was plausible."[29]

It would probably be inaccurate to say that Montague's Catholicism did not harm his public career. Under Mary he was well on his way to becoming a figure of national prominence, but Elizabeth never allowed him more than the political domination of his own county, and then only in association with a Protestant and only until the outbreak of war with Spain in 1585. Still, his career shows that even open adherence to Catholicism did not necessarily lead to total ruin —indeed, it did not bar some degree of political influence. Apparently, several reasons account for Montague's success. His willingness during part of Elizabeth's reign occasionally to attend Anglican services undoubtedly contributed to the favor with which he was treated.[30] In addition, Montague was not a convert to Catholicism; his offense lay not in abandoning the official religion for a hostile one, but in refusing to abandon a religion that he had always held. But most important, he was never caught in anything politically suspicious. In any case, Elizabeth was apparently convinced, for whatever reason, that Montague's religion did not make him politically untrustworthy.

The loyalty of Montague and his family to the queen brought very obvious benefits to the Catholics around his estates in Sussex. His houses at Cowdray and Battle served as links in the network by which priests moved around the country and as centers of Catholic worship and life, virtually immune from government action. Lady Montague's chaplain, Richard Smith, has left a vivid description of the religious life in the house of Montague's widow shortly after his death:

> She built a chapel in her house . . . and there placed a very fair altar of stone, whereto she made an ascent with steps and enclosed it with rails, and, to have everything conformable, she built a choir for singers and set up a pulpit for the priests, which perhaps is not to be seen in all England besides. Here almost every week was a sermon made, and on solemn feasts the Sacrifice of the Mass was celebrated with singing and musical instruments, and sometimes also with deacon and subdeacon. And such was the concourse and resort of Catholics, that sometimes there were 120 together, and 60 communicants at a time had the benefit of the Blessed Sacrament. And

such was the number of Catholics resident in her house and the multitude and note of such as repaired thither, that even the heretics, to the eternal glory of the name of the Lady Magdalen, gave it the title of Little Rome.[31]

The extraordinary openness of the Catholic life at Lady Montague's seat and its resulting notoriety were apparently typical of the family, whose loyalty guaranteed a great deal of immunity for their coreligionists in the neighborhood.[32] The protection of the family was probably a major reason that Sussex retained one of the largest concentrations of Catholics of any county outside the North of England.

Montague and Arundel are both extreme cases. Probably no other Catholic under Elizabeth did as well as Montague, and few laymen suffered as severely as Arundel. But although the cases are extreme, they do represent tendencies in the crown's treatment of Catholics, and the prominence of the two men must have lent influence to their examples. The Catholic who compared the two men's careers could decide that adopting Montague's attitude was the best way to guarantee his personal safety and interests. But one should be skeptical about explaining the behavior of people who deliberately adhered to a persecuted minority religion completely in terms of self-interest. The Earl of Arundel gave a very edifying example of suffering for the faith, but he was never able to serve as a protector of a Catholic community. It is Arundel, not Montague, whom the Catholic church recognizes as a saint. But it is at least not obvious that Arundel made the greater contribution to the survival of the Catholic church in England.

Montague's situation, however, raised the problem of what moral and intellectual authority could justify his loyalty to both the pope and the ruler of Europe's leading Protestant power. Montague's speech on religious policy in the House of Lords in 1559 is not directed specifically to that question; the point is to persuade his hearers that England should remain Catholic. But the speech helps in understanding the attitude underlying Montague's dual loyalty.

Montague bases his adherence to Catholicism on the central Catholic principle of the authority of a universal church that has continued through the centuries. He believes his teachers ''because they teach me the ancient faith of the Fathers delivered and received from hand to hand by continual succession of all bishops in the church of Christ, and the same wherein all the holy martyrs, patriarchs, confessors lived and died, wherein, what cause have I to doubt, if I do not think that all the world is damned, saving a few that believe and profess this new doctrine." As head of the church, God has appointed "neither emperor, king, or temporal governor," but "certain prophets, certain apostles, certain bishops, certain doctors, unto whom he hath given charge as St. Paul saith to the same: yet was there never prince nor region, that durst in using this, destroy the other neither in refusing the obedience to the pope to take to themselves the supremacy of their own churches."[33]

Montague adds that he feels he must stand up for his faith simply because it is true; if he does not do so God will disown him at the last judgment. But he says that if "religion and the fear of God" had not moved him to speak, he would be "almost as hardly driven by duty to my prince and country." He warns his hearers of the perils that he believes a Protestant England would face from hostility abroad and dissension at home. He is worried not, he asserts, for his own sake, for he will readily spend his life in defending England against any of these perils; but "I fear my prince's sure estate and ruin of my native country: may I then being her true subject see such peril grow to her highness and agree to it?"[34]

Montague believes that he is especially obliged to warn Elizabeth of the dangers of her policy because of his vocation as a nobleman and therefore as a natural counselor to the prince. God, he says, has "placed noblemen to be in dignity before others, but to this end that they should be more careful of the honour and safety of the prince and country, than others, and for any of these to be ready and willing to sacrifice themselves."[35] Montague makes it clear that he is obliged to speak against the Supremacy Bill by his duty as a royal counselor, and this has a very important effect on the tone of his speech. It enables him, in spite of his affirmation of Catholic principles, to appear not as a stern figure pronouncing the judgment of God on his enemies, but as one of a group of colleagues expressing a strong dissent from others on a matter of policy; a matter of great moral importance, to be sure, but one that need not destroy the mutual respect of himself and his opponents or affect the loyalty of any of them to the state that they all serve. Much of what Montague says contributes to this impression; he claims that he speaks with great reluctance, "not willing to impugn the judgment of others which have spoken therein, whom otherwise I honour and love . . . in whom I doubt not either certain wisdom and knowledge, nor zeal to the true Religion of Christ."[36] For a Catholic to express his belief in a

Protestant's "zeal to the true religion of Christ" implies that the difference between them is a difference of judgment between people seeking the same goal, not a deep moral split making further cooperation· on other matters impossible. Montague's disapproval of the queen's policies, one might conclude, does not absolve him of his duty of loyalty and obedience to her.

But although Montague believed that he owed allegiance to his sovereign in spite of religious differences, he also believed that there were limits to the demands that could properly be made on the queen's subjects. In 1562 Montague spoke in the House of Lords against a bill by which a second refusal of the oath recognizing the royal ecclesiastical supremacy was made treason. In this speech, he prudently disclaims any intention of pronouncing on the truth or falsity of the established religion, although his attempt to demonstrate that it was uncertain makes his stance fairly clear.[37] He does claim that the law is unnecessary, since the Catholics are loyal and quiet subjects, and that it is dangerous, since it may drive people to desperation.[38]

But Montague's most eloquent arguments against the bill are based on the belief that it is an unjustified invasion of the rights of conscience. He uses two arguments here. One is that "since the doctrine of Protestants is so uncertain . . . there is no reason nor justice, that doth permit or suffer that men should be forced to take it for certain, true, and sure, and affirm the same." This statement defends freedom of conscience in only a very limited sense. It leaves open the questions of whether there is such a thing as certainty in religious doctrine and whether people could legitimately be coerced into accepting such certainty. But elsewhere Montague defends freedom of conscience in much less equivocal terms; the proposed law, he says, "is repugnant to the law of nature, and all civil laws: the reason is, for that naturally no man can or ought to be constrained to take for certain that that he holdeth to be uncertain: for this repugneth to the natural liberty of man's understanding: for understanding may be persuaded, but not forced."[39]

How strongly Montague would have endorsed this position if a Catholic regime had remained in power is anybody's guess. However, the fact that he set limits on the extent to which the crown could properly invade its subjects' consciences is significant, if only as an indication of the way in which Catholics loyal to the Elizabethan regime were almost bound to resolve the moral dilemma in which they were placed. Loyal as they were, they were bound to insist that the loyalty that could rightly be demanded of them had limits. Their problem consisted largely in trying to convince the government that one could be loyal to the queen while reserving part of one's conscience from her jurisdiction. Montague's speeches in the House of Lords give some idea of the attitudes with which the English Catholic nobility and gentry approached the problem. But he did not really get very far in explicating it. The Catholic gentleman who has left perhaps the best record of his thoughts on the matter, Sir Thomas Tresham, provides a fuller idea of how an English Catholic magnate could define and justify his loyalty to both the crown and the papacy.

Sir Thomas Tresham was one of the most eminent and active of the Catholic gentry whose support was necessary to the survival and success of the Catholic mission.[40] He was the head of one of the wealthier gentry families in Northamptonshire, a family with a history of local prominence and royal service stretching back to the reign of Henry V. Two Treshams had been speakers of the House of Commons in the fifteenth century. Sir Thomas's grandfather, who had been a member of the House of Commons, three times sheriff of the county, and, under Queen Mary, prior of the Order of St. John in England, died in 1559, leaving his fifteen-year-old grandson heir to the family's wealth and position. Tresham's grandfather was a convinced Catholic, but Tresham conformed to the established religion (and served as sheriff of Northamptonshire in 1573–74) until 1580, when he was reconverted to the Roman church, apparently by Robert Parsons.[41] From then until his death in 1605 he was a consistent recusant and shelterer of seminary priests and, in consequence, suffered several imprisonments, heavy fines, and the increasing hostility of many of his neighbors; this last was perhaps intensified by his tendency to go in for rack-renting and enclosure.[42] Tresham was acutely aware of how much his religion had cost him; in his letters and elsewhere he frequently complained of the loss of reputation, status, wealth, and liberty that he had incurred. But in the midst of one such catalog he wrote, "But when I consider from whence this and all these springeth, I am not a little comforted in them. Had I remained a worldling these had not mishapped me."[43] However much suffering the confession of his faith had brought, Tresham apparently had no regrets.

His position as a member of a persecuted minority religion does not seem to have disturbed Tresham's sense of the social position and obligations of a gentleman. His correspondence shows a large sense of the personal loyalty due to both inferiors and superiors, a loyalty by no means limited to his coreligionists. When his brother William, also a Catholic, suddenly left the country without official permission early in 1582, Tresham wrote to William's patron, Sir Christopher Hatton, then the queen's vice-chamberlain and a privy councillor, denouncing his brother's "inconsiderate act, in regard of his own estate and credit; an unthankful office of him towards your honour (his dear, good friend) not to acquaint you therewith . . ." and adding that "an undutiful and most forgetful extraordinary demeanour the same was unto her majesty, our worthy queen and his most gracious mistress . . . to depart her majesty's service upon the sudden, without license first obtained."[44] Tresham's papers contain numerous other letters that presume friendly relations with Protestants.[45] There is even a draft in Tresham's hand of a letter from his wife to the wife of the Puritan earl of Bedford, asking her to secure her husband's assistance in getting Tresham transferred to a more convenient place of house arrest.[46] This letter goes so far as to attempt to arouse the countess's sympathy by reminding her of her family's sufferings during the tribulations that her husband underwent for his religious convictions under Queen Mary. Clearly, Tresham did not think that the religious difference between himself and others of his class should affect the basic amicability of their relationships. If he or the earl of Bedford was in trouble for their religious views, it should be regarded as a regrettable misfortune, but not in itself as a cause for shame or hostility.

There is some indication that Tresham (not surprisingly) strongly resented some of Elizabeth's policies, and a memorandum written under James I hints that her claim to the throne was inferior to that of James's mother.[47] But to whatever extent these private musings represented Tresham's real views, he wrote and acted as if his loyalty to Queen Elizabeth was one of the most important of his obligations. His papers abound with conventional expressions of loyalty and affection for her, and he constantly reiterates his willingness to "serve and defend her with life and goods" with as much zeal as any of his ancestors "did bear to any of her highness' most worthy progenitors, under whom they were dignified with many noble offices and advancements and lived in high prosperity; and at whose feet and in whose service sundry of them (even hundreds of years since) have faithfully ended their lives with honor in the field."[48]

Tresham clearly believed that service to the prince in peace and war was a very important part of his function. In a long letter to the Privy Council he poured out his resentment and shame that he and his fellow Catholic nobles and gentry, "who daily go armed with weapons as a badge of our vocation,"[49] are not allowed to serve in the queen's forces against the Spaniards, whom they are as anxious as anybody to repulse in their attack on "our sovereign queen and famous realm of England." He bemoaned the fact that "yet is there what inexplicably grieveth us, and sinketh us up in sorrow, to think thereon, which is that in valorous repulsing the enemy to their shame and foil, we are culled out and discarded as the world's wonders, unworthy to be partakers of so behoof-ful a service and renowned victory."[50] Tresham was constantly and painfully aware that his Catholicism cut him off from the full exercise of the role which he considered both his duty and his right. Apparently, he devoted a great deal of attention to arguing that this should not be so.

The fullest exposition of his feelings on this point is in a petition that a group of Catholic nobles and gentry, led by Tresham and a few others, apparently drew up in early 1585 to be presented to the queen. The petition has two main objectives: to assure the queen of the Catholics' loyalty, and to ask for a mitigation of persecution. In particular, it requested the rejection of a bill then working its way through Parliament, which defined as treason the presence in England of English Catholic priests ordained since the first year of Elizabeth's reign and made it a felony to give them aid or shelter.[51]

The petition expresses loyalty to the queen primarily in terms of sentimental traditionalism, but it is based on an explicit rejection of several principles often held by (and even more frequently attributed to) the politically aggressive faction of the Catholics. The petitioners' views of conspiracy against Elizabeth are expressed in a violent denunciation of the most recent one, "the late most horrible example of that monster Parry, whose detestable endeavors do give evident testimony that the cruel viper (ever temporizing, and making shipwreck of all faith and religion) hath thereby at length lost both taste and habit of the grace and fear of God. Let such diabolical dissimulation, and traitorous thirst after hallowed blood, sink both him and his confederates according to God's judgments, to their deserved doom of deep damnation." Tresham's ideas on the killing of rulers remained consistent over the years; writing to a fellow Catholic, Lord Henry Howard, in 1603, he expressed his willingness to act if necessary as a public executioner, "which otherwise no worldly gain should hire me unto," if it were necessary in order to prevent conspirators, Catholic or otherwise, from escaping their due reward. But much more basic for the issue facing the English Catholics in 1585 was his view on the right of the church to intervene in the relationship between subjects and rulers. "We for our parts utterly deny that either pope or cardinal hath power or authority to command or license any man to consent to mortal sin, or to commit or intend any other act *Contra Jus Divinum*. Much less can this disloyal, wicked and unnatural purpose by any means be made lawful, to wit, that a native born subject may seek the effusion of the sacred blood of his annointed sovereign. Whosoever be he therefore spiritual or temporal, that maintaineth so apparent sacrilege, we therein do renounce him and his conclusion, as false, devilish, and abominable."[52]

Logically, these three sentences are the base on which Tresham's loyalty, as a Catholic, to a Protestant and excommunicated queen is built. But the small space that he allots here leads one to believe that in Tresham's mind, the chain of thought went the other way: that his rejection of the pope's right to interfere with temporal rulers is the result of his loyalty to the queen, and not vice versa.

This loyalty, as already implied, is predominantly that of a traditionalist gentleman. But loyalty is a religious duty as well. In a letter to the Privy Council, Tresham says that "we [the English Catholics] ever have demeaned ourselves in all actions of civil duty . . . as becometh faithfullest true English subjects . . . not for dread of punishment, but simply for very native and entire Christian affection which we inseparably bear unto her excellency." One of his reasons for wanting to help defend England from foreign enemies is the "desire of a heavenly reward." He appears as confident as any Protestant that God helped defeat the Armada. "The Spanish forces no sooner appeared on our coasts, but by the mighty hand of God were discomfited and marvelously dispersed to the unspeakable joy of the whole realm and principally to us [i.e., Tresham and his fellow Catholic prisoners]."[53]

Tresham's idea that God watches over England and defends her and her rulers (even when Protestant) from enemies (even when Catholic) is perhaps most interestingly expressed in his third-person account of his proclamation of James I at Northampton on the day after Elizabeth's death.[54] Tresham apparently took this step on his own initiative. As a Catholic and an "improving" landlord, he was not overly popular in the Puritan hotbed of Northampton; that and his rather imperious behavior[55] may account to a great extent for the surliness and foot-dragging with which the officials and citizens of Northampton apparently responded to Tresham's loyal speeches of support for the heir apparent and urgings that he be officially proclaimed.

In any case, Tresham after several adventures found himself addressing a roomful of people in the mayor's house, where, after Tresham requested the company to pray for the new king, "one who stood next Sir T. behind him said, 'Let us pray that the king prove sound in religion.'"[56] Tresham considered this "distasteful and untimed" comment unworthy of reply; but when Tresham suggested that "we had very great cause to praise God for it" [James's accession], the same man "again carped out, saying, 'so as the king prove sound in religion.'"

This last comment was too much. Tresham turned upon the offender, saying, "*Quasi diceres* (as though you would say) if the king be not of your religion . . . then you owe him not duty and loyalty." This barb must have given Tresham considerable satisfaction, and he made sure his opponent understood its implications. "For confirmation of that reproof, Sir T. avouched express witnesses forth of the precepts of the apostles that we should give to Caesar what was due to Caesar, and did not only so teach but themselves gave ensamples thereof by their civil obedience to pagan and bloody persecuting emperors, under whom they lived. Therefore, said Sir T., though you differ in religion from the king, yet in so much as he is a professor of the Christian religion, you upon a far stronger argument are bound to obey him as your king in civil loyalty and obedience."[57]

The man admitted that Tresham's arguments had some force, but asked, "What if the pope would excommunicate the king?" Tresham, however, was not to be lured onto that dangerous ground. "Here Sir T. interrupted him and suffered him not to proceed in that objection, and took him by the shoulder and asked him what factious companion he was who first used such dubitative speeches of the king and now would enter into dispute about the pope, when no speech at all was of the pope or tending to the pope." Tresham then "wished the justices of peace to command him to silence, else he would put him to silence and turn him down the stairs. Wherewith he rested without after using any speech to Sir T. or in his hearing whatsoever. He is the preacher of that town. His name is Cattelyne, a factious fellow."[58]

The belief underlying Tresham's conduct during this colorful episode is clear in his first reply to the Protestant preacher. The example and precept of the apostles teach us that we must submit to all rulers. The obligation is especially binding when the ruler is a Christian—as Tresham has no apparent hesitation in labeling the Protestant James. The pope, he implies angrily in his reply to the preacher's question, has nothing to do with it. It is purely a matter for Tresham, his king, and his God.

It may seem strange that a man with Tresham's ideas on the obligation of subject to ruler and on the powers of the pope over rulers suffered so much in imprisonment, fine, and opprobrium for disobedience to his queen. Yet the behavior that brought the queen's displeasure down on him and the justification that he offers for it are not really inconsistent with Tresham's conception of his loyalty to the queen. For the clearest exposition of Tresham's beliefs here, we must return to the petition of early 1585.

Tresham refused to do three things throughout the Catholic part of his life. One, the refusal "to accuse himself or any other Catholic in matters of conscience,"[59] is a necessity for defending the other two, which are explained in the petition. First, he will not attend Anglican services unless it can be proved to "the learned of the Catholic church" that Catholics could do so without mortal sin—a most unlikely possibility in the sixteenth century. This refusal "is not grounded in us upon any contempt of your majesty's laws, or any other willful or traitorous intent, but altogether upon mere conscience and fear to offend God."[60] But although it is the refusal to attend church "which hath devoided us of all your [the queen's] wonted graces and special favors,"[61] it is the second point that calls forth Tresham's most elaborate and eloquent pleadings.

He begins, after a heartrending account of the sufferings to which Catholics are already subject, by begging the queen to "hear the unfolding of one greater and more dangerous calamity hanging over our heads." He is referring to the parliamentary bill defining the presence of Catholic priests in England as treason. Tresham begins his appeal for the rejection of the bill by reminding the queen of

the frailty of man, and how apt and prone we are to all sin and wickedness, for the stay and remedy whereof our Lord and Saviour Jesus Christ hath instituted and left behind him most holy and blessed sacraments for the comfort of mankind, and hath commanded the use of them to be continued, and practiced in his Catholic church as the conduits of his Grace, without which the benefit of his dear passion can not ordinarily descend or be applied to us . . . whereof the ordinary ministers are and always have been Catholic bishops and priests lawfully called and annointed to that charge and spiritual authority, whom by divine ordinance we are bound to hear, receive and obey with due honor and reverence, and to seek unto them . . . for council and help, how to live and die in the love and favor of him who hath power to cast both the body and soul of his enemies into perpetual torment of hell fire.[62]

Given the fact that Catholic priests are the only bearers of the divine grace that is necessary for man's salvation, what, Tresham asks, is a Catholic to do when a priest turns up at his door asking for shelter in return for the exercise of his spiritual functions? The proposed bill puts Catholics in an intolerable dilemma:

If we receive them . . . it shall be deemed treason in us: if we shut our doors, and deny our temporal relief to our Catholic pastors in respect of their function, then are we already judged most damnable traitors to Almighty God, and his holy members, and are most guilty of that curse threatened to light upon such as refuse to comfort and harbor the apostles and disciples of Christ, saying, *And whosoever shall not receive you nor hear your words: Truly it shall be easier for them in the land of Sodom and Gomorrah in the Day of Judgment;* against which irreprovable sentence we may in no wise wrestle.[63]

Although Tresham never says in so many words that he would refuse to imperil his eternal salvation even at the cost of being held a traitor to his queen, his words and subsequent actions indicate quite clearly what he regarded as the right choice. But the passages just quoted also illustrate a theme that reappears every time he touches on the subject—that it is a violation of the proper order, both human and divine, to force him to choose between salvation and loyalty.

It is clear from numerous passages in Tresham's papers that he thinks he has, in some sense, an absolute obligation of loyalty to the queen. The passages just quoted make it equally obvious that he believes he has at least as absolute an obligation of loyalty to his church. But ecclesiastical and civil authority should not come into conflict because although each is absolute within its sphere, the areas in which they ought to exercise their authority do not overlap. The church must explain to its flock their obligation of obedience to their rulers and must not otherwise interfere in civil affairs. Tresham claims that all Catholic priests with whom he is acquainted pray for the queen and urge obedience to her, and he offers to be the first to turn in to the government any priest who does otherwise.[64] Beyond this, the clergy's responsibility is to administer the sacraments and otherwise care for the souls of Catholics. Their absolute authority within this sphere should offer no threat to the state, which has absolute authority in temporal affairs but whose interference with the clergy's efforts to save their subjects' souls is as unjustified as would be the clergy's interference in the temporal realm.

Tresham's attempt strictly to separate religious and temporal concerns was, of course, unacceptable to the English government, which regarded reconciliation to the Roman church as ipso facto evidence of disloyalty. Equally inevitably, it placed him at odds with the more militant of his fellow Catholics, to whom the overthrow of Elizabeth and the reestablishment of Catholicism were the only acceptable program. The sheltering of missionary priests and steadfast refusal to have anything to do with the state church of men like Tresham helped guarantee the survival of Catholicism as a sect in England. But if Tresham's views on the proper attitude of Catholics to the English state were accepted, Catholicism would have very little chance to become more than a sect. The best that Catholics could hope for was, as Tresham requested from the queen, "the calm and safe haven of indemnity of conscience."[65]

How one saw Tresham's position, therefore, depended on one's definition of the goals of English Catholicism. Thomas Hill, a missionary priest in prison awaiting execution, who as a student had been one of the leaders of a student rebellion against the Jesuit management of the English seminary at Rome, wrote to Tresham, "I have an incredible desire to behold the amiable countenances of all our worthy confessant Catholics, and especially of yourself who by the singular grace and assistance of God have opposed yourself in that cause."[66] Henry Tichborne, S.J., a professor at the English seminaries at Seville and Rome and a great admirer of Robert Parsons, took a different view in a letter written in 1598 from Rome to his fellow Jesuit, Thomas Darbyshire, at Pont-a-Mousson in France. Among other things, Tichborne said that liberty of conscience in England would be a moral and practical disaster for English Catholics, and just before closing the letter he warned, "I must advise you that Sir Thomas Tresham as a friend to the state is holden among us for an atheist, and all others of his humor either so or worse."[67]

Montague and Tresham, of course, belonged to that majority of the Catholic landowning classes who remained in England. One might expect the Catholic nobles and gentlemen who fled the country to be friendlier to the politically militant wing of English Catholicism than those who remained behind. Some of the laymen among the Catholic exile community did cut all their ties with the Elizabethan regime and enter wholeheartedly into the efforts of Spain and the Allen-Parsons party to overthrow Elizabeth; Mary Tudor's former privy councillor Sir Francis Englefield was the most prominent of this group. But even among the exiles, there were many who often opposed the plans of the Allen-Parsons party and proclaimed their loyalty to Elizabeth; Thomas Wilson, Elizabeth's representative in the Spanish Netherlands, wrote home in 1575 that a majority of the English Catholic exiles in the Netherlands claimed to be loyal to the queen; and their own letters to the queen and her ministers are full of protestations of loyalty.[68] These "loyalist" exiles undoubtedly included many adventurers and opportunists of various sorts, as well as some outright spies of the English government. But even an exile did not have to be particularly unscrupulous or hypocritical to claim to be loyal to Elizabeth; a host of material and moral considerations could prevent him from wanting to sever all possible ties with the English crown. These considerations may be illustrated by the career of one well-known exile, Sir Thomas Copley.

Copley belonged to a prominent gentry family whose main estates were at Gatton in Surrey and Roughey in Sussex. Born in 1534, he sat for the borough of Gatton, which his family controlled, in every parliament from 1554 to 1563. Under Mary he was apparently a strong Protestant and in 1558 was briefly in trouble for expressing apprehension that Mary might attempt to grant the succession to the throne away from Elizabeth. Around 1562, however, Copley ruined whatever prospects of advancement Elizabeth's reign might have held for him by converting to Catholicism. His fortunes in the 1560s are rather obscure, but he may have spent some time in prison for recusancy, and he seems to have attracted the strong animosity of the powerful Lord Howard of Effingham (father of the Armada hero). For whatever reasons, by 1570 Copley's situation apparently became too much for him, and he fled overseas. He spent the rest of his life in exile (he died in 1584), mostly in the Spanish Netherlands, with interludes in France and possibly in Spain.[69]

From abroad, Copley sent a stream of letters to the queen, Burghley, Walsingham, and other influential people, complaining of the injustice with which he had been treated and seeking redress. He tried to persuade the government not to confiscate his lands and begged to be given some employment in the queen's service, abroad if not at home.[70] Like Tresham, but to a much greater degree, Copley gives the impression of a man cut off from the world of landowner-ship, kinship, and royal favor within which an Elizabethan magnate would expect to prosper. Like Tresham, Copley devoted considerable effort to attempting to persuade the most powerful people in that world to let him play at least part of what he considered his natural role in it.

Copley made it very clear that he would not abandon his Catholic faith in order to regain his natural place in the social order. In terms quite similar to those of other Catholics, he says that although "na-ture and all honest duties" oblige him to love "my country, friends and kinsfolk," yet "I must be content patiently to forbear the comfort of them all, as I am taught by the express words uttered by the mouth of our Saviour himself rather than to forsake him." He emphasizes the traditional authority of the Catholic church, which, he holds, is "a surer pillar indeed to lean unto in those matters, than the divers changeable confused doctrines of contrary teachers, yea, or any act of Parliament which hath not always, nor any long time used to judge and decide causes of faith, or to prescribe ecclesiastical laws."[71]

But Copley's Catholicism did not prevent him from expressing the natural love and loyalty that he owed to his country and his queen. From Rouen he wrote to Sir Francis Walsingham, "I find the saying so true *dulcis odor patriae*, that already me seemeth, the air I shall breathe on the hills near to Rouen, looking towards England, will be sweeter than I can draw from any other part."[72] But his loyalty goes beyond sentimental attachment to a sense of obligation. He repeatedly proclaims his loyalty to Elizabeth and asserts that his troubles come only from his fidelity to his conscience, not from any real fault toward the queen.[73] He claims that his military service for Spain against the rebels in the Netherlands, into which he was com-pelled to enter by his poverty and Elizabeth's refusal to employ him, is compatible with his loyalty to Elizabeth.[74] Indeed, he says, it should be pleasing to her, since it is directed against rebels.[75] He tells Burghley of his refusal to deal with the queen's enemies among the exiles and of the dislike with which many of the exiles consequently regarded him.[76]

But, Copley hints, his loyalty has been ill rewarded. He is forced into the service of a foreign prince only by "the unkindness of my country,"[77] which has cast him abroad and into poverty. He protests at the loss of revenues from his lands, asking whether adherence to "the religion holden and practised by the universal church ever since His ascension . . . is that become of late so heinous a crime, as may admit no favour or remission of rigour?"[78] Although Copley never directly accuses the queen of any offense against him, clearly he thinks that he should not be persecuted for the sake of his religious convictions; like Montague and Tresham, he believes that the religious differences between himself and the queen should not affect the basic working relationship between them.

Copley argues that it is not only right for the queen to employ the services of subjects of different religions; it is in her interests as well. If he were a royal adviser, he says, he would "rather seek to win to my prince's service all the able persons I could, than advise the rejecting of any (whatsoever religion he were of) that should offer his service with such faith as God knoweth I have done."[79] His Catholicism, he claims, might even be an advantage in dealing with Catholic rulers.[80]

Copley's belief that the queen should use the services of all her loyal and able subjects implies, of course, that religion is of little political relevance and therefore none of the state's business. "Other politic and civil nations," he declares, "do find means to accommodate well enough with modest and Christian moderation, to the conservation of public peace, and civil conversation amongst the subjects in amiable and friendly sort, each leaving to other the charge of his own soul, which if any man by wrong believing bring to a wrong place in the world to come, *suo damno*."[81]

Peace, order, and amiable relations among members of the community are much more important than doctrinal unity. Indeed, true religion itself commands charitable relations among those of different beliefs. In appealing for the friendship of that ardent foe of popery, Sir Francis Walsingham, Copley urges, "Let us think as well as we will on the one side or the other of the faith we like best, yet can that be no true or lively faith which is void of charity, for God is charity and whoso dwelleth in charity dwelleth in him, etc."[82]

These remarks clearly separate Copley from the political beliefs of the Allen-Parsons party. But in a letter to Walsingham's wife (who happened to be Copley's cousin) he reveals the theological basis of his views on political and personal relations among those of different churches:

And good madam, let not (I beseech you) a little difference of our opinions in the choice of our several ways to Heaven, be any let to the loving fruits, which the strong bond of nature bindeth us mutually to yield to each other's comfort in whatsoever fortune. I doubt not but Heaven is the place whereto we all tend. We believe in one Creator, in one Redeemer, in one Holy Ghost three persons and one God, which is the principal foundation of the faith whereby we must be saved. What a pity is it then to see such a miserable dissension about particular points of less importance among us that profess all to believe in one Christ and be members of his mystical body.[83]

Copley was not a theologian, although he was apparently interested enough in theology to be converted to Catholicism by the alleged weakness of John Jewel's defense of Anglicanism.[84] But the theological implications of this statement are sweeping enough to destroy the Allen-Parsons program, as well as all the coercive machinery of the sixteenth-century churches. Copley strongly implies that a Protestant can be a member of Christ's "mystical body" and says outright that a Protestant can be saved as well as a Catholic can. The "principal foundation of the faith whereby we must be saved" is simply belief in the Trinity. Copley classifies all the differences between Catholicism and Protestantism, over which thousands of his contemporaries wrote, disputed, killed, and died, as "particular points of less importance." What Protestants and Catholics have in common is more important than their differences, and there is no reason for them not to be friendly with each other and to cooperate as subjects of the same kingdom. If the choice between Catholicism and Protestantism is not the choice between salvation and damnation, then there is little point in anyone's being compelled to accept either, and no point at all in marshaling fleets and armies to establish either in England.

Copley's views of the obligations of the individual in society seem to be a somewhat more systematic version of views that are present in Tresham and (somewhat less clearly) in Montague. Allen and Parsons in effect identified the natural law and the will of God, the ultimate source of human obligation, with the doctrine and discipline of the Catholic church. The church was, therefore, the ultimate judge of the validity of merely human laws and institutions, and the primary criterion for judging such laws and institutions was their value in achieving the goals of the church. The ideas of Tresham, Copley, and Montague (and, probably, of many members of the English Catholic upper classes) were less consistent, more vague, and more complex. Divine and natural law bound one to different authorities in different spheres of life; one had obligations to king, friends, and country that were independent of one's obligations to the church. And since the church was only one of many allegiances, the laws of political and social morality were not entirely derived from its laws. Members of different churches could be bound together by their roles of queen and subject, of cousin and cousin, of fellow members of the House of Lords, and a host of others. The political and social views of Montague, Tresham, and Copley all presume that Catholics and Protestants are bound together by a moral law that (although perhaps they would not have accepted the proposition in this form) is higher than anything peculiar to either Catholicism or Protestantism.

The Catholic laity, at home and abroad, had the strongest apparent reasons to find alternatives to the Allen-Parsons program. But views explicitly or implicitly inimical to the Allen-Parsons program had, by the early 1590s, begun to emerge among some Catholic priests as well. The priests were, of course, more likely to write coherent works of the sort that might be intended for publication; they were thus more systematic than the laymen discussed here, and they developed some issues that the laymen did not. Two of the more interesting clerics who devoted some attention to the subject were Thomas Wright and Robert Southwell.

Thomas Wright was a member of a recusant family in Yorkshire, who went into exile at an early age in 1577 and was educated at Douai and at the English college in Rome.[85] He was one of the first English students to become a Jesuit, but in a variety of academic posts on the Continent he proved a difficult subordinate and was nearly expelled from the society for setting forth some "extravagant propositions."[86] The approximate content of those propositions may be guessed from the fact that in June 1595 Wright, after somehow being released from the Jesuits, returned to England as a secular priest in an attempt to win toleration from the government for English Catholics, a mission that had complex but, on the whole, not very impressive results. Probably shortly before his return, he wrote a short Latin tract entitled "Whether it is right for Catholics in England to use arms and other means, to defend the queen and the realm against the Spaniards,"[87] which sets forth what apparently was the justification of Wright's later career.

The piece claims to be an answer to three objections that the author had heard raised against the rightness of a Catholic's actively siding with Elizabeth against Philip II.[88] The first objection was that since the Spaniards are sent by the pope, anyone who resists them resists the pope and therefore commits the sin of disobedience. Second, the queen has committed many wrongs against Philip and his subjects (he mentions English support of the rebellion in the Netherlands and the far-ranging English activities against Spain at sea), and he is therefore fighting a "just war," which it is sinful to oppose. And third, the king intends to restore Catholicism in England, and Catholics "are bound not to resist him, who endeavors to restore and amplify Catholic faith."[89]

Wright's reply to these objections is in some respects similar to Tresham's justification for his loyalty to the queen, although Wright expresses himself far less emotionally. He claims that the queen has ample just cause for her war with Spain, alleging a string of Spanish provocations ranging from interference with English commerce and instigation of conspiracies to murder or kidnap Elizabeth to support of rebels in Ireland and attempts to invade England.[90] He casts doubt on the lawfulness of Philip's war against the Netherlands rebels, thereby implying the rightness of English aid to the rebels.[91] But his most important argument is that in all doubtful cases the subject "may with a safe conscience fight for the prince."[92] Wright absolves the subject of any moral responsibility for national policy by pinning it on the ruler. "Nor is he [the subject] bound or is able to examine the causes of wars. . . . For it is known that a prince, being set in a watch tower, seeth very many things which are secret from subjects, who dwell in the valleys."[93] Later, he quotes Augustine to the effect that "perhaps, when the unrighteousness of governing will make the king guilty, the order of serving will render the soldiers innocent."[94] The tone is very different from Tresham's, but the effect, the obligation of the subject to obey the ruler, is the same. If differences in religion between subject and ruler impose any limits on the obedience that the subject owes, Wright does not mention them.

The limits on the subject's obligation of obedience to the temporal ruler are more clearly spelled out in Wright's discussion of the other side of the same question, namely the authority of the pope over temporal rulers. The question first comes up in a discussion of the Spanish possession of the West Indies, which Wright claims the Spaniards hold illegally. After discussing several other possible religious justifications for the Spanish conquest of the West Indies, he asks, "Perhaps did the pope give him dominion, or [sic] the Indian?"

and answers, "But by the common doctrine of Catholics, neither can he grant it, nor can it be proved that he hath ever granted it anywhere." Wright does not immediately draw any general conclusions from this somewhat overstated generalization. But when the reader looks back a few sentences and sees that "it was not lawful for Catholics to deprive of his kingdom a lawful lord, though an infidel, for the sake of religion,"[95] it would not be surprising if he drew the conclusion that Wright had his doubts about Pius V's supposed deposition of Elizabeth.

The limits of the pope's authority are laid down somewhat more precisely later in the tract. Wright asserts flatly that "the pope may err in sending the Spaniards into England. It is proved . . . from the common doctrine of Catholics, that the pope may err in all those degrees which do not belong to faith and the measures of the universal church. But the sending of the Spaniards into England doth not belong to measures, nor to the faith of the universal church." This theoretical statement is all that Wright really needs to effect the same separation of the spiritual and temporal realms in which Sir Thomas Tresham believed. However, he makes the case even more clear by pointing out the disaster that would befall English Catholics if they took the pope's command seriously. "For all the Protestants will esteem them as betrayers of their country, and to proceed against them. Wherefore if they understand this before the fights, undoubtedly they will destroy all. If the Spaniard doth not obtain the victory, who doth not see how hateful the name of Catholic will be throughout all England?" The pope could not have intended these disasters, Wright thinks, "for we know he ought to carry the bowels of a father, a pastor, Christ's vicar; not to expose his son, his ships, his subjects, to so many and so great dangers."[96]

These passages effectively eliminate the need for English Catholics to pay any attention to papal pronouncements on political affairs. If such pronouncements adversely affect the situation of English Catholics, they cannot be truly intended by the pope and are based on false information. But the core of Wright's position is the limitation of the pope to dealing with the "faith and measures of the universal church." Wright never defines precisely what he means here, but he apparently does not include the right to depose temporal rulers. When a controversialist stresses the pope's role as "a father, a pastor, Christ's vicar," one may guess he is about to try to reduce the pope's power in political affairs.[97]

But Wright does not limit himself to theoretical discussion about which side in the Anglo-Spanish conflict is fighting a just war and what are the powers of the papacy toward secular rulers. In some ways the most acute part of his tract is his analysis of the actual motives of Spanish policy and of the likely effects of a Spanish conquest of England on the balance of power in Europe (he does not, of course, use the phrase), on the position of the church, and on the position of English Catholics.

The English Catholics should not, Wright warns, believe the claim of the Spaniards that they are fighting for the restoration of Catholicism in England. On the contrary, they are fighting "either upon the account of revenge, or for extending his [the king of Spain's] empire." If Philip II really had been concerned with religion, he would have intervened early in Elizabeth's reign, before Protestantism had taken root. He would certainly have heeded the pleas for help of the leaders of the Northern Rising of 1569. In fact, Wright claims, Philip "did not so much as think of restoring the ancient religion until the English had laid the axe to the root, and had wounded him to the quick by setting upon the Indian fleet. . . . You will say, he was not then ready [at the time of the Northern Rising]. But you had better have said, he would not be ready. For to defend his money he could presently be ready; but to defend religion he could not be ready."[98]

Wright supports his view of the selfish and worldly motivation of the Spanish war effort by claiming that their conquest of the West Indies was motivated by lust for power and by claiming (inaccurately) that Philip showed no concern for the religious profession of his Netherlandish subjects "so they refused not to be subject to him."[99]

It is naturally not surprising that Wright does not relish the prospect of any increase in the power of such a country. But his analysis of the effect on the European political situation of a Spanish conquest of England does not depend on a belief in any peculiar Spanish moral depravity. With appropriate changes of detail, the picture could have been painted by an opponent of any attempt at a European hegemony. "It is against policy, and the quiet of all Christian princes, to permit the Spaniard to invade England. . . . For if he subject England to his yoke, who seeth not that France, Scotland, Denmark, and other adjacent jurisdictions, are placed in extreme danger? . . . He will girt in France round about. His forces will be invincible by land and sea. . . . If so great forces be present with the Spaniard, who will dare so much as to whisper against him?

Wherefore to no Christian prince will there be any security, any tranquillity. All kingdoms, states, commonwealths, shall obey the will of the Spaniard."[100]

Philip II may have expected good Catholics to welcome his political domination of Europe as the only way of restoring the religious domination of the Catholic church. Probably Wright and the numerous Catholics all over Europe who opposed the Spanish drive for political supremacy would have continued their opposition even if they had believed that the supremacy of Spain was necessary to restore that of the church. But Wright points out that Spanish domination of Europe could be disastrous for the church; "for if the Spaniard so widely diffuse, if he obey not the church; if he become a heretic, if he rise up against the church and its dominions, if he favor the Moors, who may defend the church?"[101] This possibility is far from merely theoretical, Wright believes; he thinks that the Spaniards are prone to Mahometism, and even if the present ruler is orthodox, one never knows what his successors will do. Even now, he claims, the Spaniards make a habit of ignoring any papal commands that they find objectionable.[102]

Wright's views of the effect on Europe and the church of a successful Spanish crusade against heresy are not unusual; many other Catholics, including some popes, held similar views. But Wright also discusses the effects that support for Spain would have on the position of English Catholics and concludes that they would be getting a bad bargain no matter who won the war. If the Spaniards were victorious, English Catholics would gain no benefit from their religion:

I have heard myself from very many Dutch Catholics, that after the city was taken, all men were punished who appeared for three days in the city of Antwerp, no account at all being had of Catholics. For they know there are many, who, to defend their lives and fortunes, assume a shape of what religion you will. . . . I have understood from a certain person worthy of credit, who himself heard the duke of Medina Sidonia, general of the whole Spanish fleet, in anno 88, say that he thought no English man a Catholic, but esteemed them all for Lutherans; and so he would indifferently handle all.[103]

Since Wright believes that the Spaniards are not fighting for the restoration of Catholicism anyway, he naturally would not expect them to try very hard to make religious distinctions among those whom they conquer. But Wright embellishes the picture by pointing out what he considers some defects in the Spanish character. The Spaniards are a naturally cruel and bloodthirsty race, and they will be further maddened by the slaughter of their comrades that will inevitably accompany their conquest of England. This anger will add zest to their murderous assault on Englishmen of all religions. Furthermore, the Spaniards are possessed by "intolerable lust and heat towards women,"[104] and the fact that a woman or her husband, father, or brother acknowledges the pope does not make a great deal of difference.

But if Catholic support of Spain is not likely to spare them from the orgy of violence and lechery that Wright believes would follow a Spanish victory, it is likely to have equally disastrous consequences if the Spaniards are defeated, for "who doth not see how hateful the name of Catholic will be throughout all England? Who will not esteem him for the pest of his country, enemy of the commonweal, a domestic enemy, a betrayer of his own countrymen?"[105] The safest course for the English Catholics, Wright believes, is to help avoid both the obloquy of their Protestant countrymen and the disaster of conquest by the power-hungry, greedy, bloodthirsty, and lecherous Spaniards by taking up arms in defense of the country.[106]

Wright attempts to support this belief further by showing "other ways of bringing in the Catholic faith into England than by the Spaniards."[107] When Elizabeth, to whom he attributes many natural virtues, sees evidence that the Catholics are loyal subjects, she may be willing to grant them liberty of conscience. If not, Wright claims, with a perhaps understandable lack of concrete example, whoever succeeds the queen either will be a Catholic or will be dependent on the Catholics to obtain the crown; in either case he will be obliged to tolerate Catholicism.[108]

It is difficult to determine what Wright sees as the final goal of his program. He appears to have hopes that a Catholic successor to Elizabeth will some day reestablish Catholicism, but he does not appear very confident that this is likely to happen in the immediate future. All of his immediate advice is directed to the securing of toleration, but Wright never says whether the status of a tolerated minority for Catholics would be acceptable as a permanent condition.

This omission is not, however, the most significant point of Wright's tract. In the situation in which he was writing, it is much more important that he rejects the means that the Allen-Parsons party saw as essential to the restoration of a satisfactory situation in England. The English Catholics, Wright thinks, can only be hurt by the intervention of a power-hungry Spain and a pope who does not understand their situation and whose proper role is that of a pastor of souls. They must try to improve their position by operating within the context of English politics and national life, as loyal members of an officially Protestant community. Wright perhaps had an exaggerated idea of the strength of Catholicism in England; he had been out of the country for seventeen years and came from the north of England where Catholicism was relatively strong. To one who knew the situation in England, and perhaps to Wright himself, the acceptance of his methods by English Catholics led, as surely as did the ideas of Sir Thomas Tresham, to acquiescence in permanent minority status for the foreseeable future.

Because of his standing as a poet and martyr, Robert Southwell is the best known of the men discussed in this chapter. Born in 1561, he was the third son of a Norfolk gentleman who, until he openly declared his Catholicism late in life, apparently concealed Catholic sympathies under outward conformity to the Anglican church. His son, sent abroad at the age of fourteen and educated at Douai, Paris, and Rome, showed no such hesitation. An ardent Catholic from an early age, he was admitted to the Jesuit novitiate in 1578 and to full membership in the society in 1580. He was ordained in 1584 and in 1586 sent on the English mission. He exercised his ministry, mostly in and around London, until his capture in 1592 and was imprisoned for almost three years before his execution in 1595. During the early part of his imprisonment Southwell suffered days of horrifying torture at the hands of the notorious Richard Topcliffe, apparently without confessing anything but the fact of his priesthood (which he willingly admitted) and without giving any information that could be used against his fellow Catholics.

Southwell's literary achievements, devotion to the church, saintly life, and unflinching courage in the face of torture and martyrdom have made him one of the leading heroes of the English mission. He was also a friend and admirer of Allen and Parsons and an enthusiastically loyal member of the order that was soon to be identified by Protestants and many Catholics as the main instigator and agent of the politically aggressive Catholics. It may seem odd to include such a man among the precursors of opposition to the program that became widely identified with Allen, Parsons, and the Jesuits. Southwell himself would have been horrified if he had thought that any of his actions would contribute to division among Catholics. Yet the most "political" of Southwell's works does undercut the Allen-Parsons political program—an undercutting that is not as thorough or explicit as those of Tresham and Wright, but perhaps all the more significant for playing little or no role in the author's intentions.

In the fall of 1591, a particularly violent and abusive royal proclamation was issued establishing commissions against seminary priests and Jesuits.[109] It drew several replies from Catholics overseas[110] and one, *An Humble Supplication to Her Majesty*, from Southwell, then serving as chaplain in the household of the countess of Arundel, whose husband was in prison. Southwell did not publish the work, possibly because he was arrested soon after its completion, and it apparently circulated in manuscript for several years. It was first printed in 1600 (with the false date 1595 on the title page) by a press of the Appellant party operating with the connivance of Richard Bancroft, then bishop of London and supervisor of the government's dealings with Catholics. The point of tolerating the Catholic press was to embarrass the Jesuits and the pro-Spanish party, but in this case Bancroft got more than he wanted. The *Humble Supplication* contains numerous passages on the injustice of the government's treatment of Catholics, including a detailed account of how Southwell believed Sir Francis Walsingham had fabricated the Babington plot.[111] The government suppressed the book insofar as possible and executed some of those involved in its distribution. Except for a brief appearance at a debate between the Appellants and their opponents at Rome in 1602,[112] the work seems thereafter to have dropped from view—perhaps because its argument did not completely serve the interests of any of the parties that might have used it.

For several reasons, the *Humble Supplication* could not serve the interests of the English government or of any Catholic who wanted to arrive at an accommodation with the government. Most vitally, Southwell repeatedly emphasizes that the persecution of Catholics in England was religious in inspiration and that the martyrs of the cause were, with very few exceptions, not guilty of treason.[113] Not only is the persecution religiously inspired, but it is directed against the one true church, outside of which there is no salvation[114]—the church in which all the English saints, all of the queen's predecessors, and all previous generations of Englishmen have lived and died. In a passage of great rhetorical power, Southwell asks the queen to imagine the astonishment of all past Englishmen at the general resurrection to find their deeds of piety and charity and their submission to the chief pastor of the church taken for treason.[115] Southwell sees no excuse for the persecution of Catholics and avoids blaming the queen for it only by the common method of assuming that any royal policy of which he disapproved was the responsibility of wicked subordinates who deceived and misled the ruler.

Southwell's defense of the Catholics as victims of religious persecution is not much different from something that might have been written by Allen or Parsons. Southwell, however, seems to have believed that all activities of the English Catholics both were and should be consistent with the apoliticism that was the official stance of the mission.

Southwell's statements on the principles that should govern the conduct of Catholics toward Elizabeth are very carefully phrased; he never makes explicit rejections of papal authority over the temporal affairs of princes such as Tresham and Wright make. He does, however, stress that "our religion, . . . more than any other, tieth us to a most exact submission to your temporal authority, and to all points of allegiance, that either now in Catholic countries, or ever before in Catholic times were acknowledged to be due to any Christian prince." The advantages of Catholicism as a "civic religion" are even more heavily stressed shortly afterward:

It is a point of the Catholic faith (defended by us against sectaries of these days) like subjects are bound in conscience under pain of forfeiting their right, in Heaven, and in incurring the guilt of eternal torments, to obey the just laws of their princes, which both Protestants and Puritans deny, with their father and master Calvin. And therefore if we were not pressed to that, which by general verdict of allegiance, was judged breach of the law of God: we should never give your majesty the least cause of displeasure, for (excepting these points which if unpartial audience were allowed, we could prove to employ the endless misery & damnation of souls,) in all other civil and temporal respects, we are so submitted and pliable, as any of your majesty's best beloved subjects.[116]

Later, Southwell deals with the answer to the "bloody question" of which side he believes a Catholic ought to take in the event of a papal invasion of England. Southwell says that if any Catholic has said he will side with the pope, he must have answered out of pious ignorance, or, more likely, he answered as he did because under torture men can frequently be made to say anything that the torturer wants to hear.[117] Southwell deals with the rights of the matter briefly. "What army soever should come against you [the queen], we will rather yield our breasts to be broached by our enemies' swords, than use our swords to the effusion of our country [sic] blood."[118]

Southwell does not commit himself actively to oppose a papally approved invasion, but he definitely binds himself (and, he hopes, other Catholics) not to support it.

On principle, then, Southwell holds that Catholics owe the queen obedience in all that does not threaten their salvation and that they are never justified in active resistance to her. But he spends much more time on the actual behavior of the Catholics, attempting to prove that in fact Catholics are more faithful subjects than Protestants. His arguments in proof of this thesis are numerous; he mentions the willing contributions of even oppressed Catholics to the defense of the realm, the Catholic clergy's urging the laity to submit to authority, the missionaries' lack of the political and military training that would be essential to what the government considers their function, and much else.[119] Perhaps most interesting, however, is Southwell's defense of Allen and Parsons, who had been charged in the royal proclamation with trying to persuade Spain and the pope to attempt another landing in England.

Southwell replies to this accusation against Allen and Parsons with a general defense of their honorable birth and character and alleges that their "seditious" behavior is religiously motivated and has purely religious goals:

What cause have they given to this slanderer, unless it be counted sedition to gather the ruins of God's afflicted church, and to have provided sanctuaries, for persecuted and succorless souls: which forced at home, either to live with a gored conscience, or to lie open to continual vexations, rather choose to leave their country than the Catholic religion. . . . Nothing in those seminaries, is either intended, or practiced, but the relief and good education of such forsaken men, as from the storm of our English shore, fly thither for a calm road, that perfected in the course of learning & virtue, they may return to offer their blood for the recovery of souls.[120]

The only activities of Allen and Parsons dealt with here are education and charity; their political activities are ignored. Much later, Southwell pours scorn on the charge that Allen and Parsons had tried to incite the pope and Spain to invade England by promising English support.[121] The defense is based on the assumption that Allen and Parsons are too well informed and intelligent to give advice that ignores the political helplessness of the English Catholics. Southwell then defends the loyalty at least of Parsons with a not particularly relevant description of his services in mitigating the harshness with which prisoners of war and other Englishmen in Spain were treated.[122]

He and Allen would also, Southwell thinks, mitigate the fury of the Spaniards should they ever succeed in conquering England. But as for any involvement in basic Spanish policy, "it rests not in a private man's power, to stay the endeavors of so mighty a Prince, in so general, and important an enterprise, as is war with England."[123]

Southwell's account of the careers of Allen and Parsons is, of course, highly distorted; if they had little influence on the policy of the Catholic powers, it was not for lack of trying. But the direction in which Southwell distorts his account of their activities (whether consciously or not) is quite significant. He does not bother trying to convince anyone that they have a moral obligation not to engage in political activity hostile to the queen, perhaps because he was aware that they had engaged in such activities. Instead he implicitly argues what is probably the best line to take with a Protestant: that the significant activities of Allen and Parsons were educational and charitable and that their political activities, if any, were bound to be ineffective and could safely be ignored. They were doomed to political ineffectiveness because it was now clear that their main political stock in trade, the threat of a Catholic insurrection in England in support of a foreign Catholic invasion, was a possibility so remote it could be discounted.

This remoteness was largely because of the loyalty of English Catholics to the crown, which was demonstrated during the Armada crisis[124] and of which Southwell approves. But in demonstrating the impossibility of a Catholic rebellion Southwell stresses Catholic weakness as much as Catholic loyalty. "Can any imagine us to be so simple, that we cannot see how impossible it is for Catholics to do the king [of Spain] any good, though they were as much bent that way as their accusers would have it thought: do we not see that they are scattered one among thousands, and all such accurants [sic, perhaps for "occurants," occurrences] so well watched, and so ill provided: that to wish them to stir in the king's behalf, were to train them to their undoing?"[125] Much later in the work, Southwell lists the Spanish grievances against England and points out that Philip II has much better reasons to attack England "than the slender hope of a few beggarly Catholics, or the faint persuasion of two banished men."[126] He even points out how foolish (as well as immoral) it would be for Catholics to murder Elizabeth, since in the ensuing chaos they would likely be the chief victims of popular fury.[127]

It is possible that Southwell's admission of the weakness of the

English Catholics is the most important point at which he parts company with the political views of the Allen-Parsons party. The politically militant wing of the English Catholics wrote and acted on the assumption that the nation remained largely Catholic in sympathy. Dissent from this assumption meant acceptance of the view that the English Catholics could play no significant role in politics and therefore posed no threat to the interests of the Protestant majority. If the situation was as Southwell describes it, then the best that the English Catholics could hope for, for the good of their souls as well as of their material interests, would be better treatment by a government that realized that they posed no threat. This is what Southwell asks of the queen. It is perhaps because of Catholic weakness that he is so indefinite on the rights and wrongs of the Anglo-Spanish war and of the papal deposing power; since he and his fellow Catholics can do so little about these issues, it is not necessary for them to decide them. Whatever the rights and wrongs of the situation, English Catholics are a powerless, unpopular minority and will have to accept the fact that they can do little to change the situation.

The men discussed in this chapter were not members of any common movement. Their reactions to the situations in which they found themselves, however, may help to explain the political inertia of most of English Catholicism. Substantial material and psychological considerations drove many, perhaps most, Catholics to accept the legitimacy of the Elizabethan monarchy, while denying its right to dictate to their consciences on religious matters. The ideas typified by the men discussed here were most important for what they led men not to do; they helped insure that the English Catholic fifth column, which many Catholics hoped for and many Protestants feared, would never materialize. But soon after the death of William Allen in 1594, tendencies began to emerge among the English clergy that eventually led to the development of a movement that was primarily clerical, with a program that had much in common with the views of "gentry" Catholicism. The early stages of that movement are discussed next.

# CHAPTER IV

# Background: The Jesuits and England to 1594

The Society of Jesus in the first years after its foundation in 1541 had no connection with religious developments in England. The English-men who joined the society before 1558 could almost certainly be counted on the fingers of one hand, and the Jesuits played no role at all in the England of Mary Tudor. It was only after Elizabeth's acces-sion, with the arrival on the Continent of substantial numbers of Catholic exiles, that significant numbers of Englishmen began to enter the society. The recruits were largely university men, some of whom had left England upon the change to Protestantism and some of whom had abandoned careers in England and gone abroad upon conversion to Catholicism after a period of conformity to the Anglican church. By the late 1570s, there were probably several dozen English Jesuits. Their nationality, however, seems to have had little to do with the duties to which they were assigned. Most of them taught a variety of subjects in universities scattered all over Catholic Europe.[1]

For the first decade or so of Elizabeth's reign, the primarily aca-demic concerns of the English Jesuits did not set them off very much from their fellow exiles. After the missionary priests began to enter England in 1574, however, the situation changed. William Allen began to exert pressure for Jesuits to join the mission, and some sources indicate that some English Jesuits were anxious to do so.[2] In 1579 Pope Gregory XIII, at the request of the large majority of the scholars, put the English seminary at Rome under the control of the Jesuits. William Allen visited Rome soon afterward and took the opportunity to lobby for the participation of Jesuits on the mission for which they had undertaken to train the students of the seminary at Rome.[3] The general of the society, Allen's old friend Everard Mercurian, was reluctant to agree to Allen's urgings; he pointed out the dangers to the religious life that would be posed by conditions in England, and in words that appear prophetic, he pointed out the dangers of dissension between secular priests and members of a religious order in a country that lacked episcopal jurisdiction.[4] But Allen's insistence prevailed, and in 1580 the Jesuit priests Robert Parsons and Edmund Campion and the lay brother Ralph Emerson were sent to England.

The story of Campion and Parsons's mission in England in 1580–81 is one of the best-known episodes in the history of the English mission, and it caused a considerable sensation at the time.[5] The English government showed extraordinary concern in attempting to capture the two priests (especially Campion, who became particularly notorious soon after landing when his statement of his purpose in England, which became known as "Campion's Brag," became public) and in harassing those suspected of sheltering them. The mission helped to cause the introduction in the Parliament of 1581 of anti-Catholic laws of unprecedented severity. The mission appears also to have aroused a great deal of public interest; Campion reported that rumors of his capture preceded him everywhere he went.[6] And as Campion's mission caused exceptional excitement in England, his capture, trial, and execution on a trumped-up charge of treason (he was tried not under any of the anti-Catholic laws, but under the treason statute of 1352) received much attention from his fellow Catholics. Campion and the two companions who were executed with him were not the first priests executed in England, but their deaths were the first to be widely celebrated, and the accounts of their deaths provided the foundations and set the tone for the prolific tradition of Elizabethan Catholic martyrology.[7]

Edmund Campion's emergence as the English Jesuits' prototypical martyr is matched in importance by the emergence of his companion on the mission as their greatest agitator and organizer. Parsons left England in August 1581, a few months before Campion's execution. He rapidly became one of William Allen's most trusted confidants and cooperated with him both in the affairs of the English Catholic community and in the political and military plans that culminated in the Armada campaign of 1588. Parsons also was the guiding spirit in the foundation of the new seminaries in Spain, as well as the

English Catholic secondary school at Saint Omer in the Spanish Netherlands.[8] The Jesuits had been in charge of the English seminary at Rome since 1579; by the mid-1590s they controlled every English Catholic educational institution on the Continent except Douai, and after 1593 they exercised great influence even there.[9]

The heavy involvement of the Jesuits in the most important institutions of the exile community was to have important consequences for the Jesuits and for the mission as a whole. Even more important was the involvement of Parsons and his fellow Jesuits in the attack on England. Parsons and his order would eventually become, in the eyes of their fellow Catholics, the symbols of the politically militant wing of English Catholicism, its alliance with Spain, and its advocacy of military force against Elizabeth—a development that had disastrous effects ón the unity of the Catholic community.

The significance of the Jesuit mission within England is naturally much more difficult to assess. There were never very many Jesuits in England under Elizabeth; during the 1580s often fewer than five Jesuits at a time were at large in England. A list of 1593 records eight Jesuits in the country, three of whom were in prison; in 1598 there were fourteen Jesuit priests at large in England, in addition to two priests and two lay brothers in prison.[10] In comparison, secular priests in England in the 1590s numbered in the hundreds.

Several factors, however, brought the Jesuits much greater prominence and importance than their numbers alone would have warranted. The tight but flexible organization of the society could be adapted to the conditions of the English mission with relative ease; in this respect the Jesuits were far ahead of the secular priests, who had no superior within England and whose international connections were not as extensive or reliable as those of the Jesuits. Under the regime of Henry Garnet, Jesuit superior in England from 1586 to 1605, many secular priests appear to have functioned in effect as part of a Jesuit-run network.[11] But the Jesuits' reputation may have been as important as their organization, since they were regarded by many Catholics as especially virtuous and able priests. The Jesuit John Gerard tells the story of William Wiseman who, after being converted from an indifferent to a committed Catholic by his experience of the Spiritual Exercises, always insisted on having a Jesuit as spiritual director of himself and his household.[12] Some families established long-standing relationships with the Jesuits—including families of such prominence as that of Philip Howard, earl of Arundel, and William Lord Vaux.[13] The Jesuits' standing was not due entirely to the general reputation of their society; much of it was earned by the Jesuit missioners in England, who included many of the mission's most striking and impressive figures. It is not surprising that those who knew Campion, Gerard, Southwell, or Henry Garnet should have thought well of the society to which they belonged. Even Jesuits who attracted wide dislike (most obviously Parsons) were often men of great gifts.

But one could not expect the presence of such a prestigious, comparatively well-organized, elite (at least in many eyes) group of missionaries in England not to cause some trouble. Gerard records that William Wiseman's attachment to the Jesuits was at first resented by his chaplain, "one of those old priests [i.e., one ordained under Mary] who were always at odds with the young men, especially the Jesuits whom they looked on as meddlesome innovators."[14] The old priest was not alone in his feelings; some Catholics felt that the Jesuits' presence in England would simply disturb the status quo for no good reason. There were complaints about the increased persecution allegedly provoked by the presence of the Jesuits.[15] The Jesuit Jasper Heywood had to be recalled from England because of resentment over his efforts to bring into the country changes in the rules on fasting that had been introduced on the Continent.[16] Although the positions espoused by the Jesuits usually seemed to increase the demands on English Catholics, this was not always the case; the rules on fasting that Heywood wished to introduce were actually less severe than those previously in force in England. Apparently, actions perceived as illegitimate innovations were more likely to arouse resentment than was simple rigor.

Jealousy between Jesuits and secular priests may have continued through the 1580s and early 1590s; in March 1594 Allen wrote to John Mush, a leader of the secular priests in the North of England, urging him to help pacify dissensions between secular priests and Jesuits.[17] Allen does not mention what, if anything, was the focus of the dissension and gives little idea how serious it was. The Jesuits as such were not yet widely identified as the main supporters of the Allen-Parsons party's political plans. Active opposition to those plans among the exiles was sporadic and ineffective, confined largely to gentlemen whose conduct was recklessly opportunist and often motivated by little more than resentment at the dependence of the movement on

Spaniards and lowborn clerics. But within months of Allen's death in October 1594, the Jesuits were to become involved in two spectacular episodes that drew wide public attention and that contributed to the rapid polarization of the English Catholic community, over issues both political and nonpolitical.

# CHAPTER V

# The Wisbech Stirs

The town of Wisbech, in Cambridgeshire, contained a dilapidated old castle belonging to the bishop of Ely. In 1579, during an invasion scare, the government began to use the castle for the confinement of prominent Catholics, a practice that continued after the scare ended. At first, both laymen and clerics were imprisoned at Wisbech, but as time went on the prison population became almost entirely clerical. By 1595 there was only one layman among over thirty priests in the castle.[1]

Life at Wisbech in the early days did not always go smoothly. In 1587 quarrels between the prisoners and their keeper, a strong Puritan, reached such a pitch that several justices of the peace were called in to investigate. They found that Nicholas Scrope, a gentleman prisoner, had, among other things, refused to obey the keeper's orders, insulted the keeper and threatened him with violence, and tried to climb the castle wall with a ladder in order to raise the town against him.[2] This rowdy behavior was aided and abetted by some priests, who added to the confusion by such tricks as disturbing the keeper's family prayers by loud whistles and bouncing on the floorboards over the family's head. These events, however, can have had little connection with the quarrels that disturbed the prisoners after 1595. All of those involved in the early disorders except the priest George Potter were soon transferred away from Wisbech, and only one or two prisoners who were at Wisbech in 1587 were still there upon the outbreak of the later disorders in 1595.

The disorders of 1587 may, however, have helped bring about the strict regime that the Jesuit William Weston found in force when he arrived as a prisoner at Wisbech in 1588.[3] Prisoners were apparently confined to their own rooms except at meals, which they ate together in the keeper's presence, and were subject to many other regulations and petty annoyances. Early in 1592, however, the regulations were greatly eased, possibly as a result of the arrival of a new keeper, William Medeley. Prisoners were allowed to move about the castle and its grounds and to meet and converse without the presence of any of the prison authorities. The prisoners took advantage of this comparative leniency to arrange a program of sermons, disputations, and lectures. They also began to establish relations with people outside the prison. They became well known in the town and began to receive a stream of messages and visitors. Many of their correspondents and visitors were Catholics or people inclined to Catholicism; to these persons the prisoners offered instruction, counsel, and the use of the sacraments. They were reported to receive large donations of money and to win popularity by entertainment of the local people and by generous distribution of alms to the poor at the castle gate.[4] Several years later, in 1599, the government discovered that several of those who passed as servants of the priests were in fact the sons of gentlemen (the ages of those examined ranged from ten to seventeen) sent to receive instruction in Catholicism.[5]

Some Protestants, naturally enough, thought it very foolish to allow this sort of activity to go on; one hostile critic said that Wisbech was "as dangerous as a seminary college, being in the heart and midst of England."[6] Among Catholics, Wisbech in the early 1590s seems to have acquired a widespread reputation for learning and sanctity. Henry Garnet, then Jesuit superior in England, after a visit to Wisbech in 1593, described it as "a college of venerable confessors of the faith."[7] Anthony Page, a seminary priest captured near York in February 1593 and later executed, is reported to have consented to dispute publicly with Protestant ministers only "if the Fathers at Wisbech should think it convenient."[8] Even in 1599, after Wisbech's reputation had been damaged by the dissensions among the prisoners, Catholic prisoners in York Castle, resisting efforts to force them to listen to Protestant sermons, demanded that Catholic preachers from Wisbech be brought to dispute with the preachers of the established church.[9]

It is, of course, a good question how such a community was suddenly torn by severe dissension. Part of the answer may lie in the atmosphere that one might expect to result from throwing together in conditions of forced intimacy over a period of several years (almost all of the prisoners present in 1595 had arrived at Wisbech between 1588 and 1590) a group of men whose vocation would tend to attract strong personalities who had very definite ideas on how an ecclesiastical life should be lived. Richard Dudley, a priest who worked hard attempting to calm the stirs, wrote to the prisoner Christopher Bagshaw during a lull in the quarrels that "the straitness of a prison, joined with long continuance, doth make the best natural [sic] somewhat froward, and that which at first seemed but a prison, doth in time seem as it were a little world."[10] Under such conditions petty differences could quickly develop into major battles over principle. Before the development of the stirs is traced, the two protagonists whose views and personalities did a great deal to polarize the prisoners into two hostile camps must be introduced.

William Weston, frequently known by the alias of Edmunds, was born at Maidstone in Kent in 1550. Nothing is known of his family. He attended Oxford in the late 1560s; he may have been the William Weston who received his B.A. from Christ Church in 1569. By the early 1570s he had converted to Catholicism and in 1573 arrived at Douai. In 1575 he traveled to Rome to begin his novitiate as a Jesuit. A few months later he went to Spain, where he remained until 1584, studying and teaching in various colleges. He was ordained priest in 1579. Late in 1583 he was chosen to go on the English mission, and in September 1584 he entered England as superior of the still tiny Jesuit mission. He was apparently a successful missionary; a list of prisoners at Wisbech of 1595 or 1596 describes him as "a very dangerous man and in special account among the Papists."[11] Weston's fame among both Catholics and Protestants was not due entirely to his ordinary missionary work. He also gained wide notoriety as an exorcist; he claimed that his success in casting out evil spirits was a sign of the truth of Catholicism.[12] This assertion was taken seriously enough to provoke a book by the Protestant Samuel Harsnet attempting to expose Weston's exorcisms as frauds.[13]

Weston, one might conclude, was a man of great spiritual intensity, wholly caught up in a no-holds-barred war against the world, the flesh, and the devil. The impression is confirmed by what is known of his way of life. The most striking characteristic in most accounts is the rigorous and austere discipline that he imposed on himself. Parsons, writing several years later, describes how Weston once spent all his waking hours for a year in prayer.[14] Giles Archer, a fellow prisoner and friend of Weston's at Wisbech, later described how he never slept more than five hours a night and slept lying on the ground rather than in a bed.[15]

Weston's opponents accuse him of many things, but never of looseness where the sins of the flesh are concerned. What infuriates them about Weston is what they perceive as a holier-than-thou attitude. Weston clearly could inspire great admiration and loyalty; his followers at Wisbech stuck to him with remarkable devotion. But even some of his selfless acts of charity could be annoying. Archer tells how at Wisbech Weston fell on his knees before two quarreling inmates, neither a friend of his, and vowed not to rise until they were reconciled.[16] The two were indeed reconciled, but unless they were as liberated from normal human passions as was Weston himself, they might well have regarded him as a sanctimonious meddler.

Christopher Bagshaw, Weston's main opponent in the "Wisbech stirs," was certainly not free from the normal human passions. Bagshaw was born in 1552, the son of an innkeeper at Lichfield in Staffordshire. He received his B.A. from Balliol College, Oxford, of which he became a fellow in 1572. While a fellow, he helped to force the resignation after a violent faculty quarrel of Robert Parsons, who had not yet become a Catholic.[17] Bagshaw became a prebendary of Lichfield in 1578 and principal of Gloucester Hall at Oxford in 1579, but in 1581 he resigned his offices and in July 1582 he arrived at the seminary at Rheims. He was ordained at Laon in May 1583, and in August was sent to the seminary at Rome, where he was during the dissensions that disturbed the seminary in 1584–85. His opponents later claimed that he was expelled,[18] although Bagshaw and his friends denied the charge.

In May 1585 Bagshaw was sent into England. He was captured almost immediately and spent about two years in various prisons, although at one point he asked to be released on the grounds that he was "free from all practices against her majesty," and apparently at one point consented to confer with Protestant theologians at Cambridge.[19] He was apparently released from prison for a few months in late 1587 and early 1588, and during this time he lived in Lichfield. This temporary leniency and the conference at Cambridge lead one to suspect that the government hoped that he would return to the Anglican church, or at least stop active proselytizing. If so, they were disappointed. By March 1588 Bagshaw was back in prison at Wisbech, and the prison list of 1595 or 1596 comments that he "was first sent to Cambridge to be conferred withall and so to be reformed, but he was very obstinate and doth very much harm and mischief as is known by experience in Staffordshire, he is a most dangerous man."[20]

Bagshaw's Catholicism was clearly strong and sincere, and he is generally considered to have been a man of considerable ability and energy. But his career leads one to agree with George Abbot, who knew him at Oxford, that Bagshaw was "one who thought his penny good silver."[21] Richard Barret, president of the seminary at Rheims, on sending Bagshaw to Rome warned the rector there that Bagshaw was "clever and good enough at studies, but very much inclined to anger, hard to deal with, and restless."[22] He added that at Rheims Bagshaw had been unable to bear any word that sounded like censure. His behavior during the Wisbech stirs and his frequent quarrels at the other communities in which he lived confirm the impression that Bagshaw was hot-tempered, jealous of his status and dignity, and very quick to take offense.

Putting Weston and Bagshaw together in the same community may well have been asking for trouble; indeed, Giles Archer later believed that the government's sending Bagshaw to Wisbech was intended to cause dissension among the prisoners.[23] But whatever the two men may have thought of each other, open dissension did not break out until almost seven years after Weston and Bagshaw arrived at Wisbech.

The troubles appear to have begun with a growing sense of apprehension on Weston's part (and presumably on the part of those who later joined him) about the moral behavior of some of their fellow prisoners. In September 1594 Henry Garnet, who had become the Jesuit superior in England after Weston's capture, wrote to Robert Parsons that he had heard from Weston that at Wisbech "things go worse and worse, with no order but confusion and danger of great scandal."[24] It is impossible to tell with any certainty how much truth there was to the stories of scandalous behavior; all the evidence on both sides of the matter rests on the testimony of committed partisans with a strong interest in establishing their party's monopoly of virtue. But the two sides agree that shortly after Christmas of 1594 Weston withdrew to his room and refused to take part in the life of the community until steps were taken to insure proper moral order.[25] By early February eighteen of the thirty-one priests (other than Weston) in the prison had drawn up a set of rules under which they intended to live. They sent a copy to Henry Garnet, enclosing a covering letter that stated that they all wanted Weston to act as "a judge, corrector and censurer over us,"[26] but that he refused to do so without the approval of his superior. They therefore asked Garnet to approve the rules and to allow Weston to take up the responsibility of enforcing them.

The rules themselves do not seem particularly severe. Participation in the confraternity set up by the rules is to be voluntary (under the circumstances it could hardly be anything else), and prisoners are urged to refrain from behavior that could give offense to their fellows or to the outside world and to submit to censure if they fall short. All are to be present at public prayers. Major questions are to be decided by majority vote, lesser questions by deputies chosen by the group. Rules are laid down for handling money and general administration. At meals, each man is "to take his place . . . as it falleth out and none to contend for rooms but rather to contend with humility who shall prefer each other."[27]

But although these rules are not particularly severe, they were presented and defended in a manner that could almost have been calculated to arouse confusion and resentment among those who were not members of the confraternity. For one thing, Weston and his group were inconsistent in their account of the reasons for the institution of the rules. The letter which Weston's group sent to Garnet along with the rules stressed the aim of self-improvement by the members of the confraternity; "truly we do not find our justice to be such, nor our life so inculpable . . . as we may securely rest ourselves upon that confidence of saints, laws are not layed upon just men, but rather being taught by experience for our own weakness, by the event of divers great inconveniences, we do emulate and desire to have a law." Several months later, in October, Garnet wrote to Bagshaw that he had no reason to be offended at the setting up of the confraternity. "If some take upon themselves these obligations from a study of virtue, and pursuit of spiritual progress and perfection, in no way can others think themselves thereby aggrieved." The confraternity was nothing but "an undertaking, whereby some might promote by a rule of life their advancement in doctrine and piety . . . without any contempt for others, without any harm to charity and without casting the least reflection on the esteem due to anyone."[28] Garnet goes on to quote the letter that Weston's group had sent him in February in order to show that the confraternity was established to combat its members' moral vices and cast no discredit on others.

But the letter that Garnet quotes begins by saying that the writers have decided to set up a system of rules as a result of discussions about "how to bring in some better discipline for avoiding of these evils, or open scandals that have fallen out among us."[29] This statement seems to imply that there had been scandalous behavior and that those who were unwilling to join in the reformation were perhaps primarily to blame for both past and future scandals. This letter was, moreover, apparently not the clearest suggestion of impropriety. Robert Parsons later wrote that the priests of Weston's group had sent Garnet a letter in January 1595 in which they described their opponents' offenses under ten headings; the five that Parsons mentions include slackness at prayer and study, verbal and physical violence of various kinds, and intemperance in eating and drinking.[30] When Garnet reported on the Wisbech stirs to the general of the Society of Jesus, he said that Weston withdrew to his room because he "noticed that everything was daily getting worse, as was shown by abundance of quarrels and uproars when they met together, by scant modesty at table, by drinking parties and the rowdiness of many during public prayers and conferences, by doubts whether very good faith was being observed in the collection and distribution of monies, and what was worst, by suspected familiarity with women."[31]

Garnet goes on to say that when some priests of the other side came to ask Weston the reason for his withdrawal, he told them that he could not afford the appearance of scandal and refused to rejoin the common life unless rules were drawn up. Garnet says that Weston's interrogators approved his demand in principle, but temporized about putting it in effect.[32] When their reluctance became clear, some of the other priests came to Weston and drew up some rules. "Let the others, they said, live as they chose, whilst keeping charity. It might well be that by the pleasing grace of the rule and the beauty of order all the rest would be won over."[33]

In this version, the confraternity is intended publicly to disassociate its members from the behavior of those outside it and therefore publicly condemn them. The confraternity is also a means of bringing pressure on those who may not realize "the pleasing grace of the rule and the beauty of order." This rhetoric is difficult to reconcile with the profession that the only purpose of drawing up the rules is to help the members of the confraternity with their own moral discipline. To the opponents of Weston and his group (not men particularly inclined to overlook slights) it may have seemed that their opponents were holding them up to moral obloquy, while when convenient they blandly denied anything of the kind. Weston and his group may not have intended it, but the contradictions in their statements of purpose may have made the rules seem to be hypocritical moral blackmail.

Another apparent inconsistency in the presentation of the new discipline may also have helped to cause trouble. The rules themselves were predominantly democratic and egalitarian; important matters were to be decided by majority vote and less important matters by delegates chosen by the group. The only duties specifically assigned to the "agent" (the post for which Weston was proposed) were to act as chairman at meetings and to resolve the difficulties of those appointed to specific tasks by the community.[34] The letter that was sent to Garnet along with the rules implied a completely different principle. The writers say, "We desire not only a law to be bound unto for the direction of our life, but the life or soul itself of the law, that is, a judge, a corrector, and censurer over us."[35] This statement certainly sounds as if Weston is to be granted extensive powers; but if so, they are not spelled out in the letter. The rules do mention that violators must be prepared to submit to censure but do not say how and by whom the censures are to be imposed. If Weston's group had written only the rules, they might have been attacked for "popularity"; if only the letter, for unrestrained one-man rule. Their vagueness and apparent contradictions left them open to attack for both.

If Weston and his party made some mistakes in presenting their program, they certainly reaped the consequences. The rules were greeted with howls of protest and outrage by Bagshaw and the twelve other priests who did not sign them. Except for purposes of exchanging insults, these priests were soon not on speaking terms with Weston and his followers, who included the eighteen priests who had accepted the rules and the one layman among the prisoners, the Jesuit lay brother Thomas Pound. Weston and his group were, at least according to their own accounts, forcibly prevented from using the dining hall.[36] News of the prisoners' dissensions began to spread outside the prison, a development for which each side naturally blamed the other.[37] Two Marian priests, Alban Dolman and John Bavant, attempted to mediate the dispute, but each showed open sympathy for one side (Dolman for Bagshaw's side, Bavant for

Weston's) and therefore lost all credibility with the other. The mediation efforts collapsed, leaving behind little except some vituperative correspondence and further inflamed feelings.[38]

In early May of 1595 Bagshaw wrote to a Norfolk gentleman (or perhaps several gentlemen) who had asked him for an explanation of the situation at Wisbech, which he provided with typical verbal violence and confidence in his own righteousness.[39] The institution of the rules by Weston and his group, Bagshaw says, was motivated by "idle surmises, uncharitable suspicions, malicious amplified detractions." It is wrong, he continues, to defame anyone without proof, and it is especially wrong "by general infamy [i.e., accusations that do not name particular people, and therefore bring everyone under suspicion] to involve all which live in a place so famous as this hath been."[40] Plainly, Bagshaw sees the institution of the rules as a calculated insult to himself and his party.

But if the purpose of the rules is bad, their content is worse. Bagshaw points out the ambiguity in Weston's role. "The agent must be a Judex that is of absolute power and independent, and yet a delegate and deputy of the company. A censor may remove any man from his voice and place, yet here withall we have mention of voices, elections and suffrages." All in all, "it is very doubtful and intricate and diversely debated and sentenced whether the multitude be above the agent or the agent above the multitude."[41]

Bagshaw is not content merely with pointing out ambiguities; he attacks both democracy and autocracy as if each had been clearly adopted. The trouble, he says, is caused by "a separation, or as others think and say, a schism. . . . The form thereof is popular, the worst of all others, wherein any one is as good as any other, and commonly the worst (things passing by faction of voices) better than the best. A form . . . without example in the habitable world except the Sinedrical congregations of Geneva and the like."[42]

But if making decisions by majority vote is against all civilized behavior and suspiciously similar to the practice of heretics, that is as nothing compared to the suggestion that prisoners should sit at table randomly rather than in order of precedence:

A thing not practiced in any ordered place in the world. A disgrace to all degree of learning and fit for Anabaptists. A seditious mutiny and confusion against the several orders in the church. A contempt of reverend age, and therefore to be left to the revived Arians whose saying that is *nostra secta non curat canos*: [sic] a bait to draw in inferior men by hope of a show of eminence now and then which otherwise by their place and perhaps dessert should commonly be obscure and therefore a necessary cause of division against those which would not consent to such absurd innovations.[43]

Random seating, as a visible sign of the egalitarian basis of the confraternity, seems to Bagshaw an outrageous attack on the proper hierarchy of order and degree that is part of the essence of the church. Egalitarianism, however, is not the only threat to proper church order. The terms in which his supporters speak of Weston imply that he has "sovereign power" and "attribute unto him merum dominium and infallibility of judgment in all things." To set up such an authority outside the papacy is to bring things "to the nature of a proper schism . . . to make a Vindex, Censor Anima Legis without direction, limitation or exception of any principle, law, vow, canon, rule, order, or duty whatsoever." To set up the rules is "to make priests sent with more than ordinary or episcopal authority to be tied to the pleasures of such as be not their superiors." Bagshaw goes on to attack Weston's group for bringing in disorder under the pretense of establishing order, and near the end of his letter he says, "We therefore of the Unity dare not meddle with new designments. . . . Laws only can be made by princes and canons by bishops."[44]

Bagshaw, like Weston, presents himself as a defender of the proper order in the church and attacks his opponents as enemies of that order. The dispute between them rests largely on a matter of fact—namely, whether the moral atmosphere at Wisbech before the institution of the rules was as poor as Weston and his group said it was. But an important issue of principle also intrudes between Weston and Bagshaw: they do not mean the same thing by *order*. For Weston, order means the recognition and observance of certain standards of religious devotion and moral behavior. The maintenance of these standards requires explicit rules and someone with the authority to enforce them, but there is great leeway as to the exact form of the authority to be imposed. Weston's authority and the authority of the rules are to be accepted because they are a convenient way to achieve desirable goals; they are essentially pragmatic and presuppose considerable flexibility in the organization of the church, at least under the peculiar circumstances that it faced in England.[45] It perhaps reflects the priorities of Weston and his group that in their rules and in the covering letter to Garnet the prescribed norms of behavior are given more prominence and spelled out more clearly than the mechanisms for the exercise of authority.

Bagshaw, in objecting to the program of Weston and his group, poses as the defender of what might be called the legitimist principle of ecclesiastical authority. Authority for him is primarily a matter of rank, precedence, and structure. Authority is essentially hierarchical, and laws, to be valid, must be approved by those in the hierarchy with the right to do so. The hierarchy may be subverted either by disordered egalitarianism (witness Bagshaw's extreme verbal violence at the idea of random seating at table) or by the usurped authority of individuals, setting up their own judgment as a rule regardless of the canons and traditions of the church. Authority derives its legitimacy primarily not from its convenience for achieving certain goals, but from its conformity to a predetermined structure. Bagshaw does not spell out the details of his principles of church government; if he means the normal hierarchical structure in effect in Catholic countries, it is difficult to see how any effective church government could have been established, at Wisbech or in England as a whole.[46]

Questions of church order and the bitter personal exchanges of men with very strong grudges dominate the exchanges of the two sides in the Wisbech stirs. Some other issues, however, although they had little apparent effect on the earlier stages of the stirs, ought to be noted for the importance that they later assumed. The most significant are the position of the Jesuits and the relationship of Catholics to temporal authority.

Garnet, in his report to Acquaviva in July 1595, said that years before some priests at Wisbech had asked him to use his influence with the church authorities to obtain some remedy for the spreading disorders at Wisbech. He had declined to do so, regarding it as none of his business "to delate the defects of others, who were not of our own body."[47] When asked to allow Weston to act as agent for the confraternity of priests, Garnet gave his permission only with several provisos intended to restrict Weston's power and status. Among other things, he resolved an ambiguity in the confraternity's constitution by insisting that a majority of the members, and not Weston alone, should impose corrections and penances.[48]

Garnet said that he insisted on limiting Weston's authority in order to avoid jealousy. He certainly was aware that to place the only Jesuit priest at Wisbech in any position of authority over secular priests was to risk resentment against the society. In spite of Garnet's precautions, the resentment did develop. Garnet says that "the other side began straightway to publish abroad that the Jesuits were claiming, without justice, to exercise authority over them."[49] It is difficult to tell much about either the extent or the content of this publicity campaign, since letters spread around the Catholic community were unlikely to survive for very long. Alban Dolman, one of the Marian priests who unsuccessfully attempted to mediate the Wisbech stirs soon after they began, wrote at least one violent letter to Bagshaw accusing the Jesuits of defaming him; he also condemned one of the Jesuits' friends among the secular priests for defamation, sanctimonious hypocrisy, and legacy hunting on the Jesuits' behalf.[50] Garnet, besides noting the accusation that the Jesuits seek to dominate the secular clergy, says that the anti-Weston party at Wisbech has "alleged that Jesuits stood alone as sowers of discord between Christian princes, and as adherents of the Spanish faction."[51]

The accusation that the Jesuits are "adherents of the Spanish faction" plays little obvious role in the surviving documents of the anti-Weston party from the early stages of the Wisbech stirs. It is nevertheless quite likely that the accusation was widely made, as the society's enemies were soon to make the identification of the Jesuits with the Spanish interest virtually automatic. An English Catholic's attitude toward Spain was important primarily as a touchstone for his attitude toward the temporal authorities of England. Neither side seems to have addressed this question very systematically in the early stages of the Wisbech stirs, but Weston, in the only allusion made in his autobiography to dissensions at Wisbech, condemns the views of some prisoners "who asserted that all business touching priests and all their quarrels—I mean everything apart from questions of religious belief—should be judged and determined according to the laws of the realm and the decrees of the queen's council, so that it would appear altogether unexceptionable if our keeper, who had been a magistrate and a justice, heard and decided controversies of this kind."[52]

Bagshaw and his party do seem to support implicitly the idea that the keeper at Wisbech, as a representative of the queen's justice, ought to have some kind of authority over them. A document dated 12 June 1595, describes a conversation that allegedly took place among the keeper, Bagshaw, a supporter of Weston named Christopher Southworth, and some others.[53] The writer is clearly sympathetic to Bagshaw and his group. Southworth is described as asking the keeper to give Weston's group separate cooking and dining facilities from those of the other prisoners. When the keeper wants to know why,

Southworth eventually admits that it is because of horrible ecclesiastical crimes. He refuses to tell the keeper any more, claiming that as a layman he can have no jurisdiction over ecclesiastical offenses. The keeper takes the refusal to recognize him as a judge as a sign of "evil practice," and it is clear that the writer's sympathies are with him. At a later stage, there was probably active cooperation between the government and the anti-Weston party, but at first the government seems to have taken little interest in the stirs. But the anti-Weston group's apparent willingness to concede wider authority to the English government's representatives was both an extra spur to dissension and a portent for the future.

The disputes and ill feeling that broke out early in 1595 set the tone of life at Wisbech through the summer of that year. But by September, for whatever reason, passions may have cooled somewhat. In that month two seminary priests, John Mush and Richard Dudley, arrived at Wisbech to attempt to mediate the disagreements. Mush was one of the more prominent of the English secular clergy. A missionary in the North of England since 1583 or 1584, he had been given special faculties by William Allen and cooperated with the Jesuit Richard Holtby in organizing the mission in Yorkshire.[54] He had a long record of friendly relations with Jesuits, dating back to 1579 when as a student at the English seminary at Rome he had been one of the leaders of a student movement that helped bring in the Jesuit regime at the seminary. Later he was to become a strong opponent of the Archpriest Blackwell and his Jesuit allies, but at this time neither side had any reason to distrust him. His colleague, Dudley, a missionary in Lancashire, was younger and less prominent than Mush but had the great advantage of being a friend of Bagshaw's who apparently could speak frankly to him without offense.[55]

The first result of Mush and Dudley's efforts was the drawing up of a set of rules that were accepted by Bagshaw and his group.[56] Weston and his group rejected them, primarily because of a clause that all penalties should be imposed by a two-thirds vote of all the prisoners. Weston and his group, who included a majority but less than two-thirds of the prisoners, preferred that such decisions be made by a committee made up of three pro-Weston and two anti-Weston priests.

After the rejection of the rules by Weston's group, Mush and Dudley left Wisbech, perhaps resigned to failure. But Garnet, who apparently had urged Mush to undertake the negotiations in the first place, realized that the willingness of Bagshaw and his group to accept any rules was a major advance. He urged Mush and Dudley to return to Wisbech and persist in their efforts. He wrote letters to Weston and to his followers, apparently urging them to work toward an agreement.[57] On 8 October he also wrote to Bagshaw, defending the confraternity but minimizing Weston's role in it, and arguing that its institution was not intended as a reflection on the conduct of Bagshaw or anyone else. He urged Bagshaw to work for peace among his fellow prisoners.[58]

Mush and Dudley accordingly returned to Wisbech and resumed the task of mediation. Their efforts and Garnet's letters soon began to have some effect. On 22 October Garnet wrote to Mush that he wished "the whole company for the love of God and for the common cause which we are here all to advance with all our study and diligence, that they will earnestly go forward in that which to my singular joy I perceive they are beginning. That is, to set down by common consent such orders as may conserve them in mutual love and amity."[59]

Garnet wrote to Bagshaw on the same day, making it clear that his concern for "orders" was serious. "I allow not by any means an unordered peace. I commend such a peace, as is supported by certain rules and steadfast order." But in the letter to Mush, Garnet urged that both sides be willing to make concessions, "the ones relenting (if so it be needful for the glory of God) from severity, and the other (if it be thought convenient) adding somewhat to the accomplishing of their virtuous desires." In both letters Garnet said that he was commanding Weston to work for reconciliation among the prisoners.[60]

Mush and Dudley told Garnet that his letters cleared away most of the difficulties from their task of mediation. However the credit should be apportioned, on 6 November the two groups of prisoners accepted a set of rules for regulating their common life.[61] The rules made provision for anyone who did not wish to share commons with the others (i.e., take meals together) after the following Easter, although Mush later said that he had not expected anyone to take advantage of this clause.[62] The bulk of the rules laid down detailed regulations for handling money and goods and for assessing penalties against offenders. Accusations unsupported by clear proof were discouraged by the imposition of penalties upon accusers who could not prove their case. Punishments for infractions of the regulations were to be decided upon by majority vote of a committee of five members, two each chosen by the plaintiff and the defendant and a fifth chosen by lot.

The acceptance of the rules was marked by fervent scenes of mutual reconciliation and rejoicing among the prisoners. Mush and Dudley wrote to Garnet thanking him for his efforts on behalf of reconciliation, and Weston's followers wrote to Garnet praising the work of Mush and Dudley.[63] Even Bagshaw joined in the round of compliments to former and future enemies. He wrote to Garnet two days after the general reconciliation praising the conduct of both Garnet himself and Weston, and a few weeks later in another letter to the Jesuit superior he said that among the things impelling the prisoners toward peace were "the opinion of you which we have formed" and "the respect due to your order."[64]

The settlement of November 1595 and the euphoria that followed it did not last. For this reason, one may be tempted to underrate the importance of the agreement, which lies not primarily in what it accomplished but in what it shows about the English Catholic community at the time. The whole episode exemplifies the informal methods of government that, with the exception of the Jesuits, characterized the English mission. Neither Mush nor Dudley had any formal authority over anyone at Wisbech, while Garnet had no authority over anyone there except Weston and Thomas Pound. Within a few years Mush and Garnet were to be among the leading participants on opposite sides of a bitter struggle over the methods of the Catholic mission in England. Yet in 1595 they cooperated with no sign of friction and many signs of mutual respect in suppressing a major threat to the mission's reputation and effectiveness. The incident is impressive testimony to the ability of the missionary body to solve its problems by informal means. In some ways these methods were very well suited to the situation in England, where the church could hardly employ the administrative and judicial procedures used in officially Catholic countries. But informal methods of conducting community affairs depend even more than do more formal systems on mutual trust and compatibility of objectives among the people involved in making them work. In the fall of 1595, this trust and compatibility were still fairly strong. If the settlement of November 1595 had lasted, the Wisbech stirs might have been remembered by both contemporaries and later historians as an isolated outburst of high-strung personalities rather than as the beginning of widespread party feuding.

It is very difficult to tell exactly when during 1596 or why the stirs flared up again. Apparently some excitement was caused both inside and outside the prison by the suspicion that Francis Tillotson, a priest of Bagshaw's party who escaped and was recaptured, had been betrayed to the authorities by Bagshaw. From a postscript written by a government servant on a letter that came into the government's hands, the suspicion seems to have been justified.[65] Some prisoners' feelings seem to have been greatly exacerbated by a rather silly academic controversy over whether the prostitutes in Rome were there with the approval of the authorities or were merely officially ignored.[66] Bagshaw also wrote to Mush asking what he should do when he dissented from the majority of one of the committees set up under Mush and Dudley's rules. Mush replied that he could see no other possibility than that in such a situation the minority should yield to the majority.[67] Mush went on to scold Bagshaw (later to be his ally in the archpriest controversy) for his reported uncharitable behavior toward Tillotson over the escape attempt and about "your hard conceit of Philip [probably Philip Stranguish, a priest of Weston's party] and disgraceful language against him." He also lectured Bagshaw about his faults of character; according to Mush, Bagshaw was widely thought to be "vehement, restless, imperious and factious,"[68] a fact that did great harm to the reputation of his cause and made many priests fear subjection to Bagshaw more than to Weston.

All of this bickering gives some hints about the causes for the relapse of the Wisbech prisoners into two hostile camps. All of the disagreements savor more of the familiar personal clashes and jealousies than of vital issues of principle. This time, however, apparently little attempt at reconciliation was made either by outside agents or by the prisoners themselves. The bitter divisions among the prisoners continued until the last of them was transferred away from Wisbech in late 1600 or early 1601.

The lack of any serious effort at peacemaking after the breakdown of the agreement of November 1595 may have been partly a reflection of the effect that the collapse of one hard-earned agreement had on hopes of successfully concluding another one. But it also reflected the fact that during 1596–98 the friction at Wisbech became less and less an isolated problem and began to be perceived as only one of a series of connected agitations disturbing the English Catholic community. The divisions at the English college at Rome were attracting significant attention in England by early 1596.[69] The intrigues against the Jesuits centered in the Spanish Netherlands increased in intensity and became more open.[70] Perhaps most important of all, the anti-Jesuit groups in the three centers of disaffection—England, Flanders, and Rome—began to communicate with each other and to form something resembling a common program and a common view of the English mission's situation and of its proper goals and methods.

The content of the anti-Jesuit group's program and the response of Parsons and his supporters will be discussed later. It may suffice to deal here with the role played by the Wisbech stirs in the historical mythology that each side used in support of its claims to virtue.

From 1596 on, the views of the militant wing of the English Catholics on the Wisbech stirs became less ambiguous, and the clash between the two groups of prisoners was represented more frankly as a clash between good and evil. The pro-Weston group dropped the pretense that the institution of the rules of February 1595 was not a reflection on the conduct of Bagshaw and his group and plainly accused them of disorderly and licentious living. In December 1596 Garnet referred to Weston and those who joined him in the institution of the first set of rules as "twenty very good men" and described their opponents as "neither of the very learned or the very good." Weston, who throughout the dissensions had taken a sterner view than Garnet of the moral failings of his opponents, wrote to Acquaviva in March 1598 that the purpose of the rules had been to "preserve our own immunity [from scandal] and to make manifest our disapproval of the ill done by these others."[71]

But the most systematic discussion from the pro-Weston side of the moral lessons of Wisbech was by Robert Parsons, in the two lengthy attacks on the whole Appellant party that he wrote at the height of the archpriest controversy.[72] Parsons agrees with virtually everyone on both sides of the controversy that until shortly before the open outbreak of dissension Wisbech was justly revered by Catholics for the holiness of the prisoners' lives, which he ascribes chiefly to Weston's direction. Throughout Parsons's discussions of Wisbech, Weston's group is constantly offered as examples of the way in which true confessors of the Catholic faith ought to live. Weston himself is held up as a particularly shining example of priestly virtue. Although

Parsons mentions many of Weston's excellent qualities, he claims that Weston is especially esteemed "for his great severity used always towards himself, and mansuetude towards others in his manner of life." He could, he says, give many examples of Weston's virtues, but he will limit himself to one, "which a certain reverend priest related unto us, that lived with him above a year not only in one prison, but in one chamber also, avowing that F. Edmunds' [Weston's alias] perseverance both day and night in prayer, was such, as he never saw him in bed all that time, except only a little, when he was sick, nor ever slept, but either standing or sitting at his prayers, in which he would often fall down but ordinarily sit down upon some resting place, while the force of sleep did overcome him, and then return to his prayer again."[73]

Weston is praised for no virtue more than for his severity toward himself; Parsons's choice of an example of his virtues is an act of heroic mortification of the body in the interests of the spiritual and devotional life. Apparently, Parsons values strict moral discipline a great deal.

Parsons makes clear in his discussion of the collapse of order at Wisbech that effective moral discipline is essential for communities as well as for individuals. The admirable community life of Wisbech began to break down, he claims, when Bagshaw and his followers began to gain influence; "neither of them being a friend of discipline and order, they quickly had some followers, to bring in and maintain liberty and dissolution, so as . . . the whole good order of the house was altered, and brawls, dissension, falling out, fighting, idleness, banquetting, plays, and other dissolution were brought in."[74] The confraternity of prisoners under Weston's leadership was, Parsons believes, a justified attempt by the more sober inmates to keep Wisbech from total moral degeneracy, but it naturally attracted the ire of the undisciplined, and the resulting quarrels led to the collapse of the edifying unity that had previously been maintained among the prisoners.

Parsons makes it clear enough who is to blame for this disaster in his largely narrative account in the *Brief Apology*. His most remarkable comments, however, come in the latter of the two works, the *Manifestation*, in which he spends a few pages of the first chapter attacking the main Appellant account of the stirs, Bagshaw's *A True Relation of the Faction Begun at Wisbeach*. Even Bagshaw's detestable book, Parsons claims, will reveal to the right-minded reader where virtue lies, for the reader "may clearly perceive of the one side to stand not only the far greater part of the more ancient company, but that which more importeth, desire of order, discipline, recollection, obedience, modesty and temperate behavior, and on the other side all the contrary, to wit, not only the far less number, but freer also in speech and conversation more given to liberty, refusing all rules and order, but only, the common canons of the church and sacrament of penance as they profess, condemning for novelties and innovations all other helps to spirit and devotion."[75]

Rules, order, and discipline are necessary for warding off the threats to a healthy moral and spiritual life, and apparently the stricter the better. Parsons confirms this impression when he tries to show how Bagshaw is discredited by the views that he attributes to various characters in the Wisbech story. Parsons quotes Bagshaw: "He [Weston] took upon him to control and find fault with this and that, as the coming into the Hall of a hobby horse [probably part of a troupe of Morris dancers] in Christmas, affirming that he would no longer tolerate these and so gross abuses." Parsons comments in the margin, "virtuous speeches reproachfully alleged." Weston's alleged statement that he and his group wished to avoid "enormities" by separating from the other prisoners, and his supporter Christopher Southworth's alleged remark that they "wished to avoid such sins as whoredom, drunkenness and dicing, the same being too ordinary with some in this house" are regarded by Parsons as shameful to the anti-Weston group that reports them, since that group cannot match these "speeches tending . . . to virtue, reformation and reproof of dissolute and disordered life." Indeed they do precisely the opposite, rejecting all spiritual discipline and aid except the sacrament of penance, which is common to "the loosest sort of Christians in the world" and totally inadequate for priests confessing the faith in a heretical prison. Parsons sums up the position of the anti-Weston group as "a defense of disorder, liberty and dissolution."[76]

All this, of course, begs the most important question for allotting blame for the Wisbech stirs. The objections to Weston's program were not based on the claim that fighting, drunkenness, and the like were not serious offenses, but on the claim (whether true or not) that the allegations of Weston and his supporters about their opponents' behavior were false. In accusing his opponents of defending immorality, Parsons (intentionally or not) takes a disagreement over a matter of fact and turns it into a debate over principles—a debate, as it happens, that his side could hardly lose. Such transforming of the terms of the debate can be justified only if one assumes, as Parsons did, that strictly regulated discipline and unacceptable loose living are the only alternatives, and therefore anyone who opposes stricter discipline is defending loose living. The fact that Parsons shifts the debate onto these grounds shows the importance that he attaches to the whole issue. For Parsons, the Wisbech stirs are a morality play— a confrontation of many of the best moral tendencies in English Catholicism with the sort of moral slackness that must be crushed out of both the Catholic community and the individuals who comprise that community.

The adaptation that occurred in the anti-Jesuit party's view of the Wisbech stirs is more significant and interesting than the change that came over the views of Parsons and his friends. Some of the main themes of the most detailed Appellant account of the stirs, Bagshaw's *A True Relation of the Faction Begun at Wisbeach* (1601), are, as one would expect, extensions and amplifications of themes on which the anti-Weston party harped from the beginning of the disturbances. Weston and his supporters are castigated as advocates of "novelties" and "innovations," while Catholics outside Wisbech who disapproved of him "plodded in the old steps of antiquity" and his opponents defended "the canons of councils, the laws of the church and the sacrament of penance" as sufficient guides for their conduct.[77] The pro-Weston group pretends to superior virtue in order to mask their attacks on church order; Weston is "a new Donatus amongst us, to revive again that pestilent schism."[78]

The anti-Jesuit party's "legitimist" concern for the sanctity of church order (a concern, it must be said, without much content) was accompanied by an increasingly open willingness to say and do things that implied recognition of the legitimacy of English temporal authority. The priest Robert Fisher reported to the authorities in Rome that when he visited Wisbech in late 1596 or early 1597 he found Bagshaw and his followers, with the keeper's assistance, oppressing their opponents.[79] Bagshaw repeats the story of Christopher Southworth's refusal to recognize the keeper as a legitimate judge of crimes among the prisoners, and his sympathies are with the keeper.[80] In October 1598, while the first appeal to Rome in the archpriest controversy was under way, Bagshaw's supporter Thomas Bluet apparently told the keeper that Weston's group was "altogether Spanish" and regaled him with stories of the far-flung machinations of Parsons and his allies and of the risks that Bluet claimed the anti-Weston group was running by their opposition to Parsons's schemes.[81] Writing in 1601, Bagshaw recounts a speech of Bluet's accusing Weston of setting up laws without the queen's consent; he puts in the mouth of anonymous "people" the statement that the Jesuits are "proud, ambitious and vindictive persons, perturbers of states, countries, and commonwealths."[82]

Bagshaw's ideas about Weston are also in some ways a development of the themes of 1595; he is portrayed throughout the *True Relation* as a sanctimonious hypocrite masking a meddling and power-hungry nature under pretended concern for virtue. But Bagshaw charges Weston with a much deeper-laid plot for seeking superiority than he ever mentioned in 1595. He claims that Weston made two cleverly cloaked attempts to gain superiority over the other prisoners within a few weeks after his arrival at Wisbech.[83] Foiled in these attempts at a quick coup, Weston settled down to a long-haul effort to win support among the prisoners. He made sure he was the first to greet new prisoners, whom he treated kindly and for whom he did favors. He "would seldom omit to insist upon the commendation of order and discipline . . . his sighs and zeal seemed to be extraordinary: as though the perfection of true mortification had been the only thing he aimed at."[84] If this feigned humility was not enough, Weston got into his hands a great part of the funds collected by his fellow Jesuits (which, Bagshaw says, was most of the money given by Catholics to succor prisoners) and distributed it in a way calculated to attract the greatest number of prisoners to his side.[85]

Bagshaw claims that Weston long delayed striking for power because of the opposition of Thomas Metham, a widely respected prisoner, of William Allen, and of the prominent exile cleric Owen Lewis. But by the time these three men had died, Weston had by underhanded methods won over nineteen of the thirty-four other prisoners and saw his chance to seize power.[86] The beginning of the confraternity followed. Weston's conduct during the dissensions, according to Bagshaw, was of a piece with the conduct that led up to them; he continued to cloak a relentless drive for power under a feigned modesty and sanctity. Bagshaw is not deterred from making this picture consistent by mere lack of evidence to back up his claims. He simply assures the reader, for example, that "you must understand" that Garnet had approved the setup of the confraternity in advance, and that Weston's insistence that he be asked to approve the project was a mere charade.[87] Presumably, if Bagshaw knows how Weston operates, detailed proof is unnecessary; Bagshaw can fill in the missing evidence.

Bagshaw erects a major part of his historical myth of the Wisbech stirs when he changes the institution of the rules from a piece of sanctimonious and misguided meddling (which is about all his accusations of 1595 amount to) to the fruit of a long-standing and deeply laid plot by a cunning political manipulator. But the most significant part of the myth is the context in which Bagshaw puts Weston's scheming, a context perhaps best shown by the radical change that between 1595 and 1601 came over Bagshaw's portrait of Weston's superior, Henry Garnet.

The evidence indicates that during the stirs of 1595 relations between Bagshaw and Garnet were reasonably cordial. The letters from Garnet to Bagshaw during Mush and Dudley's mediation and Bagshaw's enthusiastic letters to Garnet after the settlement have already been mentioned. A letter from Bagshaw to Garnet of 23 August 1595 provides a better test of the two men's relations at the time, since it was provoked by Bagshaw's suspicions that the formation of the confraternity had been with Garnet's counsel and approval. Considering the unpromising occasion, the letter's tone is, for Bagshaw, amazingly mild. He is astonished at Garnet's approval of "a thing which I reckon is without precedent among Christians, and that this has been done without consulting or informing in any way those whom it most concerned to know what was being done." But he hastens to add that he does not "call in question in its sincerity and dutifulness, your charity, which that letter of yours breathes for me." Indeed,

it is to this charity that I appeal. . . . Effect has shown what thought did not foresee. This our separation is not less agreeable to the enemies of the church, than it is disagreeable to us. Take thought prudently, I beg, as to what will be the consequences of this action: the drawing apart of friends . . . the waste of time, the chill striking through devotion, the great and unnecessary cost of maintaining two households, the danger to our reputation, and to yours as well, and most painful of all, a scandal on such a scale that the like has not been seen since the restoration of the English church has been set on foot.[88]

Bagshaw disclaims any attack on Garnet's intentions or general policy. He merely suggests that Garnet has acted hastily and without adequate information and that perhaps his well-known charity will now lead him to change his approach. Far from considering Garnet a committed coconspirator of Weston's, Bagshaw apparently regards it as worth the effort to try to win his support.

In the *True Relation*, Garnet is transformed into a wholehearted collaborator with Weston's drive for power and indeed often appears to be the supervisor of it. Bagshaw's charges that Garnet had approved the first institution of the rules beforehand and that the letter asking him to allow Weston to become the agent of the confraternity was a farce intended to make it appear that Weston assumed superiority unwillingly have already been mentioned. This incident is typical of Bagshaw's manipulations to turn Garnet into a political conspirator. No act or word of Garnet's is what it appears to be; some subtle and malignant plot is always hidden behind an innocent appearance. He sends Weston secret orders, contradicting the admonitions given in letters sent openly.[89] Although Garnet publicly commended the agreement of November 1595, Bagshaw insists that he really resented it as a blow at Weston's position; Bagshaw dismisses Garnet's statements, "but hear the devilish politician how he transformeth himself into an angel of light." Garnet's letters in the fall of 1595 urging reconciliation at Wisbech were pure hypocrisy. "What he writ to Father Weston we know not: but craftily enough, we are assured by his practises towards us since: being as mere a Jesuit, as if he had been spit out of Father Parsons' mouth."[90]

These particular instances of alleged duplicity on Garnet's part reflect Bagshaw's idea of the Jesuit moral code. When Bagshaw expresses doubt as to just what Garnet said on a particular occasion, he claims, "It doth not much concern us, because no man is able to bind upon any Jesuits' word, they have so many shifts, and so little conscience in speaking truly, except it be one of themselves to another. Otherwise their manner is, to frame their speeches according to their company: always applying themselves to the times and occasions, as they fall out: if their designments prove well, they take the contriving of them to themselves: if not there is none will more condemn them."[91]

Truth, then, means nothing to a Jesuit; he recognizes no obligation to be honest except possibly to other members of the society. And the society aims at much more than merely to dominate Wisbech. Weston's attempt to gain power at the prison was only part of a long-standing plot to dominate the whole English mission; "the Jesuits . . . having gotten the regiment of the English seminary at Rome: our countrymen of that order no sooner came into England, but presently

. . . they began to lay their plots how they might bring the secular priests' heads under their girdles."[92]

By developing his portrait of Weston and completely changing his portrait of Garnet, Bagshaw has placed the Wisbech stirs in a context far wider than anything he seems to have seen in 1595. The attack on proper church order among the prisoners is now part of a long-standing and much wider scheme by a society that cleverly masks its ruthlessness and lust for power under a pretense of sanctity.

Bagshaw presents virtually no evidence to support his claims of particular instances of Jesuit duplicity. His method of proof (such as it is) depends on a deductive rather than an inductive principle. He thinks he knows how Jesuits operate, and therefore in any particular instance one can assume the existence of secret instructions, hidden intentions, or whatever else is required to make the evidence consistent with the hypothesis. Bagshaw (assuming that he really believes at least most of what he says) would seem to have fallen victim to political paranoia—meaning not necessarily that there is no evidence at all to support his view of the world, but that his preconceptions so dominate his view of specific situations that he sees confirmatory evidence when it is not there, or, when necessary, he invents evidence in order to make the specific situation conform to his general view of the world. Bagshaw's treatment of the Wisbech stirs is one of the best examples of the effects by 1601 of inflamed party feelings on English Catholics on both sides of the party divide. Wisbech itself contributed to the rise of party feelings, but events on the Continent, especially the student rebellion at the English seminary at Rome, probably did so even more.

# CHAPTER VI

# The Roman Stirs

In 1578 the old hospice for English pilgrims in Rome was turned into the second English seminary on the Continent. Almost from its origins the seminary was dogged by dissension more than any of the other English Catholic educational institutions. Its first rector was Morris Clennock, a Welshman who soon aroused the strong dislike of virtually all the English students, who accused him of being more interested in the comfort of a small group of Welsh cronies than in either caring for the English students or preparing them for the English mission. A large majority of the students, including men who were to be on opposite sides of later controversies, were soon engaged in a movement to get rid of Clennock and make the Society of Jesus responsible for the college. After a remarkably tenacious and intelligent campaign of propaganda and lobbying, the students induced an initially reluctant Roman hierarchy to give in to their demands. The Jesuits were placed in charge of the college, and an oath to receive holy orders and return to England at the command of the superiors was made compulsory for all students.[1]

The general of the Jesuits was apparently reluctant to add the English college to the society's other burdens,[2] and the subsequent history of the college amply justified his trepidation. There were several outbreaks of student unrest; Humphrey Ely, an Appellant writing in 1602, listed four such episodes after the one that resulted in the takeover of the college by the Jesuits.[3] Before the great disorders of 1594–97 the most serious quarrels were in 1585, when the pope found it necessary to order Cardinal Filippo Sega to conduct a visitation of the college. The discontented students' complaints, as Sega enumerated them, included charges that the Jesuits were more interested in the welfare of the society than in the success of the English mission, and that they showed great favoritism to students who wished to enter the society or who were otherwise friendly to it.[4] The students as a whole, however, do not appear to have been alienated from their Jesuit teachers at this time; in 1586 forty-nine students, a substantial majority of the student body, signed a statement opposing the rumored desire of some students to remove the Jesuits from the management of the college.[5]

The revolt of 1594–97 was much more serious and was the only one of the movements against the Jesuit regime in the seminary that had serious repercussions for the whole English Catholic community. The troubles were indirectly provoked by the death of Cardinal Allen in October 1594. The two leading candidates to succeed to Allen's position of leadership were Owen Lewis and Robert Parsons. Lewis, a Welsh canon lawyer, was bishop of Cassano in southern Italy but spent most of his time acting as a papal official in Rome. He had played a major role in the foundation of the Roman seminary but had lost much credit by his unavailing support of his friend Clennock against the rebellious students and, about the same time, by his support of a harebrained scheme to invade England by an exile named Thomas Stukely. Lewis regained much of his reputation by years of conscientious work as vicar-general to Charles Borromeo, archbishop of Milan, and in service to the papacy.[6]

Soon after Allen's death, proponents of both Lewis and Parsons began to organize support for the elevation of their man to the cardinalate, apparently in both cases with little encouragement or enthusiasm from the candidates. Much of Lewis's backing came from the largely aristocratic party centered in the Spanish Netherlands, many of whom had been attached to the cause of Mary Queen of Scots and were considered friendly to James VI's claim to the English throne. Many of them were also distinguished for feckless political opportunism and resentment of the control that foreigners and lowborn clerics frequently had over the affairs of the exiles.

In the spring of 1595, Lewis's friends in Rome decided to look for support among the students at the seminary. Lewis was popular with the students; he had donated money to the college, visited it frequently, preached in its chapel, and often entertained students in his quarters.[7] Edward Tempest, one of the senior students of the college, asked the rector, an Italian Jesuit named Jerome Fioravanti, for permission to work for Lewis's promotion. Fioravanti, who was not a severe disciplinarian, consented.[8] This consent led to disaster, for the students used the occasion as an excuse for agitation about much more than the promotion of Lewis. Tempest made the rounds of the students' rooms, stirring up resentment against the Jesuits and particularly against a new and more rigorous system of examinations that had just been introduced. Three petitions were apparently drawn up: one to Pope Clement VIII; one to Cardinal Caietan, the cardinal protector of England; and one to Lewis himself. The last, signed by thirty-seven students (fewer than fifty students attended the college), described the Jesuits as more interested in the welfare of the society than of the secular clergy.[9] When Lewis turned this document over to Caietan, the students had some explaining to do, but they managed to escape without serious harm.

The students' attempts to help Lewis's cause received a setback when Caietan was given control over faculties for priests on the English mission that Allen had formerly exercised. This development did not, however, put a stop to the students' secret meetings. Fioravanti was either unaware of the meetings or willing to overlook them, but the college minister, an English Jesuit named Edmund Harewood, was not. He began patrolling the college, breaking up unauthorized meetings and otherwise trying to tighten up discipline. This campaign of Harewood's began a series of confrontations between students and administration in which many causes of resentment came out in the open. Both sides spread propaganda and sought the support of powerful figures outside the college. The administration attempted to tighten up the rules and structure of the college in order to strengthen their control, while the students tried to thwart these efforts and gain as much control of the college as possible for themselves. Study and teaching virtually ceased as these struggles kept the college in a state of more or less continuous uproar for about a year. Anthony Kenny has written a good narrative of these events; there is little point in rehearsing the whole story here. Some observations about the causes of the troubles, however, are in order.

Robert Chambers, one of the few students loyal to the Jesuit administration, claimed that the rebellious students were men of slack morals who could not abide discipline and took advantage of an easygoing rector.[10] Chambers was scarcely an unbiased witness, but most of the students at Rome had come from the seminary at Douai, which had no written statutes at the time and where life was relatively informal, and they may not have taken kindly to the more strictly regulated life at Rome.[11] Some students may have acquired a dislike of the Jesuits at Douai, where the society was becoming both more influential and more unpopular. They may also have been influenced by the complaints of enemies of the Jesuits from outside the college.[12] But several incidents from the Roman stirs and the report of Cardinal Sega, who conducted a visitation to investigate the dissensions, lead one to believe that sufficient cause for trouble existed within the college itself.

The relations between the students and Edmund Harewood, the minister whose attempt at a disciplinary crackdown seems to have provoked the state of open dissension, provide a prime example (and probably an extreme one). Harewood was apparently regarded by the students as an officious meddler and apparently saw indiscipline, and particularly sexual lapses, everywhere he looked. A number of stories about him gained some currency; he was supposed to have cut down a grove of trees where the students used to walk in pairs, to have cut off the bottoms of the doors of the privy so as to be able to check the number of pairs of feet, and to have bricked up a window through which he thought the students had too good a view of the local prostitutes.[13] Some or all of these stories may well be apocryphal, but such apocryphal stories are not told about everyone.

In any case, Harewood's preoccupations caused one of the greatest outbursts of student resentment. The students had been trying to bring about the appointment of Owen Lewis to conduct a visitation of the college. Harewood spoke to two of the students, saying that he had evidence of homosexual activity (the sources do not use the word, but the meaning is clear) among the students and that if any visitation took place, this evidence would certainly come out. It is, of course, impossible to tell how much truth there was to these charges, but the students reacted furiously. They demanded that Harewood be punished for his outrageous insults to the honor of the college, and the minister apparently tried to calm the storm by saying that the whole thing was an unfortunate misunderstanding. To the students, this reaction appeared to be a hypocritical attempt to back away from an unsuccessful effort at blackmail. A meeting called by Cardinal Caietan to deal with the question broke up in a chaotic shouting match between the rebellious majority of the students and the loyal minority. After a discreet interval, the obnoxious Harewood was transferred away from the college.[14]

Harewood here made the most fundamental mistakes that a man who wished his authority to be respected could make. He confronted the students with accusations of moral offenses in such a way as naturally to lead them to think that he was more interested in maintaining his power (i.e., preventing the visitation) than in upholding morality. When faced with substantial opposition, he backed off from his charges and tried to claim he had never made them. A similar pattern of attempted crackdown followed by swift surrender to student opposition came after the pope had granted the students' request that a confessor be appointed from among the students. The rector, Fioravanti, appointed William Blundell, one of the small group of students who remained loyal to the superiors. (Cardinal Sega in his visitation report listed ten, as against thirty-seven who joined the rebellion.) Student protest, however, soon resulted in Blundell's removal. Edward Bennet, a leader of the rebellion, was appointed confessor, and two other members of the discontented faction, Edward Tempest and Anthony Champney, were appointed tutors.[15]

These episodes are somewhat extreme examples of apparently general tendencies of the administration of the Roman college under Fioravanti. Both incidents began when the administration took actions, on questions of serious moral consequence, that the students were likely to see as mere attempts to help maintain or strengthen the administration's control of the college. In both cases, the administration's hard-line policy caved in easily under student pressure. The administration reaped the disadvantages of severity, laxity, and indecision; the governing officials were neither loved, nor feared, nor respected.

The students' lack of respect for the administration was largely due to its own inadequacies, but the fact that the superiors' attempts to establish discipline were constantly being undercut by forces outside the college compounded the disrespect. Perhaps the most spectacular of many examples of the inability to maintain control occurred in the fall of 1595, when four of the leading rebels failed to obey the command of the vicegerent of the college to appear before him. They were declared contumacious and were ordered to be expelled from the college and banished from Rome. The four students' fellows attempted to leave the college along with them, but the vicegerent had arranged for a detachment of the Roman police to be on hand, and the students found the exits blocked, to their great dismay and (so they say) to the Jesuits' obvious glee. The police kept the college cordoned off to prevent the students from plotting with their allies in the city, and when the expelled students' papers were examined, documents were apparently found revealing plans to expel the Jesuits from all the English seminaries on the Continent.[16]

The authorities' high-handed tactics certainly demonstrated a less than ideal student-teacher relationship. But if the administration and its supporters had been able to enforce a firm policy consistently, they might well have ridden out the storm with their power (if not their credit) intact. However, their whole plan was destroyed by one instance of clever lobbying by a friend of the students outside the college. A Dominican named Sacheverell, a friend of the students, told the pope that such harsh treatment could cause the four expelled students to apostasize and tell the English government all they knew. Alarmed, the pope ordered their reinstatement. As if the college administration did not have enough to worry about, two other rebellious students who had been ordered to England were allowed to stay in Rome, and the pope promised a full investigation of all the points in dispute. One could hardly imagine a better way to make the superiors of the college look silly. After this, rumors began to circulate that the Jesuits would be removed from the college. In fact, Acquaviva, quite possibly disgusted with the whole business, had asked permission to withdraw the members of the society from the government of the college.

The students were apparently delighted with the idea of a visitation, which they had been trying to bring about for a long time. But they could scarcely have been pleased with the appointment of Cardinal Filippo Sega to conduct it. Sega was a veteran papal diplomat and administrator, who had conducted a visitation of the Roman college in 1585 and submitted a report very friendly to the Jesuits. He had also been a strong advocate of military efforts to conquer England, and while nuncio in Spain he had replied to an inquiry by some English Catholics by telling them that the assassination of Elizabeth would be morally permissible.[17]

The report on the English college that Sega submitted in March 1596 is perhaps the most important document of the Roman stirs. In it Sega sums up the statements of all parties to the conflict and gives his own views. On one possible cause of dissension the report is silent.

The students' dislike of Spain was to emerge openly during 1596, and many of their allies from the beginning of the troubles were hostile to Spanish influence, but Sega's report does not mention any explicit disagreements over politics. This omission does not mean that no such differences existed, for the students were undoubtedly aware of the foolishness of parading any anti-Spanish views before Sega.

Even without mentioning political matters, the students find a great deal about which to complain.[18] Much of their discontent is rather trivial; among other things the food, the condition of the sacristy, and several old feuds of little general significance were raked over. But many of the complaints fall into a pattern. Not very much is said about harshness per se. Much more often, the students object to selective harshness and to the Jesuits' playing favorites. The students mention many examples of Jesuit favoritism. The Jesuits have "by private junketings, presents and other cajoleries . . . drawn over to their interests some of the students, whom they style the elect, angels guardian, and the like, but who rather deserve to be branded as spies of their fellow students." These favorites are showered with favors and privileges, while the other students are insulted and can barely obtain necessities. The student confessor is insulted by being made to wait on table, and "beardless youths belonging to the society, but not in holy orders, take precedence in the refectory of the student-priests."[19]

The students claim that the unfairness in the administration of the college is a result of the Jesuits' real aim in running it. Since the Jesuits are a separate body, the students say, they do not really care about the welfare of the students or of the English secular mission, both of which they seek to control for their own good. The students claim that the Jesuits in England slander and oppress the secular priests and put the alms of the faithful to their own selfish purposes, while their fellows at Rome seek to lure the best students into the society, prevent the students from acquiring enough knowledge to appear as learned as the Jesuits, and generally oppress the students who do not belong to the small group friendly to the Jesuits.[20]

The demands of the students[21] are in general what one would expect from their complaints. Besides a whole list of particular changes, they ask that no student intending to enter a religious order be allowed to remain in the college and that the confessor and tutors be elected by the students from among themselves. The replies of the Jesuits and their supporters among the students are also predictable: the rebellious students are only malcontents who cannot abide discipline, their charges against their superiors are false, and their demands are contrary to the requirements of good government.[22]

Almost half of Sega's report sets forth the cardinal's own views on the causes and cures of the dissensions. He supports the Jesuit authorities on every important point, but his general analysis of the situation is much more revealing of his way of thinking than are his recommendations on particular points.

Sega begins his report by asking what caused the problems. He observes that other colleges under Jesuit management have been quiet and concludes therefore that "the disturbances . . . cannot be accounted for by any defect in its government by the Fathers, or by the native peculiarities of the English character." The causes of the trouble, he holds, lie outside the college; "these turbid streams flow from an unclean source, stirred up by the wiles and envy of the foul fiend."[23] Sega supports this contention with a lengthy account of the intrigues of spies and traitors inspired by the English government against the English Catholic cause since the foundation of the Roman college. William Allen and the Jesuits are set up as heroes of the exile movement, motivated solely by concern for religion and their country. Their opponents among the exiles are portrayed as ambitious, greedy men, spurred on either by the bribes of the heretics or by their innate malignity.[24]

Many of the people whom Sega denounces as spies, traitors, or selfish opportunists were what he said they were. The problem with his catalog of espionage, apostasy, and treachery is that none of it has any apparent direct connection with the dissensions at the Roman college, which Sega was purportedly investigating.[25] Sega himself virtually admits as much when at the end of his denunciations he denies "that what I have hitherto stated concerning these wicked and criminal men, is meant to involve any of those now studying in the college." All he can say about the present students is that, "though satisfactory in most respects, their readiness to excite disturbance is, to my mind, a symptom of no slight malady of heart."[26]

This lame conclusion to Sega's tirade naturally leads one to ask why he considered a long history of conscious and usually treasonous sabotage of Catholic enterprises relevant to the problem of the rambunctiousness of a few students. This lumping together of apparently distinct problems is the most obvious example of part of Sega's attitude throughout his attack on the opposition to the more militant of the Catholic exiles; he explicitly or implicitly lumps together activities inspired by conscious treason, personal pique, and other motives. To him, all such opposition seems part of a common pattern; the motives of the people participating in it are not the main point.

As a high papalist, Sega was probably predisposed to regard all challenges to ecclesiastical authority as the work of the devil. However, in his report on the Roman college Sega seems less inspired by his concept of ecclesiastical authority than by his conviction that the church is engaged in a war to the death with the English government, a war not less real for being fought largely by spiritual means. Sega's long account of "Jezabel's"[27] wily schemes against the true church gives the impression of a desperate conflict. But perhaps the most striking instance of Sega's attitude is the evidence by which he proves the effectiveness of the Jesuit mission in England. "The results of this suggestion [to send Jesuits to England] are sufficiently obvious in the sanguinary laws passed by that Jezabel, not only against the fathers of the society and the seminary priests, but against all who should harbor or in any wise favor them, and in the numerous martyrdoms which followed on these blood-stained edicts."[28]

The Jesuits' strongest Catholic enemies later frequently made exactly this claim, that the Jesuits' involvement in the English mission brought down increased persecution on English Catholics. They argued from it that the Jesuits should be withdrawn from the mission. Sega, of course, draws exactly the opposite conclusion. To someone fighting a total war, it is ridiculous to withdraw one's best forces from the campaign because their presence brings on a few extra casualties. If the enemy reacts vigorously to an attack, it must be because he fears its effectiveness. If one is interested primarily in destroying the enemy, obviously the attack should be pressed; casualties may be regrettable, but they must be accepted if necessary.

If this situation is typical of what the church faces, it can stand no insubordination in the ranks, whether motivated by deliberate treason or by youthful heedlessness. Sega thinks that several steps should be taken to tighten up discipline at the Roman college. The rebellious students should be expelled, although he thinks some of them should be given a chance to reform elsewhere.[29] Admissions to the college must be carefully controlled to prevent further outbreaks. Most important, the students must realize that they do not have either the time or the maturity to participate in the government of the college, which must be kept in the hands of the superiors.[30] The superiors ought to control strictly the students' intercourse with each other and with outsiders; it was laxity in this area that allowed the rebellion to get started.[31] The prefects should not be chosen from among the students, since students think it dishonorable to report infractions of the rules.[32] Student confessors and tutors are also unreliable and should not be allowed.[33] Sega says that the students should not complain of strict discipline, since strenuous self-mortification is necessary to cultivate the virtues necessary to the martyrdom that they claim to seek.[34]

Sega is predictably hostile to the idea that the Jesuits should be withdrawn from the government of the Roman college. The priests sent to England so far have "sucked in the learning and virtue they are possessed of at the breasts of the society."[35] Every Englishman who cares about religion and his country admires the Jesuits; to remove them under pressure would merely encourage sedition and contempt for authority at all seminaries.[36] Even less should the pope consider withdrawing the Jesuits from the English mission. Sega agrees with the students that the Jesuits in England have gained some authority over the secular priests, but he thinks that this authority was acquired by their superior virtue and that it is necessary to the mission's effectiveness. The secular priests are sent into England as individuals, with no structure of authority, "hence in the war they wage against heresy they would be as soldiers without a captain, did not the fathers, by the example they set of godly conversation and religious observance exert a kind of authority, and maintain them in the path of duty."[37] One of the Jesuits' most important functions is that of telling Catholics frightened by the frequency of apostasy among seminary priests whom they should and should not trust. In sum, Sega says that there is "no question that to deprive that ill-starred country of the services of the Society of Jesus were to rob it of the salt of the earth, to eclipse the sun of its afflicted church."[38]

Sega's report, which was presented to the pope on 14 March 1596, may have been his last official act; he soon fell ill and was dead within three months. Cardinal Caietan, the protector of England, was absent on a prolonged diplomatic mission to Poland. Within a few weeks after Sega's death, the pope appointed Cardinal Francisco Toledo as vice-protector of England, with immediate jurisdiction over the college. Toledo was a Spaniard and a Jesuit, but he was unfriendly to the ambitions of the Spanish crown and frequently opposed the leaders of the Jesuits. During Toledo's brief vice-protectorship (he

died in September 1596), the Jesuits were retained in the management
of the college, and the ineffective Fioravanti was replaced as rector
by Alphonsus Agazzari, who had served as rector during 1579–86.
Toledo's general policy, however, was directly contrary to that recom-
mended by Sega. Far from attempting a stern assertion of authority,
he tried to kill the rebellion with kindness. Edward Bennet, a leader
of the rebellious students, was allowed to confer with Toledo once a
week about the affairs of the college and to send and receive uncen-
sored letters. Students were appointed to two of the three tutorships,
and Toledo obtained a papal brief placing the Jesuit staff of the college
directy under his jurisdiction rather than under the superiors of the
society.[39] Under this regime the anti-Jesuit students were only too
happy to yield at least surface obedience to Toledo's eloquent exhor-
tations to obey their superiors. The pro-Jesuit students were less
enthusiastic,[40] while Agazzari was afraid of the consequences of
the vice-protector's unwillingness to offend the factious students by
taking strong measures against sedition.[41]

Toledo's policy produced surface calm during the spring and
summer of 1596; there is no parallel during these months to the spectacular public scandals of 1595. But the appearance of calm is decep-
tive. In a less flamboyant way, the struggle over the fate of the Roman
college continued and spread out to involve a wider section of the
English Catholic community and therefore to promote the polarization
that was already beginning to affect the community.

That Sega's report on the dissensions identified the Jesuits with
the cause of virtue and order, both on the mission and at the seminaries has already been mentioned. Others besides Sega felt the same
way. To Acquaviva, whose perspective was presumably conditioned
by his care for the worldwide activities of the society, the English
college may have seemed a sideshow that was more trouble than it
was worth, and his requests to be relieved of it may have seemed
reasonable. The members and friends of the society who were primarily concerned with the English mission saw the society's continued role, and particularly its control of the Roman college, as vital.
Joseph Cresswell, a Jesuit resident at Madrid influential in the affairs
of the English exiles in Spain, had since September 1595 been sending
a stream of letters to the pope's influential nephew and secretary of
state Cardinal Aldobrandino, deploring the behavior of the rebellious
students and blaming it on the machinations of the "Scottish" (i.e.,
supporters of James VI's claim to the English throne) Morgan-Paget

party.[42] In February 1596 and again in November, at times when the removal of the Jesuits from control of the college appeared to be a serious possibility, Cresswell wrote urgently about what a disaster for the Catholic cause removal of the Jesuits from the college would be.[43]

Richard Barret, the secular priest who had succeeded Allen as president of the seminary at Douai, was even more active, perhaps partly because the Jesuits in England collected and sent much greater donations to his seminary than did the secular priests.[44] In December 1595, Barret and some of the other priests at Douai wrote to Acquaviva urging that he not withdraw the society from the government of the Roman college.[45] By April 1596 Barret was in Rome, where he stayed until sometime after 28 September. He may have made the trip partly to defend his own position at Douai; his administration had not been very successful and was under attack.[46] But while in Rome Barret investigated the situation at the college and sent a report on it to Robert Parsons in Spain. Barret criticized many aspects of the college's management that he found too lax or permissive, but he had no doubt that the removal of the Jesuits would lead to "wonderful shame and the undoing of God's cause in our country." Barret urged this view on the pope in April and again in September shortly after Acquaviva had again requested that the society be relieved of the government of the college. On the latter occasion, Barret urged his views with such vehemence that the pope asked him whether he thought the world would perish if the Jesuits were removed.[47]

Barret continued his work on behalf of the Jesuits at Rome after his return to Douai in late 1596. Some hostile sources from early 1597 complain that in choosing students to send to Rome he was attempting to pack the college against the rebels.[48] But Barret's main efforts in the Spanish Netherlands were in defense of the position there of William Holt. Holt was an English Jesuit who had acquired a prominent position at the court of the Spanish Netherlands; among other activities, he dispensed Spanish pensions to English exiles in that part of the Spanish dominions. Holt had made many enemies and by 1597 was defending himself against a determined intrigue to bring about his downfall.[49] As frequently happened, the attack on one Jesuit soon involved his society, whose enemies joined the attack on him while its members and friends came to his defense. Barret and his enemy (and eventual successor at Douai) Thomas Worthington, each in a different way, collected signatures to petitions in favor of Holt and the society.[50] Naturally, supporters of Holt in the Netherlands and of

the Jesuit regime at Rome regarded each other as allies. Barret's activities in Rome and the Spanish Netherlands are one of the clearest
cases up to this point of the connections between the pro-Jesuit
groups in different areas of Europe, but Cresswell's letters from Spain
and the views that Henry Garnet expressed in England show that the
party view of the Roman stirs had spread to those countries as well.[51]
Instead of a collection of discrete factions concerned with local issues,
a perceptible party was growing in all the centers of English Catholicism, a party that explicitly regarded the continuation of Jesuit influence as necessary for the good of the English Catholic community
and viewed opponents of that influence as traitors or rebels.

Meanwhile, the students at Rome, although outwardly more
placid than before, were no more reconciled to the Jesuits than ever.
Their main overt sign of defiance during Toledo's rectorship seems to
have been their increasingly open hostility toward the Spaniards. Barret commented on the students' animosity toward the Spaniards and
toward pro-Spanish Englishmen,[52] while Agazzari wrote to Parsons
that the students

show themselves to oppose the Catholic king's enterprises, of which they
give many clear signs; they speak often and bitterly against the book of
succession to the English crown [i.e., the *Conference About the Next Succession*],
and against its author, whom they suppose to be Parsons, whose name they
can scarcely bear to hear mentioned. They are seen to rejoice at all Spanish
defeats, such as that lately at Cadiz, and to mourn at their successes, such as
that at Calais. I do not know whether they hate the society because of the
Spaniards, or the Spaniards because of the society, or indeed both because of
the Scots, the French, or something worse.[53]

The students may have limited their public demonstrations of
feeling primarily to anti-Spanish gestures because they realized that
they did not have to indulge in flamboyant public gestures in order to
get their way on matters pertaining to the administration of the college. The students appeared as confident about their position in the
college as Agazzari was gloomy about it; Edward Bennet, confident of
Toledo's favor, bragged that if the rector misbehaved toward the students he would be driven out of the college.[54] The students' confidence that the assistance of ecclesiastical superiors outside the college
would enable them to withstand any efforts by the rector to control
them apparently lasted into the period following Toledo's death in
September 1596. Toledo's death was followed by another request
from Acquaviva for the withdrawal of the Jesuits from the college and

a period during which the affairs of the college were generally up in the air. On 7 November Thomas Hill, one of the leaders of the rebellious students, wrote a letter that gives a remarkable insight into at least one student's views on the college's affairs.

The letter was to William Gifford, a seminary priest in exile since about 1573. Gifford had at one time been a propagandist for the duke of Guise, but he soon lived down his antimonarchical past; he was destined to end a long and eventful career as archbishop of Rheims in the 1620s. During 1595–97 he led the attack on the position of Holt and the Jesuits in the Spanish Netherlands. From early 1596 on, he sent frequent letters to the students in Rome, urging them on in their rebellion and denouncing the Jesuits and their alleged attempts to dominate English Catholicism.[55]

Hill begins his letter with a long and vague but fiery passage on the importance of all friends of the students supporting them at this crisis. "We see and feel so much here of their [i.e., the Jesuits] preparation towards that monarchy whereof you have said much." The death of the good Cardinal Toledo has been a blow to the cause of defeating the Jesuits' "monarchy"; "he would have done it for us & our country with great facility and expedition, which we hope to obtain at last, though with much labor and solicitude." The Jesuits "threatened us hard after his death, but behold he is dead & we yet alive, not devoured up of the Jesuits as was feared, but in good terms to have that which we desire, if you in Flanders and elsewhere will lend us your helping hands." The students' good prospects of resisting their superiors are due largely to the friendly attitude of the pope, "who hath been, & will, I doubt not, continue, most benevelous [sic] and propitious unto us," and of the new vice-protector, Cardinal Borghese, who "restraineth the rector from troubling us with innovations, and peremptory proceedings in the college, who otherwise would be intolerable: for notwithstanding that we have access to the cardinal . . . yet he troubleth us exceedingly; but I hope it will be to his confusion shortly, if he amend not, for we observe him in all his actions, & complain of all; and many times he getteth most shameful repulses, we always keeping ourselves out of his danger."[56]

Hill shows no respect for his superiors and no intention of obeying them; he is confident that he and his fellows have enough support and enough mastery of political manipulation to resist having to obey them. For a seminary student, he seems to be engaged in a lot of political wheeling and dealing, and the latter part of his letter shows that his concerns spread beyond his main interest with the Roman college. The cardinal, he writes, "putteth us in great hope that Holt shall smart for it, if it be true that is written." He writes about the students' efforts to discredit Barret in order to stop his scheming with the rector to pack the college with docile students and asks Gifford to arrange to send some fit students to the college. He urges that two priests who have recently left the Roman college for Flanders should go to England. The letter demonstrates the linking of anti-Jesuit factions in different parts of Europe into a conscious anti-Jesuit party parallel to the pro-Jesuit party that was emerging at the same time.

The students at Rome vigorously aided the formation of this party by methods other than their correspondence with Gifford and others in the Spanish Netherlands. In May 1596, the student leaders decided to send one of their number, a priest named Robert Fisher, to the Spanish Netherlands and England. According to Fisher himself, the purpose of his trip, which lasted well into 1597, was to "publish in England against the fathers of the society the objections made against them here in Rome, and that I might procure informations to be sent there against the fathers from any there who were in any way opposed to them."[57] Fisher passed time in the Spanish Netherlands conferring with Charles Paget, William Gifford, and others of the anti-Jesuit party there; Paget and Gifford told him whom to seek out for help in England and gave him several letters and messages to be delivered to various opponents of the Jesuits there. He spent several months in England, spreading and collecting stories discreditable to the Jesuits and generally acting as a courier for the anti-Jesuit group among Wisbech, London, and the North of England.[58] After leaving England, Fisher went back to the Spanish Netherlands and contacted Gifford and other members of the anti-Jesuit group there; during this visit he may have composed a long memorial summing up his party's charges against the Jesuits.[59] From Flanders, Fisher returned by very slow stages to Rome, where he probably arrived early in 1598; he later claimed that he returned as the result of a change of heart and with the intention of changing sides.[60] He found the pro-Jesuit party much more influential in Rome than when he had left, and the authorities put him through an extensive four-day examination that is the most important source of information about his travels. This scrutiny was not the first sign that Fisher's activities were of interest to his enemies as well as to his friends. Henry Garnet had reported to

Acquaviva about Fisher's activities in England, while Richard Barret had reported to Parsons about his attempts to have Fisher examined in the Netherlands and the results of a search of Fisher's baggage.[61]

Fisher's journey makes the magnitude of the disarray in English Catholic affairs in 1596–97 even more obvious than it would otherwise be. In the widespread emerging struggle between pro-Jesuit and anti-Jesuit factions the Roman college was clearly a vital position, and Toledo's death in September 1596 once again put the college's future in question. As has already been mentioned, Acquaviva renewed his request that the Jesuits be relieved of responsibility for it. The pro-Jesuit English Catholics regarded this possibility as disastrous. Only slightly less devastating to them would be a continuation of the sort of regime that existed under Toledo's vice-protectorship: a Jesuit administration hamstrung by an effective alliance of contemptuous and defiant students with people outside the college. The leading English Jesuit, Robert Parsons, had long watched the situation with dismay and in January 1596 had asked the pope to let him attempt to restore harmony. In November he was called from Spain, where he had been since 1589, to Rome. Soon after his arrival, the pope asked him to move into the college and see what he could do about restoring harmony there.

Anthony Kenny has pointed out that it oversimplifies matters to say, as some have, that Parsons instantly restored permanent peace at the college as if by magic.[62] But, considering the recent history of the college, what Parsons did achieve is amazing enough.

He apparently began with the support of the pope and many of the Roman authorities who, Parsons claims, were so disgusted with the continual imbroglios at the college that "many great and wise men began to suspect that the sufferings of our blessed martyrs also and confessors in England was not so much of virtue and love to God's cause as of a certain choler and obstinate will to contradict the magistrate there."[63] This support and the shift of the leadership of the English community in Rome from anti-Jesuits to pro-Jesuits[64] greatly strengthened Parsons's position. But Parsons's success was due largely to his winning the confidence of the students. Parsons himself describes how he conferred with the dissatisfied students at great length, pointing out the importance to the Catholic cause of ending the dissensions, reasoning with them when he thought they were wrong, conceding the point when he found they had just cause of complaint.[65] Edward Bennet confirms this impression of sweet reasonableness in a letter to the anti-Jesuit agitator Hugh Griffin, provost of Cambrai. Parsons, he says, "whom we most feared, and whom we accounted for our greatest enemy, hath been our greatest friend; yea, and the only man that hath satisfied us, and put an end to these troubles."[66] Bennet goes on to describe the new atmosphere of friendly cooperation between the students and the Jesuits, an atmosphere reflected by Bennet's own resignation of the position of confessor and by his urging Griffin to make peace with the Jesuits for the good of the cause. A new set of rules was drawn up, in general very favorable to the students.[67] Soon Agazzari was replaced as rector by Mutius Vitelleschi, who during a previous term as rector had been both popular and effective.

Parsons, however, remained in general control of policy at the college, and the rapport that he apparently established with the students helped him carry out, in a way that his predecessors could never have done, a policy aimed at preventing any recurrence of disturbances. Some of the leading troublemakers had been sent to England shortly before Parsons's arrival, and during 1597 many more were transferred elsewhere. In the fall, Parsons took advantage of an incident in which some students were caught frequenting taverns to initiate a thorough disciplinary crackdown. Regulations of unprecedented severity were imposed on the students, and in November 1597 Parsons himself was appointed rector. He held the post until his death in 1610.

Parsons's success in quelling the dissensions at the Roman college increased his stature and quieted a major trouble spot. But, as time would show, he reversed comparatively little of the damage that had been done to the English Catholic community during the years 1594 to 1597. During the Roman stirs open dissension had spread throughout the community, and the pro-Jesuit and anti-Jesuit parties had become much more self-conscious and more clearly defined than before. The quarrels between the students and the Jesuits at Rome accelerated the growth of this split in many practical ways, but their greatest importance may have been as a stage on which each party believed it saw its ideas about the other demonstrated and confirmed. The Jesuits were shown, to their opponents' satisfaction, to be selfish, hypocritical, and power hungry, while their opponents obligingly provided confirmation for the pro-Jesuit party's belief that they were turbulent, undisciplined, contemptuous of authority, and (whether consciously or not) serving the aims of the heretics. The quarrels in

England and the Spanish Netherlands had the same effect, but the Roman stirs were on center stage and seem to have attracted the most attention.

The quarrels of 1594–97 did make one point clear. Since Allen's death the papacy had largely let the problem of the English Catholic church government drift, either out of inertia or out of hope that problems could continue to be handled with the relatively informal methods used in Allen's lifetime. This policy had been a disaster. It turned out, as is frequently the case with great men, that Allen's system was very fragile, because it required his presence to function effectively. Since Allen's death no one had been able to exert comparable authority over English Catholics, and the collapse in confusion of the English Catholic community seemed very likely. Clearly some new method of government was needed, one that would be more formal and institutionalized than before. But while dissension within the English Catholic community made evident the necessity of a more definite plan of government, it also made the institution of such a plan more difficult. Every new party battle increased hatred and distrust within the community and made it harder to devise any solution that would not appear to be the instrument of one party, with consequent suspicion and mistrust by the other party. The system of government that was instituted in March 1598 fell into the trap in the worst way and led to the most fundamental and bitter struggle of Elizabeth's reign over the constitution, purpose, and nature of the English mission.

# CHAPTER VII

# Background: Narrative of
# the Archpriest Controversy

Long before the appointment of the archpriest George Blackwell on 7 March 1598, the two emerging parties within English Catholicism had taken some steps to remedy the lack of organization within the Catholic community. The efforts of the anti-Jesuit party to establish a formal organization were limited largely to England, where, sometime during the second half of 1596, several priests attempted to set up an "association," voluntary in membership and electing its own heads, for the purpose of handling alms, settling disputes, and general mutual assistance.[1] These plans seem to have been dropped before the appointment of the archpriest, for a number of reasons. Alban Dolman, and perhaps other priests sympathetic to those who planned the association, thought that even the most innocent organization of priests might appear to the government as a suspicious plot and therefore lead to increased persecution.[2] Bagshaw later listed among the reasons for dropping the association the "fear of sinister interpretations or suspicions . . . lest the endeavor of stopping practices might seem some dangerous practice."[3] He also mentioned lack of money, differences of opinion among the organizers, and the desire of the "wisest lay Catholics" that "the actions of priests should not extend beyond their spiritual functions." This last reason may mean, as J. H. Pollen has suggested,[4] that the Catholic laity feared the threats to their security that might result from the meetings, correspondence, and other business that the association would involve. It may also reflect hostility on the part of the Catholic nobility and gentry to anything that would threaten their control over the priests in their households; the rules of the association would clearly have strengthened its members' position against their hosts. Included in the rules were detailed regulations by which the association would control the placing of its members in Catholic houses and even provision for clerical boycotts of houses that failed to abide by the regulations. A critique of the association rules, apparently written before the appointment of the archpriest, makes both these points—the dangers caused by the need for frequent meetings and extensive record keeping, and the undesirable infringement on the rights of the laity that the rules involve.[5]

The association was also weakened by the circumstances of its origins. Operating in a hostile country, without the approval of any higher ecclesiastical authority, such an organization could hardly be anything but voluntary. Not only was it unsanctioned by higher authority, but at least one of its leaders, Bagshaw, had already made quite a name for himself as an opponent of the Jesuits. Almost inevitably, the association would be seen by many as an organization not of the English secular priesthood, but of the anti-Jesuit party within it—and as a potential rival to the network run by the Jesuit superior, Henry Garnet.[6] Some of those involved in the association were aware of this problem; John Mush and Richard Dudley apparently opposed forwarding formal charges against the Jesuits to Rome partly because "it might appear that the associations or fellowships . . . were inspired, not by zeal for religion, but by jealousy of the fathers."[7] But others in the association may well have intended the group to be directed against the Jesuits. It is difficult to believe that Bagshaw regarded the association and the anti-Jesuit campaign as completely separate causes, and one Appellant propagandist later wrote that the association was intended partly "for the checking of some exorbitant, and unnatural courses, taken by the Jesuits against their prince and country."[8]

The association was inevitably disliked by the Jesuits and their friends. John Mush, in a letter of June or July 1597 which marks his wholehearted conversion to the anti-Jesuit cause, denounces "the foul dealing of the Jesuits which bend themselves thus mightily against our association."[9] Little is known about just what the Jesuits in England and their friends did to sink the association; with all the other weaknesses under which it labored, they may not have needed to do much. But their motives are clear enough. The association was bound to appear as a rival organization to that of the Jesuits and their friends. To persons who believed that the strong influence of the Jesuits was necessary to the value and success of the English mission, such an organization, especially one unsanctioned by any higher ecclesiastical authority, was bound to seem subversive. Parsons, in his later attacks on the Appellants, denounced it as an attempt to usurp offices and authority.[10] The Appellants subsequently showed sensitivity to the charge; in the book written to sum up their case to the pope, John Mush claimed that the organizers of the association had intended to seek papal approval, and the Appellant Humphrey Ely makes the same claim in response to Parsons's charges.[11]

The association, in any case, seems never to have gotten very far and was apparently dropped before the appointment of the arch-priest.[12] Its limitation to lower-level voluntary organizing in England and its general ineffectiveness form a strong contrast to the efforts of Parsons and his friends in Rome. The archpriest system was not Parsons's first choice for a system of government for the English mission; in 1597 he drew up a plan for the appointment of two bishops, one to reside in England and the other in the Spanish Netherlands, to supervise English affairs.[13] For reasons that are not clear, the Holy See was unwilling to put the English mission under episcopal rule. But although the archpriest system may not have been Parsons's preferred form of polity for the English mission, its structure certainly reflected his concerns. The archpriest was given authority only over secular priests trained in the seminaries and not over the remaining Marian priests or members of religious orders, of whom the Jesuits were the only ones on the mission. Over the seminary priests he was given authority to "direct, admonish, reprehend, and even to punish,"[14] to settle controversies, to assign places to live and work, and to assign penalties up to suspension and deprivation of faculties. This last power was especially serious in a country where the Catholic church had no benefices and priests without faculties had no way of earning a living. But potentially the most obnoxious feature of Blackwell's instructions was contained in a covering letter to his letter of appointment, in which Cardinal Caietan, the protector of England who issued the letters, ordered Blackwell to consult with the superior of the Jesuits on all important matters, while Garnet was placed under no corresponding obligation to consult Blackwell.

The offense that these provisions were bound to cause to Parsons's opponents was compounded by the character of the man appointed to the office of archpriest. George Blackwell had worked in England since 1576, creditably enough, but with no great demonstration of ability as a leader. The main point that distinguished him from many other priests was his great expressions of admiration for the Jesuits. He wrote one ardent letter to Caietan in praise of the Jesuits in January 1596;[15] in December 1597 he wrote another, in which he expressed his views of the Jesuits' opponents with the comment that "nothing can be more perverse than to be the enemy of the best."[16]

A standard charge of Appellant propaganda asserted that Blackwell was a mere front man for the Jesuits, foisted on the English clergy by the influence of the arch-schemer, Parsons. In all fairness, it is hard to see any reason for Blackwell's appointment other than his friendliness to the Jesuits. It was natural that Parsons should have had great influence with the Roman hierarchy in late 1597 and early 1598; he had just settled very effectively the long-standing scandalous situation at the Roman college and as far as English affairs were concerned he was the man of the hour. But it was ultimately disastrous for Parsons's cause that the erection of the archpriest regime appeared to be a blatant attempt by his party to suppress its opponents and control the English mission.

Some of the priests of the anti-Jesuit party were naturally reluctant to accept Blackwell's authority; an excuse was provided by the fact that his authority rested on the letters not of the pope but of the cardinal protector, whose authority was more open to doubt.[17] Therefore, while most English priests submitted to Blackwell, some of them, including several of the most prominent, refused to accept his authority, pending an appeal to the pope. These priests sent two of their number, William Bishop and Robert Charnock, to Rome (where they arrived in December 1598) to point out the drawbacks of the archpriest regime and to obtain the pope's own word on whether or not he approved it.

The appeal was conducted with staggering political naiveté. Bishop and Charnock may have been effective missionary priests, but they seem to have been babes in the woods in the world of Roman officialdom. Although they attempted to enlist the aid of the French ambassador at Rome, they brought no credentials from the French government; therefore, the ambassador could do nothing for them. With no influential support visible at Rome and having brought little evidence of much support in England, the two priests were left to the tender mercies of Parsons, and that veteran of church politics mobilized his connections and made mincemeat of Bishop and Charnock.

The two Appellants were imprisoned in the English seminary in Rome under Parsons's supervision and prevented from communicating with each other; their papers were taken away; and they were condemned at a highly partial trial before two supporters of Parsons —Cardinal Caietan, the protector of England who had appointed Blackwell, and Cardinal Borghese, the vice-protector. The Appellants were denied all access to the pope, who issued a brief on 6 April 1599, confirming the system of government set up by Caietan and declaring it valid from the beginning. Bishop and Charnock were banished to Paris and Lorraine, respectively, and forbidden to return to England without express permission.

The treatment of Bishop and Charnock caused great bitterness against Parsons among the members of their party. Nevertheless, even the most strongly anti-Jesuit and anti-Blackwell priests submitted to the archpriest upon reception of the pope's brief. The matter might have ended there if Blackwell had been content with the recognition of his authority, but he had already endorsed a pamphlet by the Jesuit Thomas Lister, which accused those who had refused to accept the archpriest at once of (among other things) schism, rebellion, and disobedience to the Holy See.[18] Shortly after the reception of the papal brief of April 1599, Blackwell, moved by what he described as "a resolution from our mother city" (which, unfortunately for him, later turned out to be merely the private opinion of some members of Parsons's party at Rome), declared that those who had refused to accept his authority from the first had been guilty of schism and demanded that they acknowledge their fault and seek absolution from him.

J. H. Pollen, who is generally sympathetic to Blackwell's side, has said that the accusation of schism against the Appellants was unjustified.[19] It was also a major tactical error, which gave the Appellants a new issue and which made Blackwell and his supporters appear as the extremists. Many of the Appellants indignantly denied that they had been guilty of schism, and some of them appealed to the University of Paris for an opinion on the question. Considering both the merits of the case and the strong anti-Jesuit tendencies of the university, it is not surprising that the decision issued in May 1600 absolved Blackwell's opponents of schism.[20] Blackwell, however, forbade any priest under his authority to defend the decision of Paris and suspended many of his opponents for maintaining their innocence in this and other ways. Violent quarrels disturbed the English clergy throughout 1600 and 1601, and the Appellants began to publish tracts on the issue around the middle of 1601. Some of these books were at least partly designed to support an appeal to the pope, which was signed by thirty priests on 17 November 1600, detailing Blackwell's offenses and asking for changes in the ecclesiastical government in England.[21] This appeal was answered by a papal letter of 17 August 1601, which dismissed as unfounded Blackwell's accusations of schism, reproved the archpriest for excessive severity, and sternly lectured his opponents on the duty of Christian obedience. All controversial writings on both sides were condemned, and further publications on the subject forbidden.[22]

Like the papal brief of April 1599, this temperate and evenhanded document might have put an end to the controversy if Blackwell had been content simply to make the brief public and leave it at that. The letter, however, arrived at what he considered a very bad time, since Parsons was engaged in writing an extensive defense of Blackwell's conduct as archpriest and an attack on his opponents.[23] Blackwell therefore kept the letter secret for several months and made it public only after the publication of Parsons's book. This device was quite transparent and caused the pope's brief to be regarded as a dead letter by both sides. The propaganda battle continued through early 1603 with hardly a pause and expanded from a discussion primarily of Blackwell's appointment and conduct to an increasingly ill-tempered debate on the whole range of issues separating the two parties.

During the summer and fall of 1601, the Appellants were organizing a mission to Rome in support of their second appeal, unaware of the pope's letter answering it. It was at this stage that the Appellants established a strong working relationship with the English government. Some of the more intransigent members of the Appellant party had approached the government as early as 1599, but both the government and most of the Appellants had been cautious about establishing a real alliance. Sometime in 1601, however, the Appellant priest Thomas Bluet convinced Richard Bancroft, bishop of London and coordinator of government policy toward religious dissent, to grant passports to him and three others to go to Rome to pursue their appeal. Bluet was also given permission to travel unmolested around England, raising money from sympathetic Catholics to support the appeal.

In backing the Appellant party, the government probably expected at the very least to sow dissension in Catholic ranks and may have hoped that the appeal to Rome would result in the withdrawal of the Jesuits from England, the lessening of their influence at the English seminaries on the Continent, and a prohibition of political activity by the English clergy—all items in the Appellant program. In return for their cooperation in getting the mission out of politics and the Jesuits out of the mission, the Appellants apparently expected the government to grant some kind of toleration to Catholics whom it considered politically loyal. The government quietly encouraged this expectation, probably in order to add zeal to the Appellants' advocacy of those aspects of their program that coincided with the government's desires.

In addition to the quiet support of the English government, the second appeal to Rome had the open support of France. Having learned the necessity of powerful friends in Rome from the experience of Bishop and Charnock on the first appeal, the Appellants stopped at Paris on their way to Rome, and persuaded the seigneur de Villeroy, Henry IV's secretary of state, to instruct Philippe de Béthune, French ambassador at Rome, to support the Appellants' cause if it seemed advisable to him.[24] Béthune, a very able diplomat anxious to reduce Spanish influence at Rome and elsewhere, adopted his instructions with a vengeance. He took the four Appellant representatives (Thomas Bluet, John Mush, Anthony Champney, and John Cecil) under his protection when they arrived at Rome, and he seems to have conducted much of the negotiations with the pope and other Roman authorities on their behalf.

The governments of England and France both backed the Appellant party because of their opposition to the political militants who had become identified with Spain. One might have expected the English Catholic gentry and nobility to support the Appellants for the same reason; the Appellants' views on political matters bear a great resemblance to those of many of the gentry.

Some connections may be traced between the Appellants and individual gentlemen. Charles Paget and Sir Thomas Copley's son Anthony both wrote pro-Appellant propaganda, while in 1602 Christopher Bagshaw lived in Paris with Henry Constable, a gentleman who had written a fierce attack on Doleman's *Conference About the Next Succession to the Crown of England*.[25] William Gifford, a priest who came from a gentry family, wrote to his sister in England warning her not to trust "these violent and bloody spirits who continually and unnaturally practice against their prince and country, and seek to expose to the spoil of foreigners by unjust invasions and conquest all sorts of people of what religion soever."[26] Several early Appellant works express distress at the fact that the Catholic laity have the wrong ideas about the controversy because they have not been fully informed of the nefarious schemes of the Jesuits and their allies.[27]

But the concern expressed in these early Appellant works indicates that the Appellants were not entirely sure of the support of lay Catholic opinion. Several considerations may have held some of the gentry back from active support of the Appellants. The Jesuits, the Appellants' main scapegoats, and their accomplishments on the mission commanded widespread respect. Many Catholic gentry may also have disliked the fact that the Appellants were challenging the position of their superior—a testimony, their opponents claimed, to their generally insubordinate disposition. Some may have regarded the organizers of the clerical association as more of a threat to their position than the Jesuits were. But the greatest barrier to lay involvement may have been simple inertia and incomprehension. The archpriest controversy was an argument over the organization of the clergy, conducted largely abroad, within a framework of church law and administration that was remote from the lives of most laymen, involving a complex set of issues on which many laity probably had divided minds. Divided minds may have added to the natural reluctance of many Catholic gentry to become involved in anything that might get them into trouble. But for whatever reason, no evidence of any widespread gentry support for either side in the archpriest controversy is apparent—even though on the political front, the Appellants may appear to have been fighting the gentry's battle for them.

The Appellants' requests at Rome included their acquittal of the charge of schism, the removal of Blackwell, and either the abolition of the archpriest system in favor of episcopal rule or its modification so as to limit the power of the archpriest and strengthen the clerical rank and file. The Appellants of 1602 presented more detailed plans for the reform of the constitution of the English church than had Bishop and Charnock, but their demands in this area were similar to those of earlier Appellant agitation. The Appellants' political demands also contained little that was really new, but the interest of their allies in the English and French governments in reducing the Jesuit and Spanish influences in the English mission and in separating the mission from politics gave the demands a new urgency and caused more attention to be devoted to them.

The struggle over the second appeal was long (the final papal letter on the subject was issued on 5 October 1602) and complex, and the details need not be recounted here. The result left neither party fully satisfied.[28] As was surely to be expected, all writings of both sides were condemned and all future discussion of the issue prohibited. Parsons's side had reason to feel upset by the facts that the priests who had refused to recognize Blackwell's authority at the first reception of Cardinal Caietan's letters were cleared of the charge of schism and the faculties of those whom Blackwell had suspended were declared to have been valid during their suspensions, which were declared null and void. In addition, Blackwell was ordered to fill the next three vacancies on his staff of twelve assistants from the ranks of the Appellants, and, perhaps most distressing of all to Parsons and his allies, Blackwell was forbidden to consult any English Jesuit on the affairs of the mission.

These results were major achievements for the Appellants, but they were much less successful on the issues of greatest concern to the English government. The papal letter of 5 October forbade all dealings with heretics to the prejudice of Catholics—a clear allusion to the Appellants' suspicious involvement with Bancroft. The Jesuits were not withdrawn from England or from the management of any of the seminaries on the Continent. The letter of 5 October said nothing about the involvement of the clergy in politics or about the possibility of accepting religious toleration from a Protestant government. When this silence was considered in the context of the hostility to their political program that the pope had expressed in interviews with the Appellants,[29] it clearly meant that there would be no immediate change in the church's official stance of complete denial of the legitimacy of the English government and refusal to seek a modus vivendi with it.

Soon after the pope's answer to the appeal, the English government apparently decided that it had gone as far with the Appellants as it cared to go. On 5 November 1602 (six weeks after the papal letter of 5 October, because of the ten-day difference between the Julian calendar in use in England and the Gregorian calendar in use in Rome) a royal proclamation was issued that disappointed all the Appellants' hopes of winning better treatment from Elizabeth's government. It denied in the strongest terms that the queen had ever considered allowing the toleration of any but the established religion. Although the proclamation said that the Jesuits and their adherents were more dangerous to the state than the Appellants, it probably was cold comfort to the Appellants to be accused merely of "disloyalty and disobedience" while the word "traitor" was reserved for their opponents. The Jesuits and their adherents were given thirty days to leave the country, and the Jesuits' opponents were given until the first of February. Priests were given the option of presenting themselves to any one of several named officials, acknowledging their allegiance to the queen and submitting to her mercy, upon which "we will then . . . take such further order, as shall be thought by us to be most meet and convenient."[30]

Since the allegiance that Elizabeth considered due to her involved recognition of her authority in spirituals as well as in temporals, it is not surprising that few priests either left the country or turned themselves in in response to the proclamation. A group of Appellant priests around London, however, signed a protestation of allegiance that is one of the clearest statements of the basic Appellant position on the relative authority of queen and pope.[31] Most of the signers of whom anything is known were members of the moderate wing of the Appellant party; some of the more extreme advocates of royal authority did not sign. The queen, the protestation held, had the same claim upon the priests' allegiance in civil or temporal matters as any of her predecessors. They were morally bound to reveal plots against her and to resist invasions aimed at overthrowing her, even if sponsored by the pope in the name of the Catholic religion—even if their loyalty to the queen led to their excommunication. On the other hand, they acknowledged that the pope was the legitimate successor of Peter and that in spiritual matters they owed him obedience, "which, we doubt not but will stand well with the performance of our duty to our temporal prince, in such sort as we have before professed. For, as we are most ready to spend our blood in the defence of her Majesty and our country, so we will rather lose our lives than infringe the lawful authority of Christ's Catholic church."[32]

This statement may be regarded as a futile gesture, since its main assumptions had already been rejected by both of the authorities to whom the signers expressed loyalty. In any case, Elizabeth died soon after, and although old animosities were not forgotten, the accession of James I and the acceptance of the latest papal ban on further controversy opened a new stage in the history of the English mission.

# CHAPTER VIII

# The Archpriest Controversy:
# The Problem of Church Order

Attempting to extract coherent philosophies out of the propaganda barrages of the archpriest controversy is, to some extent, a misleading exercise.[1] Much of the material is mere invective, and more of it is taken up by the writers' nit-picking examinations of the conduct of their own side and that of their opponents. The documents are frequently dishonest and usually ill-tempered, verbose and repetitious. The writers are usually more concerned with scoring debating points or otherwise embarrassing their opponents than with precise, consistent, and systematic statements of their beliefs. Frequently this propaganda is more valuable as an illustration of habits of mind than of precisely worked out doctrinal positions. But the mental habits and doctrinal assertions of both sides are consistent enough to make it possible to analyze the nature of the parties' general views on the question of authority within the church that separated the two parties.

The only writer of much importance against the Appellants was Robert Parsons. Late in 1601 or early in 1602 he published *A Brief* (463 pages!) *Apology or Defence of the Catholic Ecclesiastical Hierarchy.* In 1602 he published an appendix to the *Brief Apology*, which he soon followed with *A Manifestation of the Great Folly and Bad Spirit, of Certain in England which Call Themselves Secular Priests.* All three works were published anonymously.

Throughout these works, Parsons assumes that the three superiors whose authority is in question—the pope, Cardinal Protector Caietan, and Archpriest Blackwell—have done nothing wrong and have commanded nothing that is not clearly within their authority. Indeed, Parsons's ideas about the authority of ecclesisastical superiors make it difficult to say that anything could be outside their authority. "The interpretation of this will of God unto us," he says, is the "will and voice of our Superior whereunto we are bound to harken and obey, for obtaining all grace & blessing." We know that "the resisting of our superiors' wills be accounted the highest sin of all others, by holy men's opinions." The "principal point in this affair" is "the resistance of power and God's ordination descending unto us from our superiors." Blackwell is "God's substitute among them [the English secular priests] . . . our spiritual superiors are most of all other men to be respected by us, yea before angels themselves . . . for that these men's authority is known evidently to be from God, which in angels is not."[2]

Parsons's image of ecclesiastical authority is of a hierarchy in which each superior speaks with the voice of God to those under his authority.[3] This high view of the authority of ecclesiastical superiors is drawn largely from revelation (as from its nature it must be). He is particularly fond of applying to the hierarchy Christ's words to his apostles, "He that heareth you heareth me; and he that despiseth you despiseth me."[4] But he also uses pragmatic arguments to justify the subordinate's almost total lack of any right to question any superior's orders. If persons may demur at receiving their superiors' commands, Parsons claims, it will spell an end to all obedience, and the church will dissolve in chaos.[5] The Appellants' claim that all superiors except the pope may err and that the pope may err in some things is merely a crafty trick to lead the English Catholics to believe that Blackwell's appointment was one of the cases in which the pope could err.[6] Elsewhere, Parsons attacks this Appellant claim on more remarkable grounds. The Appellants' doctrine,

which albeit in some senses, meanings & interpretations, they may endeavor to verify and defend, yet how dangerous, and scandalous it may prove, to teach the people in this general manner against their superiors, is easy to consider, seeing it teacheth men to doubt, whether & how far they be to be obeyed yea his Holiness himself in some points for that they say he is not warranted in all and consequently may err also in some of his ordinances and commandments, and by the same argument, which they use against the archpriest and other higher superiors, a man may argue against his Holiness & men are taught by this doctrine to examine everything coming from their superiors, by their own judgments, and admit what they please, and leave the rest.[7]

Heresy, Parsons goes on to say, began in this way; people were taught that they might differ from and disobey their superiors in some cases, "which though it were true in it self, yet these cases not being put down nor observed in particular, but the doctrine only delivered in general, wrought infinite hurts in God's church."[8]

This passage exemplifies Parsons's persistent interest in results. He does not, strictly speaking, try to prove the Appellants wrong. He argues instead that certain interpretations of their statements could lead and have led to the most undesirable consequences: to disorder, to disobedience, and ultimately to heresy against the divinely instituted hierarchy that speaks for God on earth. Clearly, logical gaps can be detected in Parsons's position,[9] but as is often the case, his views can be accounted for by the overwhelming importance that he attributes to certain goals—particularly to the maintenance of unity and discipline in the church.

Parsons, then, attempts to persuade the reader of the general proposition that in virtually all cases unquestioning obedience to ecclesiastical superiors is both a commandment from God and a practical necessity. He also attempts to undermine the Appellants' position by disposing of many of their particular justifications of their refusals to obey Blackwell. They say, for example, that the pope was misinformed on circumstances in England; Parsons says that a superior's commands are valid even if some of his reasons for the action are based on erroneous information.[10] Parsons quotes canon law to prove that in spite of the Appellants' claims to the contrary, a cardinal's letters patent ought to be accepted on the cardinal's word.[11] He quotes Thomas Aquinas to prove that a subordinate should obey a superior's commands even if he is not sure that the order is within the superior's authority; it is enough if the subordinate does not know positively that the command goes beyond the superior's authority.[12]

Parsons complements his views on the legitimate grounds of disobedience with a very broad idea of what constitutes disobedience. He says that if the Appellants had, as they claimed, really been interested in finding out whether the archpriest's appointment had the approval of the pope they could simply have inquired by letter. Sending Bishop and Charnock to appeal to the pope was obviously a seditious attempt to get the decision changed.[13] Later Parsons says that the Appellants' urgent requests that bishops be placed in charge of English affairs is an insult to the pope, who has not done so.[14] In

Parsons's view it is sometimes subversive not only to resist or disobey one's superior, but even to try to persuade him to change his mind. The tendency of Parsons's ideas on the constitution of the church extends his views discussed earlier on the relationship of the church and temporal matters. He believes that the church, and more particularly the hierarchy of the church, represents God's will in a way different from any other institution. Both direct divine sanction and the practical need for unity and effective action require obedience to the rule of authoritative leaders, from the pope on down, whose commands are to be obeyed without question. In the *Conference About the Next Succession* Parsons (or Doleman) attempted to clear away the obstacles placed in the way of his program by a system of political morality that he believed to be false; in the *Memorial for the Reformation* he planned the clearing away of obstacles within English society. The Appellants' activities provoked him to attack potential obstacles to effective action within the church itself.

The Appellants, of course, did not accept Parsons's characterization of them as seditious, disobedient, and intent on overthrowing all ecclesiastical order and authority. John Bennet expressed his party's common position when he said that they "have behaved themselves in all dutiful manner to all superiors, which they knew, and how far they were bound to show obedience."[15] Many Appellant writers argue that their action in appealing to the pope demonstrates their recognition of the pope's authority, and they point out that all of Blackwell's opponents submitted to his authority upon the reception of the pope's brief confirming him in office. One Appellant writer claims that Blackwell's opponents were not schismatics, for "we protest and vow all obedience due unto God's church, and her lawful authority. . . . If they urge against us that we obey this [Blackwell's] authority: let them show us that it is a lawful act of the church and we obey."[16]

But even in the act of protesting their loyal obedience, the Appellants demonstrate the difference in mental orientation between themselves and Parsons. The burden of proof is put on the person who wishes to prove the obligation of the subordinate to obey the superior. The obedience owed to the church is hedged around with potential modifiers: obedience *due, lawful* authority, *lawful* act of the church. Whereas Parsons draws a picture of the divine will descending through the church hierarchy, the Appellants, here and elsewhere, usually portray a church run by rules and regulations independent of the will of any of its members; their view is essentially legalistic and, one can sometimes say, constitutionalist. This frame of mind, unlike Parsons's, leaves a great deal of room for dispute about the rights and duties of people within the church and about the limits of superiors' authority.

The Appellants do a great deal of disputing, on many issues. Much of their argument is on what might be called narrow grounds. To defend themselves against the charge of disobeying Cardinal Caietan's orders by their initial failure to submit to Blackwell's authority, they claim that the unsupported word of a cardinal protector is not enough to bind them to obey the archpriest under the circumstances.[17] This claim is supported primarily by attacks on the circumstances of the archpriest's appointment. The Appellants portray the pope and other authorities at Rome as the victims of a conspiracy to misinform and mislead them about the situation in England. Parsons and a few friends, they claim, spread the false story that the secular priests were quarreling with the Catholic laity, concealed the rift between seculars and Jesuits, falsely told the authorities that the archpriest system was favored by the clergy as a whole, and concealed the secular priests' desire for episcopal rule. The archpriest's appointment is thus founded on false information and therefore is no real reflection of the will of the pope or any other superior.[18] Attempts to get the system changed are, therefore, fundamentally loyal attempts to provide the authorities with information that will enable them to make a correct decision.

All this reasoning should sound very familiar to any student of early modern European political history. The claim that a ruler's obnoxious actions were due to the influence of evil counselors who deceived and misled him was a commonplace feature of practically all opposition movements. In the ecclesiastical sphere as well as in the temporal, the evil-counselor theory has obvious advantages. It makes possible some degree of ostensibly loyal criticism of policy in a system in which outright and open opposition to the ruler's will is considered subversive by many theorists and usually by theruler himself. It therefore allows competing groups to air their differences and struggle for influence, at the same time maintaining the possibility of future cooperation with the ruler or with each other.

But criticism is risky even when the evil-counselor theory provides a respectable facade, for it is very difficult to oppose a policy solely on the grounds that it was procured by misinformation. One is almost inevitably led into criticizing the policy itself (indeed, that is probably the real purpose of the exercise) and from that point one can easily be led into at least touching on the fundamental basis of the ruler's authority. The Appellants are only too eager to criticize the archpriest system itself; they point to its badness as evidence that the pope would never have approved of it if he had not been misinformed.[19]

Several themes emerge from the Appellants' discussion of the shortcomings of the archpriest regime in general and Blackwell's conduct in particular. They frequently charge that the authority given to Blackwell gives him power only to punish those under his jurisdiction and not to bestow any benefits on them; it therefore "carrieth evident remonstrance of an intolerable burden without any commodity at all, and not without manifest suspicion of a plain plot or stratagem, to take away all ecclesiastical hierarchy and ancient approved government in our church."[20] The "ancient approved government in our church," which (among other things) is threatened by the punitive nature of Blackwell's authority, is episcopacy. The request for episcopal rule in the English church was a constant plank of the Appellant platform, and the appointment and powers of a bishop were to be one of the most important issues between the Jesuits and their opponents through much of the seventeenth century. But although some Appellant tracts pointed out the virtues of episcopacy, the lack of it under the archpriest regime seems to have attracted less of their ire than several other manifestations of what they regarded as a tyrannical disregard for the rights of the English clergy.

Perhaps the most obnoxious such manifestation was Caietan's instructions to Blackwell to consult the superior of the Jesuits on all important questions. The Appellants constantly emphasize the dignity of the secular priesthood as, by Christ's ordinance, the church's principal pastors of souls, a vocation that they consider higher than those of members of religious orders.[21] It is therefore a grievous attack on proper order and degree to place secular priests under the rule of regulars, which is what the Appellants interpret Caietan's instructions as doing. One of the wilder Appellant tracts, probably by Christopher Bagshaw, sums up the significance of the archpriest system. "All Catholics must hereafter depend upon Blackwell, and he upon Garnet, and Garnet upon Parsons, and Parsons upon the

Devil."[22] In a somewhat more moderate tone, an anonymous author in the *Copies of Certain Discourses* says that the archpriest system has been

established in such sort by them [the Jesuits] that the superior must needs remain a puny, and inferior to them, and by that mean be an instrument to execute what they shall think good . . . so that our superior being subject to them, consequently all we must be their apprentices, and stand at their command, which is to pervert all true order in God's church. For oftentimes, and by the late general council of Trident [*sic*, for Trent] it is decreed, that the secular clergy shall have power over the religious, as to visit them, reform and correct them, &c as the bishop doth, but seldom or never hath the religious clergy any jurisdiction over the secular clergy.[23]

The Appellants consider the archpriest regime an insult to the dignity of the secular priesthood not only because they think it effectively subordinates them to the Jesuits but also because it was instituted uncanonically, without the advice or consent of those over whom the archpriest was given authority. Of course, the participation of the clergy in the selection of their superiors had long been, in most cases, purely nominal; but it was quite typical of the Appellants to make a legal formality into a constitutional principle. William Bishop asks rhetorically, "Was there no means to be found for appeasing of all parties, than to cast upon us without our privities and consents, contrary to the canons of the church, a platform of government, never before seen or heard of in the church of God?" The pope, he claims to have heard, had said "that he would not establish and set any superiority among us in England before he had heard from us of our good wills and likings, which was fatherlike, lovingly, and wisely spoken, conformable unto the ancient canons."[24] Anthony Champney charges that Blackwell's authority was procured "contrary to the canons of holy church, which prescribe that priests should have the election of their archpriest."[25] An anonymous writer alleges that the pope approved the archpriest system only when he was falsely persuaded that the priests in England wanted it. "For whose advice, consent, and allowance, are required to the choosing of a superior, if not theirs that are to obey and live under the same superior?"[26]

Other Appellants claim that the appointment of Blackwell without the clergy's consent was not merely a simple violation of canon and tradition but prejudicial to the rights of the clergy placed under Blackwell's authority. John Colleton asserts that the priests' rights were prejudiced in that the archpriest was not chosen by the whole body of priests or at least by those who were chosen as the arch-priest's assistants. Surely, he says, the pope has enough respect for the secular priests who endure the dangers and discomforts of the English mission to allow them to choose their own superior and not to leave the choice to Caietan, a foreigner and a friend of the priests' enemies, the Jesuits.[27] Humphrey Ely, the Appellants' canon law expert, claims that while the priests were not obliged to obey Caietan's letters in any case, their refusal to obey was further justified by the fact that "every superior . . . by the ordinary and common course of law ought to be chosen by those, over whom they are afterwards to govern." That the pope asked Parsons's friends whether the English priests wanted the archpriest system established was, says Ely, "an evident sign and token that his Holiness meant not to give them a superior without their consents, nor to take away the right of election that was due unto them by his predecessors' decrees and constitutions. For to use Gregory IX his words . . . It is not credible that the bishop of Rome (who doth defend the laws) would with one word overthrow, that which otherwise with much pain and care hath been excogitated and invented." Besides, Ely goes on, the pope's decrees are always to be interpreted in a manner "saving other men's right and without the hurt and hinderacem [sic] of others."[28]

Some of Ely's remarks here bear on the crucial issue of the relationship between the pope and the canon law, which will be discussed later. But when dealing with the right of election the Appellants' statements generally focus (prudently enough) on the rights of subordinates rather than on the powers of the pope. Ely's phrasing here does not make clear whether the pope can override the normal requirements of canon law. But in the usual course of events, priests have the right to choose their superior or at least to consent to his appointment.

A subordinate's possession of a right implies, when viewed from the other side, the existence of a limitation on the authority of a superior. If priests ought normally to have the right of electing their superior, one would expect the superior's authority to be limited after the election as well. The Appellants do repeatedly argue that there are limitations on ecclesiastical superiors and that subordinates are not required to obey any command that a superior may give. Many of their arguments are aimed specifically at limiting Blackwell's authority, but in the process of doing so they present an alternative to Parsons's view of the nature and authority of the ecclesiastical hierarchy.

The Appellants certainly do not share Parsons's image of divine inspiration passing down the hierarchy from each superior to his subordinates. They stress that superiors are fallible human beings, who may err as easily as other men. Those who accuse them of disobedience, rebellion, and schism, one of them says, "must be put in mind that authority is not an infallible rule of truth in all who have authority, and consequently that no man is bound in all things to believe or execute what every man in authority over him shall put upon him."[29] When Parsons accuses the Appellants of being "disunited from their lawful superior, and consequently from God also," Robert Charnock replies, "What bad man in authority will not think himself much bound to this author for this his consequence? . . . cannot a lawful superior do amiss? And in that misdoing may he not be forsaken by those, whose superior he is, without incurring a just suspicion, that they are disunited from God?"[30]

Parsons, it will be remembered, attacked the Appellants' views on the obedience due to superiors by saying they would lead to general disobedience and chaos and open the door to heresy. He is not willing to state flatly that superiors are infallible, but he argues in effect that they should be treated as if they were; when he considers the institution he really cares about, he shows the authoritarian's fear that if any dissent is tolerated the institution will collapse in chaos. Charnock's remark on the comfort that bad superiors will draw from Parsons's remarks exemplifies the Appellants' frequent displays of the opposite fear, that of unbridled power. A book that has been attributed to John Mush shows particular awareness of the temptations to which those in authority are subject. "It is no rare thing for superiors, which list not to forgoe their rooms, but delight to see themselves aloft, and perhaps would ever be mounting higher, to challenge more than their due; and where their own interest may enter, to encroach also what they may." It would be very bad for subjects to yield to such encroachments; "the subjects' sufferance, and yielding to the force and injury, is often taken by the superior for title good enough, for whatsoever he listeth by iniquity to obtrude and claim."[31] One should be especially careful when a superior tries to judge a controversy to which he himself is a party, when he can scarcely be expected to be indifferent. One should also not be deceived by the pious professions of superiors; "for pretences of good ends, no superior will fail to have great store, no not in the worst things he commandeth."³²

Obviously, one would not wish to leave uncontrolled persons subject to such temptations, and Mush does not believe that in the proper nature of things superiors are left uncontrolled. "God only is absolute Lord, and independing [sic] having supreme power and sovereignty in every respect over all his creatures; all superiors under him have their authority and power limited, every one in his degree and order."³³

Mush describes two kinds of limitations on the authority of superiors, which between them include virtually all of the Appellants' manifold justifications for resistance to Blackwell. Each superior is bound, first of all, by the limitations put on his office by the laws of the church and the terms of his commission. If superiors were not limited, Mush says, they would all be equal with each other and "all equal with God himself, who may command what he will, and must be obeyed in all he commandeth." This situation is avoided by regulating the authority of all superiors, and the archpriest is no exception, as the two characters in Mush's dialogue agree:

Gentleman: no man is bound to obey him [Blackwell] in any thing he commandeth beyond the authority granted him; for he hath no more power nor jurisdiction over any, than is expressly given him by the words of his commission.

Priest: . . . then are we not disobedient to him, if we refuse to obey him in his decrees and precepts, which he hath no authority to make, by any thing appearing in his commission.³⁴

On points where the superior's commission gives him no special authority, Mush holds later, he is to submit his will to the laws of the church and proceed in all matters according to the canons.³⁵

Arguing that the archpriest may be disobeyed when he exceeds the powers granted to him is not a particularly startling claim, especially when, as is frequently the case, Blackwell can be portrayed as opposing himself to some more widely respected authority—for example, when he attempts to prevent appeals to the pope or when he forbids his subordinates to defend the hostile decree of the University of Paris. But Mush goes much farther. After the priest and the gentleman have agreed that the archpriest's authority is limited by the laws of the church and the terms of his commission, the priest brings up the next point:

Priest: . . . But yet further, let us suppose he had full authority to make decrees; doth this prove, that we are disobedient, if we refuse to obey, and resist them?

Gentleman: Me think it doth.

Priest: Doth it so? What? Will you say that unjust decrees are to be obeyed? Or perhaps think you that this archpriest is so infallibly assisted by God's spirit, that he can make no decrees but just and good?

Gentleman: No, I will neither affirm nor think either of these twain. For it is manifest, that injust & hurtful laws, as they are not to be accounted laws, so are they not to be obeyed.[36]

Superiors are not to be held merely to the limits imposed on them by the clearly spelled out positive laws of the church; they are also to be held to abstract principles of justice and morality. Mush's argument implies that these principles are not precisely the same thing as the positive law of the church, and members of the hierarchy appear to have no particular corner on them. This of course opens up the whole civil disobedience problem; if one justifies resistance to established authority on grounds of adherence to moral principle as well as on grounds of established law, how can one judge when and to what degree resistance is justified? Unless one is willing (as Parsons is) to accept the judgments of some individual or institution as authoritative, it would seem that one must leave such decisions up to the individual affected—for if the individual has an absolute right not to be compelled to do or refrain from doing certain things, no person or institution has an absolute right to be obeyed. Possibly because of the revolutionary possibilities in this position, although Mush's colleagues often seem to say things that imply the possession of natural rights by the subjects of ecclesiastical superiors, few of them state their views as baldly and clearly as he does.

Yet Mush does not go as far as he might. His discussion of the relationship between superior and subordinate is set against the background of the archpriest system, and as long as he confines the question to Blackwell and others of his level, he is not issuing any ultimate challenge to Parsons's idea of church authority. To do that, the Appellants would have to expand their constitutional and legal critique to the question of the power of the pope.

The Appellants never really go so far. They believe that the pope can err in matters of fact, but Parsons himself does not deny that this possibility does exist. As will be discussed later, they do exclude the pope from what they consider matters of a nonspiritual nature—most significantly, political affairs. But on matters clearly pertaining to faith and the ordering of the church, the Appellants frequently and loudly proclaim their loyalty to the pope. As has been mentioned, they often point to their willingness to submit to papal decisions as evidence that they are not guilty of schism or disrespect for proper ecclesiastical authority.

But in spite of the formal homage that the Appellants pay to the pope's authority in matters of faith and the government of the church, they manage to hedge him around with limitations of a sort. The assertion that the pope can err and has erred on matters of fact and can act and has acted on misinformation should not be under-estimated as a practical obstructive device; many temporal rulers could have testified to the amount of foot-dragging and outright opposition that could be covered with that cloak. There are few administrative or political decisions that do not depend on a par-ticular version of the relevant facts and that do not depend at least partly on the advice of interested parties. The possibilities for accusa-tions of malignant influence and misinformation were certainly very large, and the Appellants took full advantage of them. It might well have been possible to formulate a proposition on the pope's suscep-tibility to bad advice and liability to errors of fact that both Parsons and the Appellants could have accepted. But Parsons's image of the divine power descending through the hierarchy conveys a very dif-ferent impression from the Appellants' picture of the apparently helpless papal victim of scheming Jesuit liars and cardinals who somehow make vital decisions on the ecclesiastical government of whole countries without telling him about those decisions.

Another feature of the Appellants' criticism of the pope's posi-tion, perhaps less important in practice than their allegations of misinformation, has, however, greater theoretical implications. When talking about the internal government of the church, the Appellants rarely if ever say that there are things that the pope cannot do, but there are many things that they say are so bad that they cannot believe he would do them. Mush has one of his characters exclaim of Blackwell's treatment of his opponents, "Surely it were impiety to think, that his Holiness would give him authority to afflict and punish innocent priests in this manner."[37] John Colleton claims that "for his Holiness to increase the number of our pressures, to make the burden of our crosses more heavy, not only by denying us the choice of our own superior . . . but by imposing also a superior upon us, without all our understanding, and not with the least notice of our likes, seemeth to our judgments to be a course of much greater severity, than the mildness of his Holiness' nature, and the ripe wisdom of his aged experience, would ever design, and less enact, and put in use against us."[38]

Both Mush and Colleton assume that the pope would not violate the principles of justice that they see themselves as defending, but principles of justice are not the same as the pope's will. They are an independent standard by which, at least implicitly, the behavior of the hierarchy and the pope can be judged. But the most explicit discussion of the relationship between the authority of the pope and a standard of law external to the pope comes from the Appellants' leading canon lawyer, Humphrey Ely.

Ely's claim that election by subordinates was the normal means of choosing ecclesiastical superiors has already been mentioned. Later in his book, he takes up the issue again, in a direct reply to Parsons's attack on the idea that the pope could not appoint a superior without the consent of those over whom he was to rule.[39] Ely asks in reply, "th'ordinary [sic] means that have always been in God's church to appoint ecclesiastical superiors, was it not by election? Run over the titles De Electione and therefore the pope following the ordinary means and ways of the church canons, could not give them a superior without their consents." After quoting the relevant passage of the canon law, Ely qualifies his statement. "I speak of the ordinary way, and so do they [the Appellants] understand (else would they not have made mention of the canons) not of the plenitude of power and authority, by which he may take away all election, and alter and change all the church's canons, and constitutions, and make new in their places, but by the ordinary way of canon law, . . . the pope cannot appoint a superior without the consent of the subjects, which are to live under that superior."[40]

Later Ely makes the issue between the Appellants and Parsons even clearer; he thinks that they are not so much, strictly speaking, in disagreement as they are talking about different things. He quotes Parsons's statements defending the pope's "preeminent authority . . . in all elections, and above all that he might, and hath lawfully changed the same" and his right to "appoint an extraordinary prelate as the archpriest is, with what jurisdiction he thinketh expedient."

Ely says that the Appellants do not disagree with these views, but that Parsons's answer has nothing to do with the case:

Your answer is but a mere folly to call it no worse for they talk of cheese and you give them chalk. They talk, speak and mean of the ordinary and accustomable means of election, constituted and appointed by the canons and decrees of the See Apostolic, and you talk of the supereminent power or plenitudine potestatis that his Holiness hath over all benefices and jurisdictions to give them to whom he will and by what means and order it pleaseth him. If you think your brethren are not ignorant of this, you might have left it out, for it answereth not their canon that talketh of the ordinary means by election. And so their canon standeth still for them.[41]

Once again, it might conceivably be possible to draw up a formula on the relationship of the pope to the canon law to which both Ely and Parsons could have assented, but the images that they convey are totally different. To Parsons, the canon law means hardly anything; it is something that the pope can brush aside when he considers it expedient for the good of the church. Ely also thinks that the pope can change or override the canon law, but he implies that he will do so (and perhaps by implication *should* do so) only in very special cases. In the normal course of events the proceedings of the papacy, as of the rest of the church, are governed by known and established laws, and in all but extraordinary circumstances, the actions of the pope must be interpreted in conformity with those laws. The pope's absolute authority is in some sense preserved, but the special divine power that Parsons sees animating the hierarchy is effectively eliminated from most concrete situations with which Ely would have to deal. For most practical purposes the pope is not, as he is to Parsons, the voice through which God speaks directly in the world. He is, within his sphere, the highest guardian of the laws that God has ordained—laws that have their creation and validity largely independently of him.[42] Although the Appellants make no outright attack on the pope's supreme authority in matters of faith and church government, they certainly strip away a good deal of the divine aura with which Parsons surrounds him.

This discussion of church government has probably given an unrealistically theoretical and abstract view of the clash between the Appellants and Parsons and his supporters, but the issues involved were in fact intimately related to the situation faced by the English mission. The significance of the clash for the English mission can perhaps best be shown by looking at one of the plans for the government of the mission that the Appellants presented to the pope in 1602 and at the critique of that plan by the archpriest's representatives.

The Appellants, as has already been mentioned, considered epis-copacy the ideal form of church government and made at least a token request for the appointment of English bishops in many of their addresses to the pope.[43] But although the appointment of a bishop remained their long-range goal, in the face of the pope's apparent reluctance to acquiesce to the request they were willing to try for nonepiscopal systems of government more in accordance with their ideas and interests. Sometime in 1602 they presented a plan for such a system to the pope.[44]

The Appellants' plan called for England to be divided into a northern and a southern region, each under a syndic or visitor. The northern visitor was to have two archpriests under him; the southern, three. The Jesuits were to be forbidden to take any part in the affairs of the secular priests, "directly or indirectly, by word or writing."[45] All officers were to be elected by the priests under their jurisdiction, and elections were preferably to be annual, and at least triennial. No one was to be condemned of a crime without being duly cited and convicted. Laws and decrees were not to be binding on consciences until they had been approved by the majority of the priests within the jurisdiction concerned. Priests were to be allowed to appeal from their archpriest's jurisdiction to their visitors. The Jesuits were berated for alleged embezzlement and misappropriation of the alms of the faithful; to prevent such abuses and suspicions of shady financial dealings, each priest was to provide his archpriest with an account of all donations received. Each archpriest in turn was to provide a similar account to his visitor, and each visitor was to give an account to his successor upon leaving office.

The apparent purposes of this plan of government were to keep management of their affairs in the hands of the seculars and to make sure that no one got away with anything in the exercise of authority or responsibility. The system was admirably designed for the purpose of preventing misuse of authority, but as one of the Appellants' oppo-nents at Rome pointed out, such a structure was in many ways hope-lessly unrealistic for a church facing the situation that Catholicism faced in England.[46] The proposed government, he says, is too thick on the ground; all the gatherings, votes, appeals, and so on that it makes necessary will breed ambition, distract attention from the care of souls, and provide opportunities for heretical meddling. The necessity for frequent large gatherings will increase enormously the chances of betrayal and capture. The obligation to keep records of donations will make the Catholic laity unwilling to donate to the cause, for fear that the records will fall into the wrong hands.[47]

The writer accompanies his critique of the Appellants' program with a running attack on their ambition, disrespect for the pope, and so on. But one does not have to be persuaded by his more moralistic arguments to see the force of the writer's criticism. It is hard to see how a church facing persecution could have been run by the combination of bureaucratic accounting, constitutional legalism, and participatory democracy that the Appellants seemed to advocate. The priorities of Parsons and his friends—authority, unity, discipline, flexibility—seem much more effective supports for the sort of struggle that they believed the Catholic church was waging and had to wage against the English temporal order. The Appellants' different plan of church government was closely connected to their very different view of the nature and origins of the problems that the Catholic church faced in its relations with the English state.

# CHAPTER IX

# The Archpriest Controversy:
# The Problem of Religion and Politics

In spite of the loathing with which the Elizabethan government and the Allen-Parsons school of political thought regarded each other, their views of their situation shared a pronounced similarity. Both sides believed that an inescapable connection existed between one's religious and political loyalties. Although Allen and Parsons kept the actual operations of the mission independent of their political activities, they certainly did not think of the two as inconsistent or unrelated; both were means to the great end of restoring the faith in England. But while Allen and Parsons regarded themselves as engaged in a religious enterprise carried out partly by political means and with some political by-products, the English government tried to persuade the world that the Catholic mission was essentially a treasonous political enterprise that used religion as a cloak to beguile the simpleminded.[1] The government assumed that alienation from the official religion implied alienation from the regime as a whole. Elizabeth's last proclamation on the subject expresses the relationship neatly; it refers to "those Romish priests who were sent into this realm by foreign authority to seduce our people from their affection to religion and so *by consequence* from the constancy of their obedience to us" [emphasis mine].[2] The politically militant Catholics and the Protestant government both believed that the link between one's political and religious purposes and loyalties was an inescapable part of the world in which they lived and that to isolate one's political loyalties from one's religious commitments was neither morally acceptable nor practically possible.

The Appellants based their attack on the Allen-Parsons political program on a denial of this premise, a denial whose main practical effects were the rejection of the Allen-Parsons positions on the political supremacy of the pope, the use of force to advance religious causes, and the possibility and desirability of religious toleration. The boundary line between the spiritual and temporal powers had, of course, been a live issue through most of the Middle Ages, and many Catholic writers had defended the claims of lay rulers against the papacy. But the Appellants were dealing with a very different and more difficult situation than that of the medieval writers. The quarrels between the papacy and the temporal rulers in the Middle Ages had been between men who both claimed in some sense to be rulers of Catholic Christendom or of a part of it. The division of authority between the pope and a temporal ruler could be presented as a division of responsibility between two officers of the same community, a community in which the king as well as the pope might have some responsibility for the religion and morals of his subjects. Subjects of a queen who had completely rejected the authority of the Catholic church could not argue within that framework. There was no way in which a Catholic could portray Elizabeth as one of two coordinate or complementary authorities governing a single Christian community. Elizabeth herself had rejected any such role. If a Catholic was to claim that he owed allegiance to Elizabeth, he had to give the temporal political order a validity independent of any religious function or of any specifically religious community.

The Appellants' expression of a political world view based on this assumption predictably angered Parsons and his friends. Although Parsons's published works on the archpriest controversy were written in response to Appellant attacks, it was his policy—the policy of the militant Counter-Reformation—that was really at issue, and one must look at the ideas of Parsons and his friends on the political side of the archpriest controversy before one examines in detail the views of his opponents.

The documents that Parsons and his party presented to the pope and other officials in Rome stress very heavily the Appellants' disobedience to the pope and other ecclesiastical superiors. Much of their discussion concerns the refusal to obey Blackwell and other more or less strictly ecclesiastical aspects of the case, but the pro-Jesuit party hammers hard at the Appellants' attempts to reduce or eliminate the pope's power over princes. A list of thirty objectionable propositions drawn from the Appellants' works includes nineteen that are essentially political; thirteen of them directly concern the pope's powers over temporal rulers and the others all have implications for that power.[3] Parsons's published works during the archpriest controversy are filled with violent attacks on the Appellants' alleged disobedience to and contempt for the authority of the papacy, but he summed up the essentials of the political side of his attack in a few pages of *A Manifestation of the Great Folly*.

The attack is directed against one Appellant work, the *Important Considerations, which Ought to Move all True and Sound Catholics . . . to Acknowledge . . . that the Proceedings of Her Majesty . . . Have Been Both Mild and Merciful*. Parsons chose his target well, for the *Important Considerations* states the tenets of the Appellants' political program in just about the baldest and most extreme form possible. Bluet's work asserts that Catholics owe political loyalty to Elizabeth, attacks the idea that the pope has any power over princes in temporal affairs, and denies that the faith may rightly be spread by force. It claims that the government's persecution of Catholics is inspired by the belief that they are politically disloyal and says that while most Catholics are loyal subjects, the treasonous plots in which a small minority have engaged gives plausibility to the government view. The Spanish effort to conquer England, the work claims, is merely a selfish power play masked by pious religious professions.

Parsons replies to this attack with his party's usual argument for the power of the pope over temporal rulers. He invokes the authority of Gregory Nazianzen to support the proposition that as the body is subject to the soul, flesh to spirit, and earthly things to heavenly things, "so is the end of the civil commonwealth subject and subordinate to the end of the spiritual commonwealth, to wit the Church of Christ." As the soul is called on to restrain the body and the spirit the flesh when they get out of order, so the church is called on to discipline the temporal ruler when "he breaketh his subordination and goeth about to impugn the same and overthrow religion, whereunto he and his power ought to be subject and subordinate." To maintain that God has not given the church superiority over princes, Parsons argues, is to say that he has failed to provide the church with sufficient means of self-preservation, since it would imply that rulers could change the religion of their domains at will. Surely, Parsons says, the God who provides means of self-preservation for everything else in the world would not have left his church so ill provided.[4]

If authority is to be maintained against those who defy it, its ultimate sanction must be force. Parsons pours scorn on the idea that the faith is not to be promoted by the use of armed force. These claims remind Parsons of the teachings of Luther and the Anabaptists; he holds that the unanimous opinion of learned Catholics is on the other side. If he wished, Parsons says, he could fill a whole chapter with authoritative quotations proving the lawfulness of the use of force in religious questions.[5]

But Parsons believes that the Appellants' position on the use of force is not merely unorthodox but hypocritical as well. He quotes from the *Important Considerations* remarks to the effect that the Appellants would consider themselves bound to resist an invasion of England even if the pope led the attacking force under the pretense of establishing Catholicism. Parsons answers, "A little before they talked much of the word [in saying that the only proper way to spread the faith was by nonviolent means] and now upon the sudden they have taken up the sword, to fight against their chief pastor and bringer up, and this also in defense of heresy." Later he mocks the Appellants as "new champions that will fight even with God himself if he should come with force to root out heresy."[6]

Parsons's attack here is based on what the Appellants would consider a serious misreading of their position. They did not regard what they were advocating as the defense of heresy against the true faith, but as the defense of England against foreigners. Once again, Parsons regards the war against England as essentially a religious conflict, in which the main concern in evaluating any course of action is whether it helps or hinders the establishment of the faith. The possibility that other loyalties may sometimes take precedence over confessional ones in deciding on the right course of action either does not occur to him or does not appear to him to require refutation. Those who support the principles of the *Important Considerations*, Parsons charges, act "as public enemies to impugn their own cause, bidding war and defiance, to all those that have or do defend the same contrary to their appetite and fancy."[7] Parsons may think that some ways to advance the faith are improper, but he apparently does not consider them relevant to the discussion. If the Appellants oppose what Parsons considers necessary methods for spreading the faith, then they are plainly and simply enemies of the cause.

Parsons supports his general view of the nature of the conflict with arguments on specific points. He reasserts that the persecution is religiously motivated, that the martyrs have all died for conscience's sake,[8] and that Spain's war against England is and has always been motivated by the desire to advance Catholicism and to help afflicted Catholics.[9] The particular point that causes him the most outrage, however, is the Appellants' direct support of Protestant propaganda and their practical collaboration with the heretics. The Appellants, he complains, have adopted the justification for the persecutions that Burghley set forth in *The Execution of Justice in England.*[10] Elsewhere, he charges that they are "thought to be hired by the public adversary in religion to join with them in this capital slander against their own brethren and cause confirming herein the reports of our heretics . . . who tell strangers that no man is troubled in England for matters of conscience, but all that are punished are chastised for other delicts."[11] In presenting their case to the pope, Parsons and his allies in Rome stressed the Appellants' collaboration with the English government and portrayed it as part of a long-standing pattern of heretical espionage and sabotage that lay behind all the opposition to the Allen-Parsons party within the Catholic community.[12] The possibility that the Appellants were in some way agents of the English government did worry the pope and other Roman officials; the Appellants' representatives in Rome in 1602 were closely questioned about their relations with Elizabeth's government.[13]

The practical reasons for stressing the Appellants' ties with the English government when addressing the pope are obvious enough, but in his published works in English, Parsons also stresses the Appellants' ties to the persecutor. He describes the point of one Appellant work as "to excuse themselves from dealing with my lord of London [Bancroft] and other adversaries in religion against their own brethren." The Appellant party is "joining . . . with the greatest and most bloody enemies, that ever our cause or brethren had in our country."[14] Attractive as the issue of collaboration with the heretics may have been purely as a stick with which to beat the Appellants, Parsons's strong feelings on the matter are fully consistent with his overall outlook. He is engaged in a struggle in which the forces of good and evil are clearly and visibly divided. No rationale can make collaboration with the enemy in such a situation anything but pure, rank treason.

The attitude of Parsons and his friends toward dealings with heretics significantly governs their response to one of the key planks of the Appellant platform, the idea that the abandonment of political and military pressure on Elizabeth by the Catholic powers and the withdrawal of the Jesuits from England might lead her to grant some degree of liberty of conscience. The Allen-Parsons party's ideas about the nature of the Elizabethan government would naturally make them suspicious of the value of any agreement established with it; Parsons's supporter Henry Tichborne wrote just before the archpriest controversy broke out that if an offer of liberty of conscience were accepted it would "fall out with us as with the sheep that made peace with the wolves on condition they should remove the dogs."[15] But much of what Parsons and his friends say about the possibility of liberty of conscience assumes not only that it could not be obtained, but that it is not a particularly desirable objective anyway.

Some Catholic proponents of seeking toleration in England attempted to demonstrate its desirability and practicality by pointing to the early years of Elizabeth's reign, when the persecution of Catholics was much less severe than it later became.[16] Parsons denies that this period of comparative leniency was good for the church; "as Catholics hoping still of some change or toleration, little industry was used on their parts for preservation of religion for the time to come, nay rather the Protestants gained more to their part by gentler proceedings with Catholics, than they have done in the 34 years that have ensued by rigorous persecution, for then all (excepting very few) went to their churches, sermons, and communions, whereby infinite were infected, who since upon better consideration stirred up by persecution have made some stay."[17] It was during the period of leniency, Parsons says, that "the same devil brought in the division of opinions about going to the heretical churches and service, which most part of Catholics did follow for many years."[18]

The picture of a Catholic community much more vulnerable to damage and demoralization by a conditional toleration than by persecution is painted more strikingly by Henry Tichborne, who predicts the disasters that would ensue if Catholics accepted liberty of conscience on conditions of breaking the mission's ties with the Jesuits and with Catholic rulers. "What rigour of laws could not encompass in many years, this liberty and lenity will effectuate in 20 days. To wit the disfurnishing of the seminaries, the disanimating of men to come, and others to return; the expulsion of the society; a confusion as in Germany; extinction of zeal and fervor, a disanimation of princes from the hot pursuit of the enterprise of our reduction, will leave us hopeless and helpless . . . it will besides drive our greatest patron to stoop to a peace which will be the utter ruin of our edifice, this many years in building."[19]

Tichborne's language is not always as clear as it might be, but the general idea is clear: the extension of a conditional toleration to English Catholics would split the Catholic community, destroy the zeal that animated it, and cause the king of Spain to make peace with Elizabeth, thereby ending any chance for the restoration of Catholicism in England. The idea is therefore "neither to be allowed nor accepted if it might be procured."[20] But Tichborne thinks that it could not really be securely procured anyway, for the persecution is inspired by hatred of Catholicism and any offer of toleration is simply a device for destroying the faith. He says that when men may accomplish their ends by "Lycurgus' laws," they "put into the scabbard the sword of Draco's laws till the rigours of times otherwise require."[21] Tichborne's and Parsons's views on toleration seem consistent with the Allen-Parsons party's general approach to the problems of England. Toleration of Catholicism is not a realistic possibility; if it were, it would cause the Catholic community to lose its zeal and therefore its chances of ultimate victory. Again, the views of the militant wing of English Catholicism are conditioned by their perception of a country divided irreconcilably and for all purposes into Catholics and heretics.[22]

One would expect Parsons's views as discussed so far to be quite congenial to the pope, to Roman officialdom in general, and to the more politically militant English Catholic exiles. But Parsons also had to take into account international opinion in general, which was less likely to sympathize with political conspiracy than with religious martyrdom. He needed in addition, to consider the reactions of Catholics in England, whom the Appellants were busy trying to convince that their unenviable situation was due primarily to the meddling in politics of Parsons and his allies. He also may have considered the attitude of the English government, although he may not have worried so much about its reactions as about those of the others just mentioned. This problem of having to think about several audiences with significantly different interests and ideas may account for some features of Parsons's writings against the Appellants that may not be strictly inconsistent with what has already been mentioned, but that certainly reflect different concerns.

As has already been said, Parsons goes about as far as he could go in theoretically justifying the powers of the pope over temporal rulers and the use of force in seeking religious ends. But in handling of particular episodes, Parsons very frequently denies or plays down the political implications of Catholic activities, and in particular he denies the political and military significance of his own activities and the activities of those identified with his party within the English Catholic community. He denies that his mission in England in 1580–81 had any political purpose or that it provoked the passage of the more severe anti-Catholic laws.[23] The *Conference About the Next Succession*, he claims, has not caused any particular persecution in England; in any case, the book is nothing but an impartial examination of the various claims to the throne.[24] When the Appellants charge that Parsons's political activities have harmed English Catholics by stirring up the government against them, Parsons answers that he has done nothing to the prejudice of Catholics in England and remarks sarcastically that the Appellants' relations with the magistrates show that any anger that he has stirred up has clearly not done them very much harm.[25] Similarly, Parsons denies a host of charges implicating himself or the Society of Jesus in particular plots for assassinations, invasions, and other actions hostile to Elizabeth.[26]

Parsons thus reflects the ambivalence of much of the English Catholic exile community toward the use of political and military means to achieve their religious ends. He vigorously asserts the political supremacy of the pope over temporal authorities and the rightness of the use of force to assure that supremacy in England. But although Parsons was willing to justify levying war against the queen for religious reasons, he was reluctant to admit that he, his society, or his allies within the church had anything to do in any concrete way with the war; like most of his party, he wanted the rest of the world to treat the missionary movement and the political activities of its main organizers as distinct from each other. Even one of the strongest defenders of the Catholic attack on England may have felt he had to yield to international opinion and the views of Catholics in England in attempting to absolve himself and his friends of responsibility for putting into effect the policy that he advocated and that his principles logically implied.

Parsons's problems in dealing with the several audiences that he had to consider were not nearly as severe as those of his opponents, who were trying to achieve closer agreements than Parsons with groups whose goals and ideals were clearly contradictory. They wanted to prove to the papacy that they were loyal Catholics, an aim that, in view of their relations with the English government and their opposition to several aspects of long-standing papal policy, certainly presented difficulties. Three Appellant accounts of the first audience granted by the pope to the Appellant representatives in Rome in 1602 all describe the pope as suspicious of the Appellants' contacts with Elizabeth's government.[27] Two accounts say that he expressed hostility to the idea of expecting liberty of conscience from the queen;[28] according to one of them, he told the four priests that "you wish to be among thorns and not be pricked."[29] John Mush's diary gives the most complete summary of the pope's suspicious questioning:

[The pope] said he had heard very many evil things against us, as that we had set out books containing heresies, that we came to defend heretics against his authority, in that he might not depose heretical princes &c. That we came sent by heretics upon their cost, that we were not obedient to the see Apostolic & the archpriest constituted by him. For a toleration or liberty of conscience in England, it would do harm and make Catholics become heretics, that persecution was profitable to the church & therefore not to be so much laboured for to be averted or stayed by toleration . . . offended that we named her queen whom the see Apostolic had deposed & excommunicated. So that we knew not how to name her . . . Our protestation of obedience to him he called verba, & parole. All we proposed seemed to dislike him.[30]

Obviously, the Appellants would have been ill advised to spend much time discussing their views on the relations of the spiritual and the temporal power with the pope or with Roman officials in general.[31] In fact, the documents presented by the Appellants to the pope and other officials in Rome and the two Latin books in which the Appellants presented their case to the pope and the hierarchy[32] put little emphasis on political issues. When they did bring up politics, the Appellants usually concentrated on pragmatic considerations —on the actual effect of Catholic political and military activities rather than on the theoretical rights involved.

The Appellants' attempt to win the support of Rome and of their fellow English Catholics was, however, based largely on the hope that their way of dealing with the English government would win more lenient treatment for English Catholics. If this hope were ever to be realized, the government would have to be convinced that Catholics could be reliable subjects. The most obvious method of establishing such credibility was wholesale repudiation of papal policy toward England since 1570 and probably of the moral and political assumptions underlying that policy as well. It would clearly be difficult for the Appellants to persuade the English government of their loyalty as English subjects without providing ammunition for their opponents to use in casting doubt on their loyalty as Catholics.

The Appellants' problem was complicated by their relations with the English Catholic laity. At least some of the Catholic laity appear to have been scandalized by the Appellants' resistance to Blackwell. Several Appellant works, particularly among the earlier ones, begin by bemoaning the misunderstanding and erroneous information that have led many Catholics to regard Blackwell's opponents as disobedient to the church; these works announce the intention of setting the record straight.[33] The Appellants' arguments on the constitution of the church and their attacks on Blackwell's conduct in office were necessary parts of this process, but these issues tended to put the Appellants on the defensive in the argument and may not have been good issues to hold the interest of the Catholic nobility and gentry. The Appellants' best chance of gaining the support of the Catholic gentry and nobility was probably the issue that at Rome was their greatest liability—the charge that Parsons and his allies were disloyal subjects whose activities were not only morally objectionable but were responsible for provoking the persecution of English Catholics.[34]

The Appellants were thus faced with the fact that the propaganda emphasis most likely to gain them favor with the English government and perhaps with the important Catholic laity—violent attacks on Parsons, the Jesuits, Spain, and Catholic conspiracies and invasions, and strong loyalty to the crown and to the basic structure of English society—was also the most likely to lose the sympathy of the papacy. This situation probably accounts for much of the confusion and bifurcation in the Appellants' approach to political propaganda. The Latin works intended for the hierarchy and the arguments used by representatives of the Appellants in Rome are generally restrained in tone and pragmatic in their arguments, tending to avoid issues of basic political principle. They are quite different from the unrestrained attack on the theory and practice of the politically militant wing of English Catholicism that appears in many of the Appellants' English works. The Appellants' representatives in Rome in 1602 disowned a collection of pro-Appellant books out of which Parsons and his friends had culled a list of allegedly objectionable propositions; they claimed to base their case entirely on the two Latin works.[35] Both

Christopher Bagshaw (from Paris) and William Bishop (from Rome) wrote to the wildest Appellant writer, William Watson, warning him that his bitter style and (according to Bishop's letter) his extreme propositions were doing the cause more harm than good,[36] and one of the Appellant representatives in Rome reportedly told the authorities that Watson deserved to be whipped through the streets of Rome for his book.[37]

These and other disagreements among the Appellants may tempt one to divide them into "moderates" and "extremists" and to conclude that only the extremists made a really fundamental critique of the Allen-Parsons party's political program. This temptation is increased by the fact that many (although not all) of the authors of the works making the most enthusiastic attacks on the Allen-Parsons political program were among the more irresponsible or bizarre personalities of the Appellant party. A certain amount of truth is reflected in the distinction that some historians have made between the more responsible (or, if one prefers, "moderate") members of the Appellant party such as John Mush, John Colleton, and William Bishop, and others such as the erratic and self-important Thomas Bluet, the intriguers Christopher Bagshaw and John Cecil (who appears on occasion to have betrayed his fellow priests to the government), and the possibly deranged William Watson. But it is hard to support the proposition that the distinction lies in the realm of fundamental political ideas. For one thing, the works of the generally responsible Robert Charnock and (if he really wrote the *Dialogue Betwixt a Secular Priest and a Lay Gentleman*) the very responsible John Mush are among the strongest political critiques of the Allen-Parsons policy. Other evidence is provided by Richard Blount, a Jesuit apparently living in London, who wrote to Parsons on 5 May 1602, that the Appellants in London were still cooperating amicably with Watson in spite of the repudiation of him by their agents at Rome and that one of them (apparently Edmund Calverley) had told an "honest gentleman" that they stood by "both all the books [which the agents in Rome had disclaimed] and every line in them."[38] Later, Calverley wrote to the layman Anthony Copley, one of the more violent Appellant writers, asking him to help arrange the distribution to "men of worth in the country about us" of Appellant books; the books he names all include strong attacks on the Allen-Parsons political position.[39] All these facts suggest (although Blount's evidence may be suspect as partisan) that one's desire to please a particular audience depended partly on how large that audience loomed on one's horizon.

But perhaps the most convincing evidence here is the declaration of 31 January 1603, which states clearly the basic principles of loyalty to the queen in temporal affairs on which all the Appellants' political writings were based.[40] This document was definitely the work of the more "responsible" members of the Appellant party. The first three signatures are those of Mush, Colleton, and Bishop, and with the exception of Francis Barneby none of the thirteen signers seems ever to have compromised his loyalty to the pope in strictly religious matters. Two of the signers, Robert Drury and Roger Cadwallador, were executed during the reign of James I after refusing to take an oath of allegiance that they believed infringed the pope's spiritual supremacy. The difference between "moderate" and "extremist" in political views may have been more a function of one's willingness to rush into print with lengthy and vitriolic expositions of one's position than of fundamental political values.

But although it does not seem that the differences of emphasis between various pieces of Appellant propaganda really reflect basic differences of opinion, they may partly account for the fact that Appellant political propaganda was carried on at several levels. It may be convenient here to begin with the Appellants' pragmatic arguments, before examining their more theoretical ideas about political ethics.

Several Appellant writers justify their initial resistance to the appointment of Blackwell by establishing its political context. William Watson, writing in his usual style, which could charitably be described as uninhibited, charges that it was a plot devised by Parsons "to further the Spaniard, and the most effectual means he could possibly have devised to give to the secular clergy . . . and in truth to all priests, prelates, and princes in Christendom . . . the greatest downfall that ever yet was given them by any innovation, supplantation, or other Machivellian [sic] device of infidel, heretic, or atheist."[41] The point of the device, Watson goes on to explain, is to force all Catholics to place themselves in danger of the law of praemunire by acknowledging Blackwell's authority and therefore, by driving them to despair at their situation under Elizabeth, make them more willing to join in Parsons's nefarious plots against queen and country.

Robert Charnock is perhaps more prudent than Watson and certainly more restrained, but he makes a similar point. He does not say explicitly that the archpriest regime is part of a political plot, but he does say that before the pope confirmed Blackwell's appointment, there was ample reason to suspect that it had been foisted on the

pope by the Jesuits and Spaniards and their friends. He claims that
rumors were widespread in Spain to the effect that the archpriest had
been appointed to further political plots against England, and he
points out that until the pope confirmed the appointment, the priests
knew only "that all proceeded from the Cardinal Caietan at the instances of the Jesuits, whose troublesome and seditious state-humors
were too well known in England."[42] But Charnock's main concern
with the political significance of Blackwell's appointment is its effect
on the English government. It was well known, Charnock claims,
that those who brought about the archpriest's appointment were
"such, as were also known to the council to be more meddling in
matters of state, than became them." Therefore, "they could not
shoot very wide, who affirmed that this authority was already thought
by her majesty's council to be of purpose erected, for the better ef-
fecting of such designments." In such a case, the priests "had no
reason to run further into displeasure with her Majesty & her honorable council; but rather seek to be well answered, that the ground
thereof was no state plot, but religion, for which they have been, and
are most ready to shed their blood, when it shall please God to suffer
it." Charnock adds that even a Catholic ruler might have charged the
priests under praemunire for having accepted Blackwell's authority
and that even priests willing to die in defense of Catholicism may
justly hesitate to run into danger for such a cause.[43]

An anonymous writer in the *Copies of Certain Discourses* draws
an even sharper line between causes for which a priest should and
should not be willing to die. He says that the council regards Blackwell's appointment as a political stratagem and that if the priests
accept it "so shall we, being brought within the compass of other
men's actions, be hanged for kingdoms and matters of state, and the
glory of our cause thereby diminished, if not clean extinguished, to
satisfy other men's pleasures & serve their turns."[44] Neither Charnock
nor the anonymous writer questions the glory and efficacy of martyrdom for the faith; Charnock explicitly affirms it. But Charnock
holds that no priest is obliged to risk death for what may be political
reasons if the interests of the faith are not clearly at stake, and the
anonymous writer believes that execution for political reasons would
actually detract from the glory of the missionary enterprise—and,
since the success of the mission depends largely on good public relations, presumably from its effectiveness as well. Perhaps more important, both writers believe that if the English government perceives

Blackwell's appointment as politically motivated, his subordinates will be persecuted more severely than otherwise. In effect, they partly accept the government's claim that much of the English Catholics' troubles are due to the mission's apparent connection with military and political action against Elizabeth, action that they believe has no essential connection with the purposes of the mission.

This belief plays a very important part in the Appellants' version of the history of the English mission and (usually less explicitly) their program for its future. John Mush, in a Latin work addressed to the pope, claims that before the involvement of the Jesuits in the mission, there was no pretext for accusing the missionaries of *Laesae Majestatis* and no capital laws against priests or those who sheltered them.[45] The severe persecution of priests and other Catholics, Mush claims, began only when Parsons and the Jesuits, by their political propaganda and involvement in attempts to overthrow Elizabeth, gave the government apparent cause to suspect that the missionaries were using Catholicism as a cloak for political plotting.[46] Mush made a similar argument in a speech to the pope soon after he and his colleagues had arrived in Rome in early 1602, when he pointed out the total failure of all violent methods and claimed that their main effect was to cause increased persecution.[47]

Appellant works written in English often make the same claims about the importance of political and military scheming in causing persecution; in addition, they go considerably farther in absolving the queen and her government of responsibility for any blameworthy actions and often attack Parsons and his allies as traitors to their country. Thomas Bluet argues that the queen's treatment of Catholics during the first ten years of her reign was as lenient as could be reasonably expected,[48] and he spends most of his tract trying to show how the subsequent passage of anti-Catholic laws and increased persecution were understandable (if occasionally somewhat extreme) responses to acts of treason and violence. Robert Charnock implies that the Jesuits' political schemes make them "the chief impediments . . . whereby I am persuaded, that both the common cause of religion, and of all that truly seek the promoting of it, are so hateful and odious to the present state."[49]

Parsons perhaps would not have denied that military and political attacks on Elizabeth made life more difficult for English Catholics, but he would have regarded persecution as a price that had to be paid for using all necessary means to restore Catholicism in England. The

Appellants' complaints about the suffering that the mission's political connections brought down on them would have rung rather hollow unless they could claim that the Spanish efforts against England were no necessary part of the mission's religious purpose and not intrinsically connected with it. The Appellants did try to convince the pope (who probably needed little convincing) that Spanish policy was not motivated entirely by religious zeal, while another document was apparently drawn up for what must have been the completely superfluous purpose of persuading Henry IV of the same thing.[50] Christopher Bagshaw scolds the Jesuits for their alleged efforts "to persuade all Catholics, that the king of Spain and our faith are so linked together, as it is become a point of necessity in the Catholic faith to put all Europe into his hands, or otherwise that the Catholic religion will be utterly extinguished and perish."[51] Several Appellant writers attack the motives of the king of Spain, charging that he uses religion as a pious front for schemes whose purpose is to increase his wealth and power. They go on to describe the horrible results that a Spanish conquest would bring to England: murder, pillage, and rapine throughout the country; subjection to foreign rule; and an increase in the power of Spain, which would threaten the interests of other countries and possibly the independence of the church itself.[52] Parsons, for most purposes, regards all aspects of Spanish and papal policy toward England—political and military activities, as well as support of missionaries and religious propaganda—as part of one coordinated effort. The Appellants regard the political and military efforts of Spain and the papacy as totally separate from their missionary work—as having different motives, different purposes, and different probable results. The connection between the two is made for their own selfish purposes by those who do not care how much suffering and disgrace they cause Catholics in England.

Given the fact that the Appellants saw no intrinsic connection between the work of the missionaries and the Spanish war effort, it is not surprising that their views about the moral responsibility for the persecution under which English Catholics suffered should be very different from Parsons's. Thomas Bluet's tract attempting to show that Elizabeth reacted with severity only to plots to murder her or to invade the realm has already been mentioned. After a passage in which he argues that the queen's reactions to the schemes of the early 1580s had been relatively mild, he admits that some priests were executed, "we say upon our knowledges (concerning the most of them) for their consciences: but our adversaries (as they think) do still affirm for treason."[53] This statement would imply that the executions are not the result of hatred for Catholicism per se, but of a genuine misunderstanding; the treasonous activities of a few Catholics have genuinely persuaded the state that Catholics are politically dangerous.

William Clarke, in one of the later Appellant tracts, defends Bluet's work against Parsons's accusations that it justifies the persecution of Catholics. The point, Clarke claims, is not to defend religious persecution or, as Parsons implies, to defend every action that the English government has ever taken against Catholics. "For who will or can justify, or excuse the killing of a priest as a priest, or confiscating or hanging of a Catholic as a Catholic merely for religion."[54] But, Clarke goes on, such persecution is not what the English government thinks it is engaged in. Certainly, he says, wrongs have been inflicted, as in all cases where general laws must be applied to particular cases, but the government's general approach is neither particularly unusual nor particularly unjust,

and I would but ask Father Parsons . . . whether in his conscience he do think there be any prince in the world, be he never so Catholic, that should have within his dominions a kind of people, amongst whom divers times he should discover matters of treason, and practices against his person, and state, whether he would permit those kind of people to live within his dominions, if he could be otherwise rid of them, and whether he would not make straight laws, and execute them severely against such offenders, yea, and all of that company, and quality, rather than he would remain in any danger of such secret practices, and plots?[55]

If Elizabeth's policy toward Catholics is the natural result of attempts at political subversion by a few Catholics from among a much larger community, then it is both permissible and advisable for Catholics to do as the Appellants have done in trying to persuade the queen of their innocence:

And then judge whether we, that have been innocent in such practices (as GOD and our conscience can witness, and yet have felt the smart of such proceedings) have not great cause to clear ourselves; to exclaim against such as will never leave to irritate our prince, and state, and to make known unto her Majesty, and our state, the innocency both of us, & of our ghostly children (who have been pressed with the burden of affliction, by reason of such undutiful attempts in some few unrestrained persons) most humbly craving at her sacred hands, some redress for such miseries, that the stroke may light where the offence hath been given, and not henceforth upon the necks of poor innocents.[56]

Clarke here reflects one of the crucial differences in world view between the Appellants and Parsons and his friends. The Appellants' justification of their attempts to convince Elizabeth of their innocence of any political offense and to persuade her to mitigate the persecution implies that Elizabeth is not purely a representative of evil, to be attacked without mercy. She is someone who has made a plausible mistake, but who can be dealt with in a reasonable way. The gulf between the Catholic priest or subject and the Protestant ruler is not absolute or unbridgeable; their religious differences do not eliminate all possibility of genuine ties of cooperation, loyalty, and obligation between them. Furthermore, the religious ties between the innocent missionary priests and the plotters of treason and rebellion do not mean that the priests are obliged to maintain a common front with their fellow Catholics on every issue. Confessional ties are, to the Appellants, apparently not the only determinants of morality and obligation.

This point is made very clear in the Appellants' lengthy discussions of their obligations to their queen and country. Some vent their spleen at supporters of a foreign conquest of England with emotional patriotic and monarchist rhetoric high-flown enough for any English Protestant. Christopher Bagshaw objects to the tone in which Parsons and Joseph Cresswell address the queen in a book that they jointly wrote "like two arrant companions they presume divers times to speak to her majesty (their natural sovereign) as if they were themselves two emperors, and she but a milk maid." He is even more outraged immediately afterward, as he tells the reader how moved he is when Parsons is so presumptuous as "for him so vile a rascal to deprave and extenuate the blood royal which is in her majesty's sacred person, descending from the renowned King Henry the Seventh; what true English heart can endure it?"[57]

Anthony Copley, the son of Sir Thomas Copley and one of the few laymen directly involved in the archpriest controversy, exceeds Bagshaw in fervor as he considers the possibility of a Spaniard on the English throne. The Spanish claim to the throne is invalid, he holds, because it has lain dormant so long and because foreigners are automatically barred from the throne anyway. The Spaniards can claim the throne, their supporters say, by descent from King John and from Edward III; although Copley admits that John was not the best king England ever had, "yet will we not hold him so unblessed of God, and unhappy, as that from his loin should be entitled a foreign-pretender to this realm: ne ever built London bridge for a Spanish conquerer to trample on." As for Edward III, "Much less . . . may his ghost abide to see England under a foreign rule, who subdued foreign powers and crowns to it."[58] Copley goes on to chronicle the glories of England's military history, at one point contrasting England's alleged success in freeing herself from the Danes in twenty-four years ("the Dane being a nation full of valour") with Spain's taking seven centuries to free herself from the Moors ("being a base and obscure nation"). Rather surprisingly, Copley mixes into his chronicle of martial exploits the assertions that the English nation has "performed more service for God and his church than any other" and has supplied the church with as many saints and learned men as any other. For a nation of such military and religious virtues "to cease now at length her monarchic-honour, and become vassal to Spain or any nation in the world be it by title or conquest, or whatsoever pretence, yea of religion; oh how dishonourable and abominable were it to true English-nature and valour, and scandalous to all the world."[59] This passage is hardly a model of logical reasoning or of factual accuracy, but its combination of martial and religious pride may have been more calculated to appeal to Catholic nobles and gentry than drier arguments.

The Appellants do make more abstract statements of the principles underlying their loyalty to England and her queen in the war against Spain, although their principles are often stated as axioms rather than proved as propositions. The most basic axiom is that the difference in religion between Catholic Englishmen and their queen does not significantly affect the loyalty that they owe to her or to England. Thomas Bluet bemoans the fact that Elizabeth has not remained obedient to the pope, "but seeing that God for our sins would have it otherwise, we ought to have carried ourselves in another manner of course towards her, our true and lawful queen, and towards our country, than hath been taken and pursued by many Catholics, but especially by the Jesuits."[60] Later, Bluet criticizes the refusal of Campion and his associates to answer plainly the question of which side they would take in the event of a papally sponsored invasion of England; the queen, he says, is entitled to know which of her subjects she may trust, and subjects ought to be willing to make open profession of their allegiance when required.[61]

William Clarke, in attacking Doleman's *Conference About the Next Succession* (which he assumes to be written by Parsons) accuses the author of wanting his countrymen to "suffer all the villainies, and miserable oppressions in the world by the Spaniard, because he is a Catholic: rather than to admit of the Scot for that he is not so, or of any other in his case; and will needs have all men bound, without all temporal respects whatsoever, under pain of damnation to strive to bring in a Catholic prince, against the true heir, and him that hath the best title." Clarke implies that there is such a thing as the "true heir," who possesses his right to the throne regardless of his religious beliefs. Doleman's propositions to the contrary he describes as "absurd" and "against the very law of nature."[62] Christopher Bagshaw makes essentially the same point in attacking the Jesuits' propaganda aimed at justifying subjects rebelling against their rulers and changing the succession to the crown "under pretense" (as Bagshaw puts it) of religion. "For as when religion is received into any kingdom, it medleth not with, or maketh better any king's title to his crown, so when it is banished thence, it doth not diminish any prince's right or inheritance, but leaveth (in our opinion) the same as it found it."[63] The queen's rights, and the rights of temporal rulers in general, antedate their religious commitments and are essentially independent of them. The authority of monarchs has a certain legitimacy of its own and is inherent in the monarch's own position, whether or not the monarch accepts the beliefs of the Catholic church or recognizes the authority of its head.

The Appellants' general views on the rights and status of social and political authority and the laws that support it are largely consistent with their ideas on the rights of monarchy. The Appellants and their friends portray themselves as great supporters of order and degree. Charles Paget, an exiled gentleman, experienced (although not particularly successful) intriguer and longtime enemy of Parsons, gives vent to the anticlerical gentry's supercilious attitudes when he denounces some of his opponents as, among other things, an innkeeper, a blacksmith's son (Parsons, whom he refers to as "George"), an "ordinary serving man," and a cooper's son.[64] The *Memorial for the Reformation* is frequently condemned as an attack on English rights, laws, and institutions, and particularly on the status of the nobility and gentry.[65]

The Appellants' defense of order and degree extends to their defense of the monarchy; if religious differences do not justify resistance to the monarch, neither does the people's opinion of his fitness to rule. Christopher Bagshaw provides a good example of the Appellants' ideas on the rights of subjects when he denounces the Jesuits' "very odious and seditious" proposition "that the people may depose their princes, and choose others at their pleasures: have they any or no right to the crown, that it is not material. . . . It had been well if they had left this point to some of our enemies to have branded them with, for rebellious subjects when they cannot have their wills; but it hath pleased the fathers to stain both themselves and the Catholic cause with it."[66] The Appellants' favorite word for the doctrine that the people may overthrow their princes is "popularity"; several Appellant works are full of denunciations of it as opening the door to the breakdown of all authority and the collapse of society into chaos.[67] This sort of horrified response to any challenge to order and authority is, of course, a staple of early modern political propaganda, but one would expect it to be most congenial to people for whom monarchical legitimacy formed a large part of their religion. To find such views among members of a proscribed church is more surprising.

The Appellants' views on the rights of monarchs and of temporal authority in general depend heavily on a mostly implicit hallowing of the English temporal political and social hierarchy. Since they have rejected the possibility that the legitimacy of the political order can be affected by either its members' religious commitments or the desires of the people, it would seem that the only possible source of its legitimacy is in some moral standard not dependent either on any particular human will or on the authority of any particular religious confession—in fact, in natural law. The Appellants do sometimes use the phrase, although not as often as they implicitly use the concept. To Anthony Copley, the Jesuits are "impudent transgressors . . . of the law of nature towards their country."[68] Later he argues that to interpret the pope's excommunication of Elizabeth in such a way as to permit subjects to take up arms against her "were to conster [sic] the pope's act so overmuch in religion and grace, as to the destruction of nature. . . . For a man to go against his own country, is and ever was holden in the civil part of the world an act Contra jus gentium: and also unnatural, yea and against all grace."[69] William Clarke claims that his attack on the Jesuits is justified because they are trying to bring about what would be a disastrous foreign invasion of England and that every man "is bound more to love his country than a Jesuit, yea, the whole order of Jesuits: sith unto the first he is bound by the law of nature, to the second only by the law of fraternal charity."[70]

The love of one's country and the duty toward it that the Appellants claim is part of the natural duty of man in practice amounts to a sort of "my country, right or wrong" principle; one is bound in all circumstances that the Appellants discuss to support the government of one's country (which for all practical purposes the Appellants identify with the country itself) against any attempts to overthrow it. William Clarke translates this principle into a formula when he says that even an invader with a just cause may be resisted. "For the common good of my country, and weal thereof, is to be preferred before the particular right of any person whatsoever."[71]

The Appellants' beliefs about their obligations to Elizabeth could be taken as a reply to Doleman's Conference About the Next Succession; in fact, the Appellants frequently cast their arguments as attacks on Doleman. Doleman's case, it will be remembered, rests largely on two points. One is the natural right of the people of a state to change their rulers (who are rulers by a compact with the people) upon just cause. The second is that religious disagreement between a ruler and the people is, on both prudential and moral grounds, the best possible reason for the people to change the ruler. The Appellant writers are not nearly as systematic or coherent as Doleman, and they never make as clear as he does the beliefs about the nature of man and the origins and nature of the state that underlie their political ethics. But they vehemently deny both of the main props of Doleman's argument. Neither religious differences nor the will of the people can in any way affect the monarch's rights. Those rights, then, cannot have been created by an agreement with the people, as in Doleman's model. The rights of the ruler, rather than being part of the agreement for the formation of the state, seem to be the original condition that defines the existence and nature of the state, antedating the consent of any of its members. Although probably no Appellant uses the phrase, it is hard to avoid applying the label of divine right.

Doleman's work is, however, unusual among the political writings of the Allen-Parsons party, both in the depth of its inquiry into the general nature of politics and in its emphasis on the natural rights of the people. Most of the politically militant party's writings (including those of William Allen discussed earlier) justified the party's conduct primarily by the assertion of the supremacy of the church, and particularly the pope, over temporal rulers. The Appellants' ideas on the powers of the pope and on the related issue of the right and wrong ways of spreading the Catholic faith are largely the logical consequence of their views on the obligation of loyalty to temporal rulers, but these issues also give some new insights into the Appellants' ideas of the nature of Catholicism and its relations to politics.

Allen and Parsons, it will be remembered, argue that the church, as the supreme authority in spiritual matters, has and ought to have authority over the temporal power, whose sphere of jurisdiction is by nature inferior to that of the spiritual power. The Appellants make a similar distinction between the spiritual and temporal powers, but the relationship between them is not one of superiority and subordination. Their model of this relationship resembles that of Sir Thomas Tresham. It involves two hierarchies, ideally more or less sealed off from each other, each one with absolute jurisdiction over certain aspects of life. In order to decide whether to obey the pope or the queen in a particular case, the individual must understand whether the action commanded falls within the temporal or the spiritual sphere. If the question at issue is purely religious, then a Catholic is bound by loyalty to the head of the church and to his fellow Catholics. The Appellants take considerable pains to prove their obedience to the church on religious matters. On some issues, particularly that of refusal to attend Protestant church services, they claim to have obeyed the pope more completely than the Jesuits have.[72] Robert Charnock puts the Appellant view in a nutshell in answering Parsons's charge that they have conspired "with the very enemy against their own . . . which is most false: for if matters of religion be in question, the priests are ready to join rather with the lewdest Catholic in the world, than with the Protestant: although when matters of treachery against their prince and country be handled, they are as ready to defy the plotters thereof, were they the most zealous Catholics in the world."[73] Parsons is a Catholic first, for all purposes; his Catholicism always defines the group to which he owes his primary loyalty. For Charnock, the division of the world into "us" and "them" varies according to the context, and one must consider oneself as English or Catholic according to whether the legitimate claims of England or of the Catholic church are at stake.

All the Appellants who discuss the problem are sure that this principle excludes the pope from using force in religious matters or from absolving others from their political allegiances to their temporal sovereign. Thomas Bluet attacks Allen's assertion that one must always obey the pope's commands on which side to take in wars.[74] Anthony Copley uses biblical references to try to prove that the power that Christ delegated to Peter and his successors over trans-

gressing rulers and nations is limited to announcing God's displeasure by means of excommunication and other spiritual weapons; the
actual execution of revenge for wrongdoing must be left to God.[75]
Such opinions, which appear in many Appellant works, can be exem-
plified by one relatively clear example from William Clarke's tract.[76]

Clarke is concerned in this passage with rebutting some of Parsons's objections againt Bluet's *Important Considerations*. In some cases
he says that Parsons has exaggerated the Appellants' opposition to
the powers of the pope and to the use of force. He claims not to deny
the indirect power of the pope in temporals, although he hedges it
with so many restrictions as to make it practically a dead letter.[77]
Nor, Clarke claims, do the Appellants accept the belief, described by
Parsons as Lutheran and Anabaptist, that the use of force is forbidden
to Christians; Clarke admits that temporal rulers may wage war on
each other upon just cause.[78] Force may even be used in some cases
where religion is involved; among the rights of temporal rulers is that
of using force to quell religiously inspired malcontents who threaten
the stability of the commonwealth as well as the church.[79] Even religious men and priests may sometimes use arms to defend themselves
and their possessions from attack (Clarke gives the example of monks
protecting their monasteries) or to defend Catholic countries from the
attacks of Turks, infidels, or heretics.[80] The pope himself, and some
bishops, have the right to use force on some occasions.

But, Clarke says, the pope's and bishops' possession of the right
to use force does not come from their ecclesiastical calling. They
possess that right only when temporal jurisdiction is joined to spiritual authority. Insofar as they are spiritual persons, they are obliged
to limit themselves to "praying, preaching, and the administration of
the sacraments." An ecclesiastical ruler may use force to enforce the
laws against his subjects, but only as a ruler, not as an ecclesiastic. He
may also use arms to defend himself or his country against attack,
"not as he is an ecclesiastical person, but as he is a civil magistrate,
and enjoyeth the freedom of the law of nature, which he looseth not
by being ecclesiastical, secular, or religious."[81]

Thus two limits are placed on the use of force by ecclesiastical
persons; it must be used in response to attack or to the infringement
of law, and the right to use it is not enhanced by one's ecclesiastical
status. To spread the faith by force is a completely different proposition. "But that ecclesiastical persons, as they are ecclesiastical, should
go about to reduce either Pagans, Turks or heretics by force, and dint

of sword, by poisoning, or murdering of princes, by soliciting rebellions, or invasions, to the destruction of their prince or country,
leaving thereby the ordinary means of preaching and teaching with
sufferings, and bloodsheddings commanded by Christ, and by Himself, and His disciples, and all former Christians practised, is scandalous, not religious, Pagan like, & not Christian like."[82] Christ,
Clarke goes on to say, could certainly have used the force of legions of
angels to force the Jews to accept the Gospel, and the Jews were
under at least as much obligation to obey him as Protestants are to
obey Catholic priests. Yet Christ did not use force himself, and did
not command his disciples to do so; he simply instructed them to
preach the gospel throughout the world, leaving it up to the hearers
whether to accept the offer of salvation.[83]

Clarke uses the teaching and example of Christ and the history of
the early church as major props for his arguments on the illegitimacy
of the use of force in spreading Catholicism. But Clarke realizes that
his opponents could make the traditional argument that heresy was a
different case from that of people living in the first century, since
heretics were "by their baptism born true subjects unto Christ's
church, and afterwards are revolted from their due obedience, which
they owe unto her: wherefore, they may be constrained unto their
obedience again as well, as any natural subject rebelling from his
natural prince."[84]

Whether Clarke found this comparison of religious with temporal
obedience in any of his opponents is not clear. It may well be that he
put the parallel into his opponents' mouths, since it helped him to set
up the straw man that he wished to knock down. It is still wrong, he
holds, to compel heretics by force to accept Catholicism, since the
nature of religious allegiance is fundamentally different from that of
temporal allegiance:

For why, the obedience of a subject to his temporal prince, consisteth only in
the will, which is in every man's power within himself, but the obedience of
every Christian Catholic to God's church, consisteth as well in the understanding as the will, and chiefly in the understanding, which ought to direct
the will.

Now I think all men know, that the understanding of a man cannot be
forced by any . . . but as it is informed and convinced by reason. For who is
he that can enforce his understanding to judge it to be midnight, and extreme
darkness, when the sun shineth at noon-time of the day? Whereupon it
followeth, that there is more reason, & less difficulty for a temporal prince to
enforce his subjects to temporal obedience, than for the church by temporal
force to constrain countries and kingdoms into the faith.[85]

Obedience to religious authority, then, can be demanded only on the basis of the individual's reasoned and voluntary consent to the truth by which the authority claims obedience. Although Clarke may not quite accept all the logical implications of this premise,[86] he does draw the logical conclusion as far as the church's policy toward England is concerned. The faith must be spread in England only by the means commanded and practiced by Christ and the apostles—by preaching, teaching, and administration of the sacraments, and when necessary by suffering and by shedding one's blood for the cause.[87] Clarke insists that "all beauty of the Catholic church consisteth in unity, and consent of doctrine, true, and reverend administration of sacraments, true, and sincere preaching of God's word, holy observation of the rights [sic, probably for "rites"] and ceremonies thereof, and the like. In these consist the beauty of the Catholic church, religion, and not in any arm of man, or sword of flesh."[88]

Clarke's ideas about the relationship of religious and temporal authority and about religious allegiance exclude consent to any attempts to change England's religious allegiance by force. Clarke says that natural law, which requires every man to defend his country, obliges him to defend England against a papal invasion; he says that in doing so, one cannot be said to resist the Catholic faith, since in such a case the pope would be coming to England simply as a foreign invader.[89] When the pope steps out of the vital but limited sphere in which he has authority, his actions apparently may be judged (and found wanting) just as anybody else's.

The Appellants' views on temporal and religious allegiance cast their contact with the heretical government in a completely different light from that in which Parsons puts it. Although it does not mean very much, the Appellants' correspondence with Bancroft shows no sign of any consciousness of contradiction between their religious and their political beliefs; Bluet, writing to Bancroft while on his way to Rome in November 1601, proclaimed his loyalty to "the cause that I follow & my duty unto God's church, her Majesty & my country."[90] Many Appellants also attempt, in works directed to Catholic readers, to defend their party's contacts with the English government. Their arguments are very similar to each other; those of John Mush may be taken as an example.

Mush sums up his opponents' charges fairly enough, saying that the Appellants have been accused of being untrustworthy since they deal with and find favor with "professed adversaries to God's holy

church and to all Catholics."[91] Mush replies that many Jesuits have
also won favors from the government and accuses them of distorting
the nature of the Appellants' contact with the heretics.[92] He also
rebuts some specific charges, such as that of receiving money from
the council.[93] These specific arguments are not, however, the most
important (nor on some points the most convincing) part of Mush's
defense.

Mush begins the more general defense of the Appellants' contact
with the government by having the priest in his *Dialogue* ask whether
it is "a manifest and undoubted sin, that a Catholic priest and prisoner haunt an adversaries' house, and have conference with him?"
The gentleman replies that it is not, for "many good saints . . . have
haunted the company of evil persons with great zeal and merit, and
our saviour Christ himself and his apostles used the company of
scribes, Pharisees, publicans, and the worst sinners." The only thing
that can make the Appellants' dealings with the government sinful is
"their intention and business only, or perhaps the scandal they give
thereby."[94]

The scandal in this case, the priest replies, is only taken and not
given, and certainly priests who have suffered for the faith should be
given the benefit of the doubt more than the Appellants have been
given.[95] As for their intentions in approaching the heretical magistrates, the Appellants might be seeking many lawful goals, such as
easier terms of imprisonment or banishment from the country for
prisoners. Perhaps the priests are trying to convert the magistrates or
(somewhat more plausibly) trying to win more lenient treatment for
Catholics.[96] And if the government seems more willing to consider
making concessions to the Appellants than to the Jesuits and their
friends, it is because they know that the Appellants are not involved
in the kind of subversive political activity of which the Jesuits and
their friends are guilty. But Mush's main point, and that of most of his
colleagues who discuss the question, is that dealings with heretics,
even with persecutors, are not in themselves wicked. Each case must
be judged on its merits, according to its results and to the intentions
of those involved.

The main intention that the Appellants claimed was winning
some degree of liberty of conscience for Catholics. Unlike Parsons,
the Appellants did not adopt the position that the queen and the
Protestant establishment were irreconcilable enemies with whom the
Catholics could not deal. They sometimes suggested that toleration

would help insure that loyal Catholics would actively support the queen against enemies, foreign and domestic.[97] The main point of the Appellants' argument on the possibility of religious toleration for Catholics has already been touched on several times; the persecution of Catholics is caused primarily by sincere suspicion on the queen's part of the loyalty of her Catholic subjects, suspicions that are made plausible by plotting of violence and subversion by a minority of Catholics led by the Jesuits. If the queen could be convinced of the temporal loyalty of most of her Catholic subjects, perhaps she "would at least make a distinction betwixt her natural children and subjects that in all sincerity do honor & reverence her, and those unnatural bastards that do attend to nought else but conquests and invasions."[98]

The problem of toleration was not, however, limited to the question of the likelihood of obtaining it. It will be recalled that Parsons, his supporter Henry Tichborne, and the pope all expressed doubt about whether liberty of conscience would be desirable even if it could be obtained; they were afraid that toleration would demoralize the Catholic community and destroy the dedication that had been built up during years of persecution. Here, if anywhere, the Appellants had an advantage over their opponents in the debate, since it was very easy for them to present themselves as supporters of the obvious commonsense attitude. An anonymous Appellant writer in the preface to Ely's work describes his opponents' "absurd" idea that "we notwithstanding our long endurance of manifold afflictions, should not accept of a toleration in matters of religion, no not if her Majesty of her singular clemency, should offer it unto us. Need you hear any more? Do you not think these men to have lost four of their five senses? or else that lying too long out of gunshot at their ease, have cast off all human compassion of their brethren?"[99]

Later in the same collection Humphrey Ely attacks the idea that the banishment of the Jesuits would be too high a price to pay for liberty of conscience. "I would to God they or any other could get liberty of conscience in England, under conditions that all the fathers were out, and I myself banished with them never to come in so long as I live. If you or the fathers had that zeal and charity to your country, you should not mislike of this condition, if liberty could be gotten by it."[100] One can imagine that an English Catholic, oppressed by the threat or the fact of fines, confiscation of property, imprisonment, and sometimes death, might have trouble grasping why his troubles should continue because someone in Rome thought that it was good for him. Toleration of loyal Catholics would mean merely that the queen would cease interfering in something over which she had no authority. If it was offered in return for the temporal loyalty that the Catholics owed the queen in any case, why should toleration not be accepted?

The mental habits that lie behind many of the issues discussed in this chapter may be summarized by examining three remarks dropped more or less in passing by three Appellant writers. One is by Thomas Bluet, who, after scolding the Jesuits for the refusal of some of them to give an unequivocal answer to the "bloody questions," continues, "And we greatly marvel, that any Jesuits should be so hard laced (concerning the performance of their duties, towards the fathers and kings of those countries where they were born, and whose vassals they are) considering what obedience, they tie themselves towards their own general, provincial, and other governors: unto whom they were no way tied, but by their own consents, and for that it hath pleased them voluntarily to submit themselves unto them."[101]

The second statement is by John Mush, who has just asserted that men are not obliged to obey their ecclesiastical superiors when the superiors command something intrinsically evil or when the command is outside the superiors' authority. He concludes the argument, "For otherwise I know not how our refusal to obey our temporal prince's command for going to [Protestant] church, and for practice of our religion, or any other magistrate's injust commandment, may be excused or defended from the crimes of disobedience and rebellion in the Jesuits and Arch-Priest themselves."[102]

The last remark is by William Clarke, who is lambasting Parsons as the supposed author of the *Conference About the Next Succession*. "Their full scope is: how they may set up the people against their sovereigns. Well, well, good father, when people are thrust into such courses, they are not easily stayed: and you are but a simple man for all your statizing, if you know not, that popularity in the civil state, doth not well digest a monarchy in the ecclesiastical."[103]

These three statements all have some interest on their own, but it is a common feature that is most pertinent. All three statements assume that spiritual and temporal authority are of the same essential nature, that they are governed by the same principles, and that the psychological and moral relationship between the subject and his superiors is governed by the same principles in the spiritual and temporal spheres. Such a habit of thinking is foreign to the ideas set forth in the principal works of the Allen-Parsons party. For Allen and Parsons, the authority of the church hierarchy (although, except for the papal supremacy, perhaps not its particular form) was divinely ordained, an inescapable part of the moral structure of the universe. Any temporal authority was valid only insofar as it served the church's purposes and was approved by it and (according to Doleman) insofar as it served the natural needs and rights of the people and was approved by them. Only the spiritual hierarchy was morally inevitable. Its authority, if not unlimited, was limited in practice only by its own self-restraint. Temporal authorities were contingent; they existed not of their own right, but by the sufferance of the spiritual authorities and (in some works) of the people. Order and degree are necessary to the regulation of human communities, but any particular structure of temporal authority, and the placing in a position of authority of any particular person, are essentially means to ends and can be judged by how well they serve those ends.

The Appellants would, if asked, presumably have said that religious concerns were higher than temporal ones and that the task of the spiritual authority was therefore higher than that of the temporal authority. But they do not emphasize the point as Allen and Parsons do, and they do not go on to draw the conclusion that the religious hierarchy is politically superior to the temporal hierarchy. The Appellants think of the two hierarchies as parallel, each having jurisdiction over one area of life, but ideally neither one interfering in the area of the other's jurisdiction. The subject owes absolute obedience to each authority within its sphere, but none outside it. Neither hierarchy is primarily a means to an end; each is an intrinsic part of the proper moral order, which cannot legitimately be changed by human effort. Each hierarchy is itself sanctified by divine and natural law. Order and degree are sacrosanct, not as a means to an end, or as the guarantors of a particular religious doctrine, but in their own right.

# CHAPTER X

# The Myth of the Evil Jesuit

The last two chapters may have given a misleading idea of what it is like to read the barrages of propaganda exchanged in the course of the archpriest controversy. The discussion may have given the impression of an argument over principles conducted on a relatively abstract level. The clash of principles and views of the world is certainly there, but the debate was definitely not carried on in a spirit of amiable academic give and take or even of academic courtesy. Much of the propaganda of both sides is scurrilous, abusive, and hysterical. Some of this tone can be written off as simple obedience to the conventions of late sixteenth- and early seventeenth-century pamphleteering, but at least in the Appellants' case the less abstract parts of their work are too extensive and too consistent to be so easily explained. The Appellants devote a great portion of their works to an all-out attack on the Society of Jesus and on many of its members, particularly Robert Parsons. The Appellants' ferocious hatred of the Jesuits has been mentioned before, but a closer look at it may clarify the connection between the Appellants' theoretical ideas of what the world is and should be and their emotional sense of the fitness of things.

William Clarke provides a good example of the contrast in tone between at least some of the Appellants' discussions of general moral principles and their discussions of the Jesuits. Clarke's views on the nature of religious and temporal authority and his attack on the practice of imposing Catholicism by force were discussed in the previous chapter. While it is obviously possible for a reasonable person not to agree with everything Clarke says, his argument is in general coherent, cogent, and clearly expressed. The passage would not lead the reader to see Clarke as a great thinker, but it probably would encourage most readers to regard him as reasonably intelligent and intellectually competent.

A few pages later Clarke begins to examine the role of the Jesuits in the history of English Catholicism, and the whole tone changes. Clarke wishes to reply to Parsons's assertion that Catholics had been involved in hostile actions against Elizabeth long before the Jesuits had taken any part in the affairs of the English mission.

First, for his evasion in matters attempted before their [the Jesuits'] entrance into England . . . it doth not follow, that therefore no Jesuits had their fingers in such attempts. Were there not Jesuits of other countries to step into such actions? . . . Secondly, was not Father Darbyshire a Jesuit, long before the English Jesuits came into England? And I have heard men, that knew him very well, affirm that he was a great meddler many years ago in such affairs. Might he not then have his fingers in the French matters, concerning the duke of Guise, and queen of Scots? Some will affirm, that he was an abettor therein. Thirdly, were not the Jesuits from the beginning, great with the Spaniards, whose fingers have been almost in all matters, as that of the duke of Norfolk, that of Ireland, and divers others? Is it not somewhat probable by this, that the Jesuits might be councillors, or abettors in these affairs, being men of such stirring spirits, and so forward to put themselves into prince's matters . . . were they not likewise very great with Pope Gregory the thirteenth . . . might they not then be of council in Stukely's intention for Ireland? Are not there great probabilities to induce men to think, they have been hammering from the beginning; having had such fair offers, and so fit opportunities, and themselves being so ready, and desirous to deal in such kind of affairs?[1]

The method of reasoning here resembles Bagshaw's in his retrospective account of the Wisbech stirs.[2] Clarke thinks he knows what the Jesuits are like and in general what their objectives are. From this, he can figure out how the Jesuits are involved in any particular situation; he looks around for the nearest member of the society and decides that that unfortunate representative is largely responsible for whatever objectionable political activities are going on. No specific proof of Jesuit involvement in particular political plots is revealed; the passage just cited is a hodgepodge of vague rumor, non sequiturs, innuendo, and guilt by association.

In this passage Clarke leaves his method of reasoning as an implicit assumption, but a few pages later he practically makes it into an explicit principle. After claiming that the Jesuits and their friends were responsible for the Babington plot, Clarke meets a potential objection:

That the Jesuits were not taxed of this, at the arraignments of these gentlemen, or accused by their confessions, imports little. For you must know, that the Jesuits are wise, and cunning politicians, and can tell how to manage matters by secondary, or third means, lying aloof off themselves, and being least seen or suspected, such as have been acquainted with their dealings know this, which I say, not to be void of truth. . . . That Father Parsons, Father Holt, and Father Cresswell, were at Rome, and Naples, is little to the purpose; the intercourse of letters, and intelligences from all places, being so speedy, familiar, and common with them, wheresoever they remain, as it is known to be.[3]

The passage represents a sweeping triumph of preconceived opinion over lack of observed fact. It is difficult to see how in Clarke's eyes any Jesuit could ever clear himself of any charge, since the lack of evidence relevant to the accusation cannot overcome the presumption that wherever mischief is being plotted a Jesuit must be at the bottom of it. Clarke deals with another potential objection to his account, as well as adding to its luridness, by portraying the Jesuits as masters of the arts necessary for secret political conspiracy; difficulties of long-distance secret communication that would stump ordinary mortals apparently present no problem for them. From Clarke's account, the Jesuits seem ideally qualified for the role of secret, sinister conspirators—active, dedicated to stirring up mischief, and extraordinarily cunning and skillful at covering their tracks.

The portrayal of the Society of Jesus as an incredibly powerful and clever secret conspiracy against all that is good in church, state, and society is probably the most constant single theme of Appellant propaganda. The society is depicted as a far-flung political network. Christopher Bagshaw charges, "There are few kings' courts in Europe where some of their masterships do not reside; of purpose to receive and give intelligence unto their general at Rome . . . which they dispatch to and fro by secret ciphers; having either a Jesuit or someone altogether Jesuited in the most of those kings' councils, who *propter bonum societatis*, must without scruple deliver to them the secrets of their sovereign to their uttermost knowledge." This network, the Appellants hold, is used primarily to support the overweening political ambitions of Spain. Bagshaw claims that "the inventor of their order being a Spaniard and a soldier, of what country soever any of his disciples are by their birth, in their hearts and practices they are altogether Spanish, breathing little but cruelties, garboils, and troubles."[4] Thomas Bluet uses much of the *Important Considerations* to describe the Jesuits' alleged connections with all the plots and invasions hatched against England by Spain and in the Spanish interest. In some way, virtually every Appellant writer assumes or attempts to prove the connection between the secret plotting of the Jesuits and the political ambitions of Spain.

The Jesuits, the Appellants charge, try to justify their support of Spain with pious motives; Bagshaw says that they have "labored to persuade all Catholics, that the king of Spain and our faith are so linked together, as it is become a point of necessity in the Catholic faith to put all Europe into his hands."[5] But the Jesuits' pious professions on this and other points are mere hypocrisy; in reality the society cares for nothing but its own aggrandisement, and the conduct of its members is motivated mainly by their desire to dominate the Catholic church in England immediately and the temporal and spiritual life of the country after its return to Catholicism. Bagshaw's idea that the Wisbech stirs were merely part of a widespread scheme for the Jesuits to dominate the secular clergy has already been mentioned.[6] William Clarke agrees that the events at Wisbech were merely preliminaries to an attempted Jesuit takeover of the whole English mission, while William Bishop, among others, charges that the appointment of the archpriest was a plot to bring the secular priests under the Jesuits' control.[7] Even the Jesuits' apparently good deeds are suspect; the purpose of the Jesuits' founding of seminaries is allegedly to destroy the seminary at Douai—which the Jesuits are also striving to take over.[8]

Naturally, the Jesuits' unbridled desire for power, as individuals and as an order, can be expected to make them enemies of the rigid hierarchical order in church and state of which the Appellants are such great admirers. The Appellants see the Jesuits' pursuit of power and their attacks on the temporal and spiritual hierarchies as ruthless, amoral, and characterized by the use of a feigned sanctity to cover up their wicked deeds. The Jesuits, several Appellants charge, collect alms from the faithful, supposedly for charity, and then use the money for their own dubious purposes, including luxurious living for themselves.[9] The Jesuits use the Spiritual Exercises, knowledge gained in the confessional, and their reputations for holiness to persuade wealthy Catholics to place their fortunes and their affairs in

the hands of members of the society.[10] They slander the secular
priests, the main pastors of the church, and claim for themselves
most of the credit for the achievements of the English mission; in fact,
the Appellants claim, the secular priests have run far more risks and
have accomplished far more than have the Jesuits.[11] Robert Parsons,
in Appellant eyes the arch-plotter of everything evil, is accused of
cowardice in leaving the English mission and in carrying on his
intrigues from the safety of exile on the Continent.[12]

The Appellants believe that the Jesuits' hostility to all "order and
degree" extends to the church as well as the state. Their enthusiasm
for the papacy is held to be a sham, a point proved by such evidence
as the Jesuits' alleged criticism of Clement VIII for his absolution of
Henry IV.[13] The Appellants attempt to prove the Jesuits' general
antipathy to the proper order of the church by a story that Bagshaw
and Watson both tell, with almost the same phrases. Pope Sixtus V,
they say, once called the general of the society before him and asked
why the Jesuits should appropriate to themselves the name of the
Society of Jesus, "more than all other Christians, of whom the apostle
saith: *vocati sumus in societatem filii eius?*" The pope went on to demand
why, since the Benedictines and the Dominicans were named after
their founders, "should not you be called Ignatians, according to the
first author, and also keep the choir, and rise at midnight, and in all
things do as other religious men do?"[14]

The words that Bagshaw and Watson put in the pope's mouth
(for which, they both hint broadly, the Jesuits soon murdered him)
reflect the offense that the Appellants took at the Jesuit way of life.[15]
The Appellants, like most ecclesiastical traditionalists, claimed to be
admirers of the religious life. But the Jesuits were radically different,
in goals and in methods of operation, from most religious orders.
They did not engage in a regular round of communal worship, they
were highly individualistic in their approach, they regarded prayer
and study essentially as preparation for action, and they had little
regard for the traditional forms of ecclesiastical practice and authority
if those forms interfered with effective action. Anyone who refused,
as did the Jesuits, to fit neatly into the traditional ecclesiastical categories was likely to be suspected of a lack of enthusiasm for the
traditional hierarchy.[16]

Sixtus V, moreover, is not the only person whom the Appellants
more or less explicitly accuse the Jesuits of murdering; in fact, secret
murder of high dignitaries is the logical extension of the Appellants'

ideas about the Jesuits. The Jesuits seem to have been transformed into a personification or incarnation of the Appellants' fears, a concrete embodiment of the threats to the Appellants' vision of the ideal world. To understand how this came about, one must consider how the actual position and behavior of the Jesuits may have led the Appellant party to seize on them for scapegoats, and why the Appellants needed scapegoats so badly in the first place.

For many reasons, the Jesuits fitted easily into the scapegoat role that the Appellants assigned to them. The belief that the Jesuits were deeply implicated in political plotting against England was made plausible by the activities of several very prominent and visible Jesuits.[17] The Appellants' arch-villain, Parsons, had been very involved in politics since the early 1580s as a leader of the "activist" exiles and as a political propagandist. He had if anything been more visible as an adviser to the pope (especially after his arrival in Rome in 1597) and as an adviser to the Spanish government during the eight years he spent in Spain after the defeat of the Armada. The ferocity of the Appellants' attacks on Parsons may have been intensified by their desire to clear the name of William Allen, the almost universally revered father figure of English Catholicism, of responsibility for plotting or writing against Elizabeth; several Appellants made Parsons into a sort of "evil counselor" to Allen, who either gulled the well-intentioned cardinal into such indiscretions as the *Admonition to the Nobility and People* or borrowed his name for them.[18] Although no other Jesuit came close to equaling the breadth of Parsons's political work, the activities of both William Holt in the Netherlands as adviser to the Hapsburg government in Brussels and dispenser of Spanish pensions to English Catholics and Joseph Cresswell at the Spanish court lent credibility to the idea that the Jesuits were heavily involved in the Spanish efforts against England.[19]

The Appellants' belief that the Jesuits were attempting to dominate the English mission was made plausible by several developments. The Jesuits' control over the most significant institutions of the Catholic exile community, its schools and seminaries, had been increasing ever since the beginning of the society's involvement in the affairs of the mission. The seminary founded at Douai in 1568 and the one founded at Rome in 1578 had both been set up under the rule of secular priests, but in 1579 the seminary at Rome had been placed under the control of the Jesuits. After the defeat of the Spanish Armada, Parsons took the lead in establishing Jesuit-operated seminaries in Spain at Valladolid (1589) and Seville (1592), as well as the Jesuit school at Saint Omer in the Spanish Netherlands (1592). Douai itself, under the presidencies of Richard Barret (1588–99) and Thomas Worthington (1599–1613) saw a great increase of Jesuit influence in the faculty and administration, as well as intensified hostility between the students and their superiors.[20] The fact that Douai under Barret and Worthington saw a marked decline in morale, educational effectiveness, and financial solvency was not entirely the Jesuits' fault, but nevertheless provided a handle for Appellant propaganda, including charges that the Jesuits were deliberately starving Douai of funds for the benefit of their seminaries in Spain.[21]

The Jesuits by the 1590s thus seemed to have a strong and expanding influence at the strategic political centers of the Counter-Reformation and in the most important institutions of the Catholic exile community. The situation within England may also have contributed to the impression that the Jesuits were taking over the affairs of the Catholic community. The number of Jesuits in England was growing, but not until the reign of James I did they become a large fraction of the total missionary body; as late as 1598 there were only fourteen Jesuits in England, as compared to several hundred secular priests.[22] But both sides in the quarrels of 1594–1603 agree that the Jesuits in England were far more influential than their numbers would indicate.

This importance was partly due to their reputation for sanctity, learning, and effectiveness as spiritual directors. Their position is illustrated by Sega's claim that the Jesuits rendered valuable services to the English mission by telling Catholic laymen which secular priests they could trust and which they could not,[23] a service that would have been useful only if the Jesuits as a group had been considered more trustworthy than the secular priests. The Jesuits certainly included many of the more remarkable men who served on the English mission, perhaps partly because of their more selective recruitment and their training that was more consistently thorough than that of the secular priests. The Jesuits' reputation may also have owed something to a more extensive use of the techniques of Counter-Reformation spirituality. John Gerard's memoirs of his eighteen years as a missionary in England recount numerous episodes of conversions, vocations, and other advances in the faith made as a result of undergoing the Spiritual Exercises.[24] On a somewhat more mundane level, the Jesuits may have been able to win the support of some landowners through their possession of special faculties for absolving the possessors of monastery lands.[25] Whatever the sources of the Jesuits' prestige, it was clearly a great help to them; perhaps the best evidence of this is the Appellants' constant complaint that the Jesuits hoodwinked the laity by hiding their evil deeds behind a reputation for sanctity.

The Jesuits' influence in England was also at least partly the result of their superior organization. While the secular priests operated with little apparent structure of authority, the Jesuits were connected to an international society and, within England, were under a superior (from 1586 to 1605, Henry Garnet) who seems to have exercised fairly close control over the activities of his subordinates. During Gerard's period of missionary work (1588–1606), the Jesuits in England had a regular practice of gathering every six months for a renewal of their vows, confession, and conference. Simply being in touch with a network of Jesuits scattered through England and with connections on the Continent could be a great advantage in handling the manifold practical problems faced by the mission—collecting and dispensing information, assigning priests to places of work, collecting money, arranging the passage of people and money within England and between England and the Continent. The Jesuits' network of contacts was, naturally, used by others than the Jesuits themselves. This story cannot be traced in much detail, but its importance is hinted at by the amount of time that the Jesuits and their enemies spent in wrangling over whether the Jesuits' assistance to secular priests was charitable aid or another aspect of the Jesuits' attempt to take over the mission.[26]

The resentment that may have been brought on by these general features of the Jesuits' position was undoubtedly aggravated by the roles that the Jesuits played in the particular controversies of the period between 1594 and 1603. Their part in the disturbances at Wisbech and Rome has already been discussed; these episodes served to confirm any ideas that the Jesuits were selfish, devious, and power hungry. The archpriest affair was even more disastrous; the society's opponents could use many features of the episode as confirmation of their stereotyped notions about the Jesuits. The fact that a known admirer of the Jesuits was appointed by the influence of Parsons and a few friends at Rome, with no significant consultation of the secular priests in England, confirmed the suspicion that the Jesuits were unscrupulous intriguers, using their sinister influence in the world of courts and rulers to their own advantage. The obligation imposed on Blackwell to consult the Jesuit superior on all important matters fitted in with the image of the Jesuits as clever behind-the-scenes manipulators, using front men as instruments for their own ends. The fact that Jesuits took prominent roles in Blackwell's defense, both in England and in Rome, helped to corroborate the view that the archpriest regime was a Jesuit plot. Once in office, Blackwell showed a combination of sanctimonious severity and shifty fast footwork that could have been calculated to confirm all the stereotypes about the hypocritical and domineering nature of the Jesuits and their allies. He even provided an excellent example of the abuses to which the doctrine of equivocation (to their opponents a Jesuit specialty) could be subject, when he described the private opinion of two Jesuits in Rome on the question of schism as "a resolution from our mother city"; while technically accurate, the statement was certainly a conscious attempt to deceive.

Perhaps a more general cause of the resentment that the Jesuits attracted was their attitude. Many Jesuits and admirers of the society considered the Jesuits' services indispensable to the English mission, and the society's apologists used a good deal of space chronicling the Jesuits' contributions to the mission and defending it against Appellant attacks. But these lengthy arguments may be less revealing than the occasional remarks about the society's value and role that the Jesuits drop—sometimes very consciously, sometimes hardly consciously at all—in the middle of discussions of other topics.

One of the more extravagant examples is a lamentation written by Robert Southwell, when at the age of fifteen his request to enter the Society of Jesus was met with the advice that in view of his youth he should postpone his attempt. Southwell compares his situation to that of Hagar wandering in the desert after being cast out of the house of Abraham:

This my calamity surpasses her indigence, this my solitude is greater than hers, this my misfortune exceeds her banishment. For I wander about an exile from a place, as far surpassing the house of Abraham in dignity, as a body does a shadow, or truth a fiction. Inflamed from on high with the greatest desire to join myself to their happy number who upon earth, imitating the choirs of angels, so entirely devote themselves to God as to have his glory alone in view in all their undertakings, begun and ended; I have erred from the mark at which I aimed; I am cut off from the hopes I had greedily indulged in, frustrated of the expectation upon which alone I leaned.

Later, Southwell implies that he can enjoy complete union with Christ only by joining the society; addressing his own soul, he urges, "Admit no consolation to thy grief, no mitigation of thy sorrow, till thou shalt enjoy thy Jesus, and acknowledge thyself his faithful spouse."[27]

Southwell continues in this tone for about fourteen hundred words in Foley's English translation. Some of his effusiveness may be written off as the product of a sensitive and precocious adolescent, but the idea that membership in the society brought a special outpouring of divine grace that made the recipient a better servant of God was not unique to Southwell. In the preface to his memoir of his years as a missionary, John Gerard explains that his lack of virtue and natural talents and his lack of close union with God made him a less successful missionary than many others (as his account makes clear, an unjust assertion). He declines credit for what he did achieve. "What was done, was done by God. And, I believe, he chose to do it through me, because, I was a member—an unworthy one, I admit—of that body which has received from Jesus its head a remarkable outpouring of his spirit for the healing of souls in this last era of a declining and gasping world. This is how I account for anything that God has been pleased to work in and through me." Later, Gerard describes how he was tortured in the Tower of London. The torture, he says, left him unable to walk. "I was very weak now and if I had any spirit left in me it was given by God and given to me although most unworthily, because I shared in the fellowship of the society." Elsewhere, Gerard describes the good effect on him of the Jesuits' twice-yearly meetings to renew their vows and give account of their consciences. "It braced my soul to meet all the obligations of my life as a Jesuit and meet all the demands made of a priest on the mission. Apart from the consolation I got from renewing my vows, I experienced—after renewing them—a new strength and an ardent and freshened zeal. If I failed, then, in my work it was through no fault of the society which provided me with means such as this and gave me assistance in striving for the perfection which is its aim."[28]

Gerard is a good example of the remarkable combination of individual humility and corporate pride that seems to have characterized many Jesuits. Their work shows how effective that mixture could be, but pride and confidence in the society posed problems when it shaded over into the belief that the success of the English mission was somehow peculiarly bound up with the continued participation of the Jesuits. No one explicitly made this claim (although Cardinal Sega [see chapter 6] came close), but it does seem occasionally present in the back of some Jesuits' minds. William Weston, after telling the reader of his autobiography about the imprisonment of Ralph Emerson and the deportation of Jasper Heywood, says that he was left "alone in England"[29]—meaning that he was the only Jesuit at liberty; at the time (1585) there were, of course, many secular priests in the country. Gerard describes with apparent approval a work on the spiritual life by William Wiseman, a gentleman whom he had served as chaplain, in which Wiseman "described the ideal spiritual guide in such detail that no doubt was left in the reader's mind that he meant a Jesuit, or failing a Jesuit, a priest who was friendly to the Jesuits and sought their advice in his own difficulties." Later, Gerard tells how he had to decide whether to join the Jesuit Richard Collins as resident chaplain in the household of the widowed Lady Elizabeth Vaux; one of the things that made the possibility attractive, he told her, was "that here I would be living with another Jesuit, a man whom I liked very much; elsewhere I had always been with secular priests."[30]

The idea that Jesuits were in some way special men under special divine guidance was sometimes transfigured into the idea that the opposition that they suffered from their fellow Catholics was imposed on them as a special service to God. Henry Garnet wrote to William Clarke early in the archpriest controversy, "True it is, that it hath pleased God to give our society part in many glorious [sic] which his holy church are continually achievers; so oftentimes yea ordinarily doth he make us partakers of the afflictions and difficulties which do thence arise; and if any worthy thing be accounted worthy of blame, we are lightly the first which are blamed."[31] During the Wisbech stirs Garnet, in a reference to the summary of the constitutions of the society, wrote to Acquaviva that subjection to calumniation along with so many other things offers "notable opportunity of imitating Christ, our leader, and wearing his livery."[32] William Weston, also writing to Acquaviva to reply to attacks on himself, tells the general, "I am, of course, not unaware that I may not expect to be always the object of the same savour to all men, (for even those saints of the Lord, the Apostles, were to some the savour of death, bringing death, and to others the savour of life, bringing life)."[33] Robert Parsons, in an anonymous work, also invokes an exalted comparison in reply to the Appellants' attacks on him. "And truly in this our English

Catholic cause . . . it seemeth that God hath suffered him [Parsons] to be *in signum, cui contradicetur*, as a mark or sign set up for all sort of bad people, atheists, heretics, apostates, seditious, contentious, tumultuous, disastered, and dissolute to inveigh against, and this is to the imitation of his master and Saviour Christ, who was, and is, and shall be to the world's end, a sign of contradiction in the highest degree to all wicked whatsoever."[34]

The most amazing demonstration of a perceived connection between the divine purpose and the activities of the Jesuits appears in a letter written by Alphonsus Agazzari, rector of the English college at Rome, to Parsons shortly after the death of Cardinal Toledo, vice-protector of England, in September 1596. Toledo, it may be remembered, during his short term of authority over the English college at Rome had treated the rebellious students very leniently, to Agazzari's great dismay. The cardinal's death set the rector to thinking about the evidence of God's favor on the society.

And certainly, father, this appears to me a great indication of his Divine Majesty and a great sign of the love he bears to the society, to this college and to the cause of England—the evidence that when human means are lacking, He, as it were miraculously, sets there his own divine hand. While Allen walked well in that matter with the conjunction and fidelity to the society with which he was wont, the blessed Lord preserved him, prospered him and exalted him, but, when he began to leave the path, the thread of his designs and of his life were both at once cut off. And when a much more dangerous adversary then arose, when he had almost arrived at the summit, he was the following year taken from this life—the bishop of Cassano; and two days later the same befell Throgmorton, a most ardent sharer of the same opinions. But now it appeared to those people, in Rome as in Belgium, that they had a stronger supporter than all the previous ones—as they openly boasted—but now behold them again unexpectedly spoiled and deprived of that hope. So that, father, we should not lose heart, because *Deus pugnat pro causa sua*, and the blood shed by so many martyrs and their continued intercession in Heaven must in any case give us great confidence.[35]

That this passage has become something of a chestnut does not detract from the stunning arrogance of the belief that God times the deaths of the leaders of English Catholicism for the convenience of the Jesuits. The statement is even more remarkable since it apparently was not inspired by personal malice; Agazzari seems to have worn himself out watching at Toledo's deathbed.[36] But one may begin to understand how the Appellants could believe some of their wilder accusations against the Jesuits; in one version, "so holy, so godly, so religious would they seem to be; as nothing is holy, that they have not sanctified; no doctrine Catholic, and sound that cometh not from them; no dispensation available, that is not granted by them: and which is worse, they have beaten into the heads of most, that the mass is not rightly, and orderly celebrated of any, but a Jesuit."[37]

All this discussion may help to explain how the Appellants' views of the Jesuits gained some plausibility, but it still does not account for the phenomena. The Appellants and other opponents of the Jesuits did not limit their criticisms of the society to points on which there were some grounds for reasonable criticism. Some evidence could have supported a critique of the Jesuits' position in the English mission that would have borne some resemblance to the critique that the Appellants did make. But the Appellants did not look at the evidence and criticize the Jesuits on the basis of it. They insisted that the Jesuits and their allies[38] were responsible for everything that had ever gone wrong with the English mission. When there is no evidence of Jesuit involvement in a particular incident, the evidence is invented, or its absence is declared irrelevant, or even used as an occasion for commenting on the Jesuits' cleverness in managing things while keeping themselves out of sight. The explanation for the Appellants' fears about the Jesuits is to be sought largely in the Appellants' psyches rather than in the Jesuits themselves. To make that assertion is, in a sense, to ask what psychological purpose was served by the ferocious attack on the Jesuits. To attempt to answer this question, one must step back for a moment to examine the situation in which the missionary priests lived and the psychological reactions to that situation that different groups of priests showed.

The most obvious feature of the missionary priest's life was physical danger. The possibility of prison, torture, and death hung constantly over all Catholic missionaries; the danger was much greater for priests than for laymen. This physical threat in itself undoubtedly caused great psychological strain, and the circumstances under which the missionary priests worked must have added greatly to it.

Elizabethan England was a hierarchical society. This was true to a very large degree in fact and, what is more important here, it was intensely so in theory. Great store was set by one's social roots, in family, social status, and economic position. One's position in society was manifested and secured to a great extent by external signs of status—in dress, deportment, and the way one was treated by other people. These social supports were largely denied to the missionary priest. He had no part in the ecclesiastical structure, with its hierarchy, benefices, and recognized status, which supported the pre-Reformation Catholic priest and the post-Reformation Anglican cleric. He was frequently isolated from his family and locality.[39] He was likely to be cut off from any income to which he might have laid claim and to be dependent for his livelihood (not to speak of his safety) on the generosity of those whom he served. Perhaps most important, the missionary's claim to status and respect, his priesthood, could not be avowed openly. In order to practice his priesthood he had to adopt a disguise—as steward, tutor, servant, or gentleman. The necessity for disguise, anonymity, and constant concealment of his real status and transcendent religious function must have increased the priest's sense of being cut out of the normal web of relationships that defined and gave meaning to people's lives. Secular priests, with their amorphous organization, sometimes less thorough training, and less defined esprit de corps, might feel this isolation more intensely than the Jesuits, whose methods, organization, and corporate ethos could be adapted to the English situation with comparatively little difficulty.[40]

The missionary movement did offer compensations for this situation, but the most concrete social and institutional means of countering the missionary priest's sense of isolation and vulnerability could exist only outside England.[41] Within the exile community, and particularly in the schools that were its most important institutions, the priest or candidate for the priesthood could find his status and his work supported by the structure and values of the community. Indeed, within the exile community the cleric enjoyed a higher status than either the pre-Reformation Catholic priest or the post-Reformation Anglican clergyman in England. The very existence of the exile community was entirely dependent on religious ties, and its purposes were religious purposes. The exiled gentry and nobility had been to a great extent deprived of the wealth and influence within England that accounted for their status and that alone gave them any value to the "enterprise of England" apart from their own native abilities. Laymen such as Sir Francis Englefield and Sir William Stanley could become prominent in the service of Spain and of the "enterprise," but the goals of the exile community were set essentially by clerics, its most important activities were run by clerics, and clerics played the most central roles. This situation, as Bossy points out, undoubtedly helped stimulate the splenetic anticlericalism of the more marginal characters among the exiled gentry and nobility,[42] but the period of intense Catholic creative activity that ran from the 1560s until the death of Elizabeth would probably have been impossible without it.

But the institutional structure of the Catholic exile community could not extend to England, and both in England and abroad the Elizabethan Catholic priest probably owed more of his psychic support to an idea than to a social or institutional framework. The missionary priest's life was devoted to the service of the most important cause in the world. His duty was to risk his life to keep souls from perishing in heresy, schism, and indifference; in Campion's words, "to cry alarm spiritual against foul vice and proud ignorance."[43] The belief that he was serving such a cause could, of course, provide tremendous help to the missionary priest; indeed, one cannot imagine that the missionary movement could have existed without it. The priest's position as an individual largely cut off from normal social ties could be justified by the need to serve the cause above all else. The Elizabethan missionary priests are not the only example of persons for whom ideological commitment justified and supported a largely individualist and activist way of life, in which such social and personal ties as one had were formed and conditioned on the basis of common commitment to the cause.

It is at this point, however, that the trouble starts, for as both Robert Parsons and Lord Burghley realized, the natural extension of the missionary priest's way of life is to stand in judgment on the political and social order that made that way of life necessary. If the cause is so vital that not only virtue in this life but salvation in the next depends on it, then surely the social and political order that opposes it tooth and nail cannot be particularly sacrosanct. The logical extension of this attitude is active cooperation, or at least passive acquiescence, in efforts to overthrow the Protestant regime.

Robert Parsons and some other priests followed their commitment to its natural political conclusion. For many other priests, probably a large majority of those on the mission, no substantial or reliable evidence is available to show what they thought about the political activities of their fellow Catholics. But at least a fair-sized minority among the missionary priests rejected with extreme violence the militant political program that seems the natural extension of the missionary movement's ethos and blamed the Jesuits, sometimes in the face of all the evidence, for every manifestation of it.

Any attempt to explain this reaction must be extremely tentative —or, to be a bit less high-flown, must be limited to educated guesswork. From the general view of the world that appears in their works, it would seem reasonable to guess that the Appellants and their supporters included those missionary priests who felt most acutely the strain of the social dislocation that their roles imposed on them. For all missionary priests, the situation that they faced must have given them some sense of moral disorder, but for one who did not believe that the social and political order had any intrinsic sanctity, it was comparatively easy to justify his position and organize his world around a simple dichotomy of good and evil. For the Appellant, the situation was not so simple. In his eyes, the political establishment that was persecuting the church had its own independent validity, and he had a strong sense of the obligation of loyalty that he owed to that establishment and to its head, the queen. For the Appellant, the already great strain of the exile and the mission was complicated by an internal conflict, for his sympathies could not be unreservedly with either side in the war between the English government and the militant Counter-Reformation. The Appellant felt obligations to both the church and the state, but both sides were intruding into areas where they did not belong and making demands which they had no right to make. The government took the priest's priesthood as a sign of political disloyalty, while the leaders of the church in effect insisted that his loyalty as a Catholic should at least make him acquiesce in political and military attacks on Elizabeth, if not actively cooperate with them. The Appellant wanted to satisfy both authorities, but the authorities themselves made it virtually impossible to do so.

The obvious escape from the moral conflict that the political situation imposed on the missionary priest was to admit an irreconcilable conflict and to choose sides. But for the Appellant even this was impossible, for the basis of his position was that he could not choose a side for all purposes. To admit that the all-out struggle between England and the Catholic church was natural and irreconcilable would be to accept a morally and practically hopeless situation, to admit that the proper structure of authority in the world was completely out of order and that there was little left to do but to suffer—and worse, to suffer without clear purpose or necessity.

The Jesuits provided a solution to the dilemma. The image of the Jesuit that the Appellants set forth was just close enough to the truth to make that image plausible, and the image, horrifying as it was in itself, helped greatly in keeping the Appellants' world comprehensible and manageable. The central point of the Appellant tirade against the Jesuits was that it was they—a powerful, cunning conspiracy of men devoted to nothing but the power of their order—who were responsible for the war between England and the church. It was the Jesuits who misled the pope, deceiving him into following their plans for assassinations and invasions; it was the Jesuits who misled William Allen into writing and acting against the queen; it was the Jesuits whose violent schemes provoked Elizabeth into thinking that Catholicism necessarily involved treason. Far from reflecting an irreconcilable conflict, the worst aspects of the plight of English Catholics were due merely to a series of misunderstandings. The solutions to the Catholic community's worst problems might be difficult in practice, but they were very simple in principle. The Jesuits had to be recalled from the English mission (and hopefully their power everywhere else would be reduced in the bargain) and the policy for which they stood should be thoroughly and convincingly repudiated by the papacy and the English Catholics. Elizabeth would cease to persecute if only she could be convinced that her Catholic subjects were loyal.

Bossy has accurately pointed out that the Appellants were wildly overoptimistic in their hopes for concessions that the English government might make,[44] and in general they were not greatly distinguished for short-run political realism. But their hysteria about the Jesuits is understandable, for it made the world they lived in more bearable by providing an explanation for what had gone so horribly wrong with that world and by providing some hope that something could be done. Instead of being at odds with the course of history, the Appellants could convince themselves that they were merely at odds with men. Their attitude may have resembled the one that supposedly leads people to kill the messenger who brings the bad news and it may be largely irrational, but people like to believe that they might have some control over what happens to them and that the world, if not exactly a happy place, is at least a bearable one.

# CHAPTER XI

# Religion and Loyalty

Any attempt to examine the importance of the divisions in English Catholicism under Elizabeth must begin with some clearing of the ground. A good number of those who have written on the Elizabethan Catholics are still largely interested in vindicating those whom they admire and in condemning those whom they do not—in a manner not very helpful to understanding. Before thinking about the nature and importance of the divisions, one has to deal with some possible misconceptions that this situation has created.

Writers who sympathize with Parsons and his allies tend to regard the Appellants as "troublemakers," guilty of "an insolent tone," "impudence and inveracity,"[1] and general disloyalty to the cause of the Catholic church in England. They see the Appellants' contacts with the English government and their recognition of Elizabeth's authority as the greatest evidence of that disloyalty. The Appellants were guilty of many of the offenses with which they were and are commonly charged, although they could have replied that their opponents were just as guilty of some of those offenses. The Appellants' cooperation with the government was certainly dangerous and likely to give scandal, and several individuals who participated in the opposition to the Jesuits either apostasized, as did Robert Fisher,[2] or gave information on their colleagues to the government, as did John Cecil[3] and, on one occasion, probably Christopher Bagshaw.[4]

Yet the conclusion that the Appellants as a group were disloyal Catholics can be reached only if one starts by assuming that disagreement with the Allen-Parsons party's view of the situation in England

and opposition to that party's program for action is prima facie evidence of disloyalty to the church. Most of the Appellants appear to have been unaware of the most dubious dealings of some of their colleagues. For most of them, there is no evidence that their relations with the government extended to betrayal of other priests, and there is much evidence that they thought that those relations would promote the good of the church. The principles on which they acted were very similar to those of a substantial portion of the Catholic laity, including persons who suffered considerably in the Catholic cause. One must ask why, if the Appellants and those of the laity whose views resembled theirs were not loyal Catholics, they remained Catholics at all. All of the tangible inducements bearing on one's religious choice certainly would push one the other way—not only the avoidance of the penalties of Catholicism, but also the frequent generosity with which Elizabeth's government treated apostates.

The clearest demonstration of the fact that the great majority of the Appellant party were not willing to put their loyalty to the government ahead of their position as Catholic priests came after the pope's decision on the archpriest controversy. The royal proclamation of 5 November 1602[5] dealt a severe blow to Appellant hopes of toleration. In addition, the government seems to have wanted the priests to take some kind of oath of allegiance that would distinguish the loyal from the disloyal. Most of the Appellants rejected this idea, particularly when the council attached the condition that priests would be given immunity from the penal laws only if they ceased to function as priests. The Appellants refused to consider this demand, and their declaration of allegiance of 31 January 1603[6] contained a firm statement of allegiance to the pope in religious matters. This position was unacceptable to the government, and negotiations for toleration were broken off. When James I's government came out with the theologically offensive oath of allegiance of 1606[7] there was no stampede of former Appellants to take it. John Mush was a leader of opposition to the oath, and two of the thirteen signers of the declaration of allegiance of January 1603, Robert Drury and Roger Cadwallador, were executed after refusing to take the oath. All this indicates that the Appellants "were first and foremost Roman Catholic priests."[8] Their general policy is open to criticism and they certainly made their share of mistakes in carrying it out, but merely tagging them as disloyal troublemakers distorts the truth.

The errors of most of those who condemn the Allen-Parsons party are at least as serious. Those who dislike Parsons and his allies tend to regard them as fanatics who, not satisfied with the relatively tolerant regime that Elizabeth established, engaged in traitorous schemes of invasion and violence against their queen and country, provoking Elizabeth to stern measures in self-defense.[9]

It is true that the strictly political activities of the Allen-Parsons party were essentially futile. It is also true that Elizabeth's persecution of Catholics was fairly mild compared to the policies of many other rulers. But the queen claimed, and exercised, the right to invade consciences as surely as did those other rulers. Her subjects were forbidden to participate in any way in the life of the Catholic church or to act on Catholic beliefs, even to the point of stating them. They were required to attend the Anglican church and to recognize implicitly or explicitly the queen's authority in ecclesiastical matters. To the Allen-Parsons party (and probably to many other Catholics who did not take such explicit political stands) these demands meant participation in a blasphemous rebellion against God and consent to the damnation of their own souls. The Allen-Parsons party's refusal to accept the legitimacy of a government that thus violated the true rights and interests of its subjects reflected their belief that "the king is for the Commonwealth and not the Commonwealth for the king."[10] The party's reaction to the situation in which they found themselves posed problems, but it is not merely the reaction of unreasonable fanatics or of simple traitors.

The quarrels of the Elizabethan Catholics, then, cannot be explained as a simple opposition of good guys against bad guys. The two sides were separated by difficult issues on which reasonable people could differ. The explication of the differences has been a major goal of this book; the rest of this chapter will summarize the major differences and reflect on the significance of the Elizabethan Catholics' disagreements as an example of the relationship between religion and politics in England and Europe in the late sixteenth and early seventeenth centuries.

A common theme in the historiography of early modern England is the revolutionary impact of "Calvinism" or "Puritanism" on English society and politics. (The two terms are often used interchangeably, although in fact they are far from synonymous; here "Calvinism" will be used to mean adherence to the fundamentals of Calvin's theology, while "Puritanism" will be used to mean a strong desire to reform the English church in a more Protestant direction.) The author of one study of the political impact of Calvinism or Puritanism in England goes so far as to subtitle his work "a study in the origins of radical politics."[11] Catholicism, on the other hand, is rarely seen by historians in general as anything but either a religion of passive conservatism or (when politically active) an attempt to restore a lost world. Even many specialists in Catholic history seem to view the Catholicism of Elizabeth's reign as little more than an attempt either to bring back the good old days or to preserve a little bit of them.

Clearly, something is to be said for this view. After a fringe group had a last fling in the Gunpowder Plot, Catholicism retreated into political passivity after Elizabeth's reign, and the Calvinist tradition did provide the supporting ideology for numerous changes in the attitudes and habits of the English people. Most important, it fueled the great political crack-up of the 1640s. The case for Puritanism as the great revolutionary ideology of seventeenth-century England is so obvious as not to need stating, and certainly many aspects of Puritan thinking and acting can be discovered in the reign of Elizabeth.

But if one tries to avoid looking at Elizabeth's reign through the prism of the reign of Charles I, one might begin to doubt the intrinsically and uniquely revolutionary nature of Calvinist thought. One finds Calvinist theology dominating the established church,[12] Marian exiles among the high dignitaries of the church,[13] and a Calvinist archbishop of Canterbury, Whitgift,[14] spearheading the drive against the "Puritan" opposition, while numerous Calvinists sat on the queen's council. The Puritan opposition may have worked for the further reformation of the church, refused to wear surplices or keep strictly to the prayer book services, and engaged in some political agitation and organization, but during Elizabeth's reign there was little apparent desire on the part of the Puritans to engage in directly revolutionary political action. Many Calvinists may have regarded the Elizabethan settlement as a botched-up political compromise, but most of them seem to have made their peace with it. When they went too far in trying to change the church they frequently found themselves thwarted or opposed by officials of church and state whose theological opinions differed little from their own. The effects of Elizabethan Puritanism on the ideas and habits of its followers may have been profound and may have prepared the way for opposition to the crown in the seventeenth century. But under Elizabeth the mainstream of English Calvinism was not particularly revolutionary in the political sphere. Apparently, Calvinists could settle for something less than the Puritan millennium; Calvinist belief alone was insufficient to make most Calvinists dedicated and uncompromising revolutionaries.

Indeed, one suspects that most Elizabethans, if they had thought in such terminology, would have said that the truly revolutionary component bulked much larger in English Catholicism than in Calvinism, or even in Puritanism. The sweeping implications of the political works of Allen and (to a greater degree) of Doleman and Parsons have already been discussed; their lack of reverence for the temporal hierarchy when unsanctified by right religion is as blunt as any Puritan's. Doleman gave the people about as much license to set up and pull down governments as did anyone in the sixteenth century. And these ideas were expressed not by fringe characters but by the most prominent leaders of the Catholic missionary movement. The fact that there was a long Catholic tradition behind most of their ideas does not make Allen and Parsons's ideas any less radical, in the sense that they went to the roots of the political and social order and advocated drastic action to change it.

The resemblance of the missionary movement to the conventional idea of Puritanism is not limited to ideas about social and political hierarchies. The missionaries seem sometimes to have had a "puritanical" (in the popular sense) belief in austerity and rigorous self-discipline and a dislike of what they considered frivolity; it is rather ironic that Weston (whose Catholic opponents frequently accused him of resembling the Puritans) reportedly was finally driven to separate from his opponents at Wisbech by what he considered the unseemly presence of a team of Morris dancers at Christmas. The Catholic missionaries' lives were of a sort that called for such rigorous self-discipline. For the most part, they lived not within a web of conventional social relationships, but within a movement dedicated to a cause. They had to be much more individualistic in their mode of working than clergy of more settled churches, more flexible and innovative in their methods of organizing and acting, and less tied to traditional ecclesiastical forms and procedures. For the creativity of their response to the challenge that they faced, the Elizabethan Catholics can certainly bear comparison with their Puritan contemporaries—who, after all, faced much less severe persecution. The Puritans ultimately had more effect on English society and their tradition entered more deeply into the national life, but these developments were not obvious during Elizabeth's reign. The fact that Elizabethan Catholicism was as innovative in its methods of operation and, if anything, more revolutionary in its political ideology than other English religious groups resulted primarily from its being a persecuted opposition. It was part of a pattern of rapid reversals of the correlation between religious and political thought that members of the Catholic and Reformed traditions went through in England and France in the sixteenth and seventeenth centuries. But these transformations took place under the pressure of circumstances, which should indicate that Calvinism did not lead inescapably to social and political radicalism, even when the social and political order showed no commitment to the Puritan millennium, and that Catholicism was not necessarily politically passive or simply reactionary. Calvinism and Catholicism both had radical and conservative political potential, but the strength of radicalism or conservatism in either tradition at any given time depended largely on circumstances, both on the course of events within the group involved and on its relationship with the state and society. The differences over the relationship between religious belief and the political and social order were fought out within confessional groups, as well as between them.

The confrontations within English Catholicism may provide a good example of the mental traits that divided political radicals from political conservatives within religious confessions that had strong potential for both conservative and radical political tendencies. Elizabethan Catholicism, like the Reformed tradition in England and elsewhere, produced men who were convinced that the most important thing in the world—more important, if need be, than the short-run maintenance of civil peace or of obedience to the established political and social order—was the establishment of the true worship of God. In a sense every missionary priest, by his participation in the mission, was committed to a "reformation without tarrying for the magistrate," but the distinguishing characteristic of the political radicals was their willingness to use all available methods to bring in the reformation that they desired, regardless of other obligations and regardless of its effect on the social order. The most important work of the radical group dealing with the social order, the *Memorial for the Reformation of England*, considers the social and political order widely corrupt and in need of moral regeneration, which can be brought about only by religious reformation.

The Catholic opponents of the Allen-Parsons party's political efforts might appear to be more "modern" and "forward looking" because of their greater support for the "modern" (at least in the Western democracies) ideas of religious toleration and the separation of religion from politics. But this view can be maintained only by isolating the issue of toleration from its political and intellectual context. The opponents of the Allen-Parsons political approach were much more conservative than the Allen-Parsons party in their views of the world and of society, and the idea of toleration plays an important part in maintaining their conservatism.

The strongest evident priority in the political and social ethics of the Appellants and others of similar viewpoint is the necessity of maintaining a web of social and political relationships. The relationships to be maintained sometimes seem personal (for example, the chivalric images of Sir Thomas Tresham's declarations of loyalty to the queen) and sometimes based on traditional roles (for example, the Appellants' desire for the establishment of traditional episcopal rule), but the distinction is really a false one, since relationships between persons are based on their political and social roles. The Appellants' explosive hatred for Parsons and his allies results largely from the threat to the stability of the traditional world which his kind of politics represents. Both the political ideology and the method of operation of the Allen-Parsons party very definitely shifted ties based on traditional social roles to the background; Allen and Parsons may have been willing to use such ties to serve the cause, but they cared little for them in themselves. The cause of the restoration of Catholicism established the primary ties of loyalty among those dedicated to it.

The conviction that a religious or political cause is the most important determinant of one's social and political relationships threatened to break down the stable, traditional, hierarchical social and political order that was the Appellants' ideal. To maintain their ideal in the face of Parsons's attack the Appellants had to deny his premise that their religious allegiance was the fundamental fact that united or divided people. The traditional political and social bonds had to be given their own value. If religious differences were not to destroy political and social bonds between people of different religious camps, toleration had to be considered as an acceptable alternative, in order to prevent the political ideals of dedication to a cause from unsettling the whole political world. It may have been this mentality, the desire not to have the traditional world broken up (associated, of course, with a multitude of vested interests) that as much as anything defeated the movements of religiously based political radicalism, whatever their theological base, in early modern Europe.

J. J. Scarisbrick, in an article on the *Memorial for the Reformation of England*, says that "Persons's magnificent vision never really had a chance. The quieter, even quietist, and conservative world of the Appellants won through not because it was less Christian but because it was more realistic."[15] Whether or not the Allen-Parsons party's program ever did have a chance, it is true that after 1603 English Catholics effectively abandoned the idea of direct political action to bring in a Catholic ruler. Even Parsons was soon writing a letter to James I explaining at some length (the matter did require some explanation) that he had never been an enemy of James's.[16] James's own apparently effortless succession helped to expose the inability (and in many cases lack of desire) of English Catholics to oppose a Protestant succession. The end of the war between England and Spain in 1604 and the defeat of the Holy League in France took away the main political supports of the politically militant wing. Within a few years speculation about the rights of subjects against their rulers was no longer permissible anywhere in the domains of either the Bourbons or the Hapsburgs, and the general of the Society of Jesus had forbidden his subordinates to discuss the embarrassing subject of tyrannicide. As Catholic political attitudes in western Europe grew increasingly reconciled to absolutism, the English Catholics had to give up political radicalism in order to maintain the niche in the international Catholic world without which they could not have operated in England.[17] From the reign of James I on, it was essentially the Appellant attitude that English Catholics adopted toward their government. And although the Appellants' more optimistic hopes for toleration were not realized, if their political attitudes had not prevailed, the persecution of the English Catholics would probably have been much more severe, and the survival of the Catholic community perhaps in serious doubt.

The Appellants' political approach, then, was certainly more "realistic" than that of their opponents after 1603. With the benefit of hindsight, it seems true that they were more realistic even during Elizabeth's reign. Allen and Parsons seem to have badly misjudged both the extent of Catholic sympathies among the English people and the political attitudes of such Catholics as there were.

Yet the question of which group had the more "realistic" approach to the problems of English Catholicism is broader than the purely political question. The Appellants' point of view may have been the more practical method of maintaining a stable, ongoing community with a regular supply of priests being sent in from bases overseas; a community, moreover, that (although it still had its share of "church-papists" who attended Anglican services when necessary to stay out of trouble) had at least a hard core of determined recusants clearly separated from the Protestant majority. For the first decade or so of Elizabeth's reign, it was not at all clear that such a community would come into existence. In spite of the comparative leniency of government policy in the 1560s it was probably then, as Meyer has persuasively argued, that Catholicism lost most of whatever hold it had on the English people.[18] As they saw little sign that the international church cared about them, the English Catholics naturally fell into compromise with the government's not-so-unreasonable-sounding demands for token conformity to Anglicanism; and with their Catholic tendencies unsupported and the boundary between Catholic and Protestant unclear, it is not surprising that many fell away. Even if, as Christopher Haigh has recently suggested, the surviving Marian priests should get more of the credit for the emergence of recusancy than they have been given,[19] it is difficult to see how the disintegration of the Catholic community could have been avoided without the steady supply of new priests provided by the mission.

The mission was not uniquely the work of men who shared the political views of Allen and Parsons; many Appellant sympathizers took part in it, and the Appellant leaders John Mush and John Colleton seem to have been among Allen's trusted subordinates. But one may wonder whether the mission could have been created if the Appellant outlook had predominated among the exiles. The Appellants' ideas about the proper way to run the mission were of a piece with their ideal political world: cautious, careful of the proper traditional rules and structures, generally by the book. The creation of the mission had to be carried out with a very different mentality. The men who organized the mission had to be ready to adapt their methods to new and unprecedented situations; to operate with structures of authority and attitudes toward authority designed to meet the new situation rather than to conform in detail to the traditional hierarchy.[20] The struggle over the government of the mission between the advocates of episcopal rule and the Jesuits and other advocates of methods that they believed more suited to English conditions divided English

Catholics well into the seventeenth century,[21] but until very late in Elizabeth's reign the advocates of the more ad hoc approach had their way without significant opposition. The dominance of the flexible, pragmatic, somewhat improvised approach to the organization and structure of the mission is symptomatic of a mentality that placed the highest possible value on the traditional authority of the church, but that, with the exception of the papal power, was not particularly fussy about the forms and methods through which that authority was exercised. This mentality tended to promote a more individualistic and activist approach than the Appellants, to whom the form of authority was often an end in itself.

The spirit of intense, individualist activism that was characteristic of the mission in its first decades may have faded. But it left behind a Catholic community clearly marked off from Protestant England, confirmed in its refusal to be absorbed into the established church, and supported by a network of institutions, mostly abroad, that supplied its priests, its books, and education for some of its members, and kept it in touch with the international Catholic church. Not least, it supplied the English Catholics with the memory of the Elizabethan martyrs—as well as with enough martyrs during the seventeenth century to keep the tradition fresh. The Appellants' attitude was perhaps the more realistic one for this community to adopt after 1603, and on strictly political questions perhaps their views had always been more realistic. But without the activist mentality that dominated the mission during most of Elizabeth's reign, English Catholicism might not have survived as a significant community at all.

# Appendix: Bibliographical Essay

The historiography of Elizabethan Catholicism began before Elizabeth herself died; the contrasting views of Elizabethans ranging from Burghley to Parsons depended largely on their ideas of the history of the relations between England and Catholicism. Unfortunately, the nature of those relations, under Elizabeth and for long after, has made it practically inevitable that the historiographical tradition would be largely one of polemic. Many works in this field have been little more than propaganda, with all the characteristics of factual omissions and distortions and ludicrously unfair standards of judgment that the term implies.[1] But the production of propaganda is probably not the most serious effect that the long hostility between the Catholic church and the English state has had on the writing of history. The long history of hostility has led even serious, responsible historians with a great deal of knowledge and insight to concentrate too much attention on the wrong issues. Questions of right and wrong, of justice and morality, should have a high place in scholarship, but such issues become destructive when they take precedence over the effort to understand the environment and the thought of the persons whom the historian studies. The most obvious case of this tendency in the historiography of Elizabethan Catholicism is the labored efforts of many historians to convict or acquit the seminary priests of political treason or their persecutors of religious bigotry. These questions are not irrelevant, but often they are distractions from the task of trying to understand both groups in their historical context.

The atmosphere of judgment often pushing aside history runs

through the surveys of the subject by even the best English Catholic historians of the first half of the twentieth century, J. H. Pollen and Philip Hughes.[2] In a more subtle way, this flaw affects Pollen's book on the archpriest controversy—nevertheless a fine book that is still the best introduction to the problem. Pollen is generally fair-minded in assessing the two Catholic factions,[3] but his tendency to judge his characters in terms of adherence to the ideas of high papalism sometimes makes his approach narrower and more legalistic than necessary.

It may be partly because of the polemical distractions that surround the history of Roman Catholicism in England that the best available survey of Elizabethan Catholicism was written, over sixty years ago, by a German whose own personal roots were outside all English traditions. A. O. Meyer's *England and the Catholic Church under Queen Elizabeth* is still the indispensable starting point for any student of the subject. The book has many virtues, but its greatest contribution was to leave behind the common obsession with martyrology and plots and examine the conflict between England and the Catholic church as a clash of persons, of institutions, and of ideals rather than as a battle between light and darkness. Meyer does not fail to give the protagonists on both sides their due. He acquits the seminary priests as a body of active political opposition to the crown, and his account of their heroism and their sufferings is at least as moving as Hughes's or Pollen's. On the other hand, he recognizes throughout that, brutal as the repression was, most opponents of the seminary priests were acting in defense of what they genuinely saw as the national interest; and he convincingly argues that the sharp decline of Catholic feeling among the English people owed much more to the positive attractions of Protestantism than to government persecution.[4] But most important, Meyer's main concern is to understand and explain, not to justify or condemn.

Nevertheless, Meyer's work does have its limitations, many of which, as a recent critic has said, stem from the fact that Meyer has a German axe to grind rather than an English one.[5] Meyer fits his work into a conceptual scheme in which England, as the virile prototype of the modern national state, confronts and defeats Rome, the representative of the declining but still potent "medieval" world order. This scheme, while somewhat anachronistic, does not do much harm to Meyer's account of the political and diplomatic side of Elizabethan Catholic history, nor to his account of the individual dramas of conscience that the clash of great ideals and institutions produced. It does not account for everything that happened in English Catholicism under Elizabeth, particularly the internal history of the community. For example, as John Bossy has pointed out, Meyer's dichotomy of nationalist Appellants versus pro-Spanish Jesuits greatly oversimplifies, and in some way falsifies, the issues in the archpriest controversy.[6]

One reason for Meyer's oversimplifications was undoubtedly that he was working from a much smaller base of detailed scholarly investigations than is available today. In the last thirty years, knowledge of the history of English Catholicism has expanded in two crucial areas. Our knowledge of the mentality of Elizabethan Catholicism has grown; on the political side, T. H. Clancy's study of the political thought of the Allen-Parsons party is the most notable contribution.[7] Perhaps even more important, our picture of the actual life of the English Catholics has been enormously expanded and deepened by a host of local, social, and administrative studies.[8] From these studies has emerged a picture of a Catholic community whose members varied in many ways: in social standing; in degree of commitment to Catholicism; in their relationship, both ideological and practical, to the larger society; and in the extent to which they suffered from government repression. The English Catholics, like any other human group, had their own internal social history; they were not (as even Meyer sometimes tended to treat them) simply a backdrop for the titanic struggles of great historical forces or the dramatic deeds of martyrs or conspirators.

The most outstanding interpreter of the internal history of English Catholicism is John Bossy. Bossy's influence is due to a great extent to his ability to combine his insights into the ideas and mentality of English Catholicism with his view of its social history. The combination is extraordinarily fruitful; although his published writings on Elizabethan Catholicism do not add up to any great number of pages, Bossy has probably contributed more valuable ideas than anyone else who has written on the subject. More than any of his predecessors, Bossy has recognized the radical break with the past, both in spirit, and in method of operation, that the missionary movement represented.[9] He has also greatly advanced our understanding of the splits within the English Catholic community. The divisions that he sees are much more profound than the traditional distinction between politically militant exiles whose hopes of a Catholic restoration were maintained only by their ignorance of the English situation and Catholics in England effectively cowed into political inactivity. In Bossy's view, the main distinction within English Catholicism was between a Catholicism that was activist, outward-looking, cosmopolitan, and willing to adapt the structures and practices of the church to a radically new situation and a Catholicism that was inward-looking, provincial, and most comfortable with the traditional hierarchical forms of society and the state. The first orientation, Bossy holds, was characteristic of the founders of the mission; the second was characteristic first of the Catholic gentry and later of the Appellants. The "missionary" attitude tended to be connected with political militancy, the "gentry" attitude with loyalty to the crown.[10]

Bossy's distinction seems to account for a great deal of the history of Elizabethan Catholicism, but a few points do seem to call for comment. Bossy claims that the Catholic gentry during the archpriest controversy was "on the whole too diffident to intervene but sympathetic to the Appellants."[11] The parallels between gentry and Appellant political views might lead one to expect this, but there is little apparent evidence for it, and there is some evidence that the Appellants were worried about gentry hostility.[12] Gentry hostility to the Appellants would be comprehensible if one assumed that the gentry perceived the issue not as political loyalty to the queen but as clerical obedience to ecclesiastical superiors.

But Bossy's interpretation of the archpriest controversy also involves a more general problem. In fact, he has presented two interpretations, which are not entirely consistent with each other. In an early article, Bossy ascribes the Appellants' violent anti-Jesuit tirades to a combination of "hankering after orthodox procedures" and the psychological strain imposed by the dangers of the mission. But when he moves from describing the tone of Appellant propaganda to its substance, Bossy emphasizes their political argument and program, concluding that the Appellants "adopted the language and outlook of lay supremacy" and that the Appellant vision involved a cleric who "was to be not only a gentleman, but a gentleman bound by a personal obligation to the queen which would take precedence over all others."[13]

The idea that most Appellants placed their allegiance to the queen above all others accords poorly with several facts—most obviously with the total failure to agree with the government on a mutually acceptable oath of allegiance and conditions of toleration and with the firm opposition of most Appellants to the oath of allegiance of 1606. Bossy himself, in his more recent work, has compellingly criticized the view either that the Appellants were simple supporters of gentry Catholicism or that they gave an unconditional allegiance to the queen, or indeed that their primary interests were political at all. He reminds us that the central issue in the archpriest controversy was one of ecclesiastical organization, not of political morality, and that everyone involved in the controversy accepted the pope's jurisdiction over it. He also demonstrates that in the long run the Appellants' desire for an independent, although traditionalist, Catholic church hierarchy was not much (if at all) more compatible with gentry aspirations than was the "missionary" ideal. The alliance on political questions, if there was one, between the gentry and the Appellants during the archpriest controversy appears in this account to be an essentially accidental result of the fact that the gentry's disagreements with the Allen-Parsons party were more obvious than their disagreements with the Appellants.[14] In Bossy's words, "Their Protestation [the Appellants' protestation of January 1603] far from being the central statement of their belief, was the result of a short and unsuccessful excursion into alien territory"—namely, into "a problem which primarily concerned the Catholic laity, the problem of allegiance."[15]

Much of this argument is a valuable corrective to traditional views. The Appellants were priests first, and they cannot be understood if one assumes that political objectives were uppermost in their minds. One of the main points of Appellant propaganda was the necessity of the mission's avoiding political involvement. The gentry, insofar as their views are known, believed that priests should leave politics to them, and after 1603 they were generally able to enforce that view.

Nevertheless, Bossy exaggerates when he calls the problem of political allegiance "alien territory" for the Elizabethan priests. However apolitical he may have wanted to be, it must have been obvious to any missionary priest that the mission's peculiar problems were primarily the result of English government policy. It was because of the government's hostility that the mission had to operate in secret, that it was deprived of the normal Catholic hierarchical organization, and that more than half the missionary priests spent time in prison and about one-fifth were executed. Allen and Parsons tried to remedy this situation by attempting to overthrow the hostile regime; the Appellants, by trying to mitigate its hostility.

The questions of political values with which both groups struggled were not at all peripheral to the religious goals of the mission. They involved fundamental judgments about the conduct of the mission and its relationship to its environment. If anything, the missionary priest would seem to have been more affected by official hostility than most of the laity—he had been more violently uprooted by it and was much more likely to die because of it. The main concerns of both the Allen-Parsons party and the Appellants were religious, but their religious problems could not be solved in any satisfactory way without a change in the political situation—and when a priest tried to reduce the obstacles to the mission's religious task, it is largely a matter of semantics whether his action was "religious" or "political." Considering the relationship of the Catholic community to the English political order, the question of political loyalty was bound to be central to the religious concerns of many priests.

# Notes

*Abbreviations*
CRS    Publications of the Catholic Record Society
*Douai Diaries*    T. F. Knox, ed., *The First and Second Diaries of the English College, Douay, and an Appendix of Unpublished Documents.*
ERL    Publications in the English Recusant Literature Series, facsimiles published by Scolar Press, London.
Foley    H. J. Foley, ed., *Records of the English Province of the Society of Jesus.*
Lambeth    Documents in the Lambeth Palace Library, London.
PRO    Public Record Office, London.
Stonyhurst    Documents at Stonyhurst College, near Blackburn, Lancashire. The xeroxed copies of these documents at the Jesuit Library on Mount Street, London, were the source actually used.
Tierney-Dodd    Mark Aloysius Tierney, ed., *Dodd's Church History of England from the Commencement of the Sixteenth Century to the Revolution in 1688. With Notes, Additions, and a Continuation by the Rev. M. A. Tierney.*
Westminster    Documents in the Westminster Diocesan Archives, London.

*Chapter 1*
1. For example, *The Copy of a Letter, Written by a Master of Art* [*sic* ]*of Cambridge* . . . (commonly known as *Leicester's Commonwealth*), pp. 179–84; and Thomas Bluet, *Important Considerations, which Ought to Move all True and Sound Catholics . . . to Acknowledge . . . that the Proceedings of Her Majesty . . . Have Been Both Mild and Merciful.*

2. A. G. Dickens, "The First Stages of Romanist Recusancy in Yorkshire, 1560–1590," pp. 161–63. For another example, see John Bossy, *The English Catholic Community 1570–1850*, pp. 145–46.

3. A. O. Meyer, *England and the Catholic Church under Queen Elizabeth*, pp. 68–69.

4. See ibid., pp. 68–70, and F. X. Walker, "The Implementation

of the Elizabethan Statutes against Recusants, 1581–1603," chap. 1.

5. Meyer, *England and the Catholic Church*, pp. 71–73.

6. This line of argument, particularly the last sentence, owes much to John Bossy, "The Character of Elizabethan Catholicism," and *English Catholic Community*, especially pt. 1.

7. Bossy, *English Catholic Community*, pp.12–13.

8. Ibid., pp. 12–20.

9. Ibid., pp. 168–82.

10. A. L. Rowse, *Tudor Cornwall*, p. 378; Roger B. Manning, *Religion and Society in Elizabethan Sussex*, pp. 40–41, 158–63. For other examples, see Bossy, *English Catholic Community*, pp. 174–76.

11. Bossy, *English Catholic Community*, p. 100.

12. Ibid., pp. 77–107, where Bossy gives a very comprehensive account of the geography of Elizabethan Catholicism, of which this paragraph is a bald summary.

13. Walker, "Elizabethan Statutes against Recusants," is a thorough study of the recusancy laws and their enforcement, although other anti-Catholic laws are not treated systematically.

14. Relevant portions of many of these laws are printed in G. R. Elton, ed., *The Tudor Constitution*, pp. 418–32.

15. List in *New Catholic Encyclopedia*, 9:322–29. The source also lists eight lay people as "dilati," i.e., those whose cases are still under consideration.

16. Godfrey Anstruther, *The Seminary Priests*.

17. For the exchange that began the debate, see Robert M. Kingdon, ed., *The Execution of Justice in England, by William Cecil*, and *A True,*

*Sincere, and Modest Defence of English Catholics, by William Allen*.

18. Philip Hughes, *Rome and the Counter-Reformation in England*, p. 261. In the faculties granted to Parsons and Campion in 1580, Gregory XIII declared that the bull of 1570 was not binding on Catholics as long as its execution was impossible. This well-meant gloss made the Catholics' situation more difficult, if anything, since it cast doubt on the sincerity of any Catholic who tried to prove his loyalty. For the relevant clause, see Meyer, *England and the Catholic Church*, p. 487.

19. Hughes, *Counter-Reformation in England*, pp. 246–47.

20. Bossy, "Character of Elizabethan Catholicism," pp. 48–50.

21. See A. J. Loomie, *The Spanish Elizabethans*, pp. 14–51, and Tierney-Dodd, 3:xlviii–lii.

22. Tierney-Dodd, 3:xlviii–lii; Garrett Mattingly, "William Allen and Catholic Propaganda in England," especially p. 326; L. Hicks, ed., *Letters and Memorials of Father Robert Parsons S.J.*, pp. 161–63.

23. T. H. Clancy, *Papist Pamphleteers*, deals effectively with the political thought of Allen, Parsons, and others of their party.

24. Peter John Holmes, "The Political Thought of the Elizabethan Catholics." This dissertation will be a very valuable contribution to the field when it is published, although Holmes may tend to overrate the importance of the occasional signs of loyalism from Allen and Parsons.

25. The best example may be Allen's *True, Sincere, and Modest Defence of English Catholics*.

Chapter 2

1. From the bull *Regnans in Excelsis*, in G. R. Elton, ed., *The*

*Tudor Constitution*, pp. 416–18.

2. Excerpts from many important documents in the controversies between popes and secular rulers may be found in Brian Tierney, *The Crisis of Church and State 1050–1300*. See also Walter Ullman, *Medieval Papalism*, pp. 114 ff.

3. See William Allen, *An Apology and True Declaration of . . . the Two English Colleges*, pp. 51b–65b, especially p. 54b.

4. Ibid., p. 55.

5. Ibid., pp. 65b–66.

6. Ibid., p. 4b. In this and other quotations from original sources in English, spelling and capitalization have been modernized.

7. William Allen, *A True, Sincere, and Modest Defence of English Catholics*, p. 59.

8. Ibid., p. 56.

9. Ibid., p. 60.

10. Ibid., p. 195.

11. Ibid., pp. 8–9. Allen is justifiably unimpressed by the fact that the queen had not actually assumed the title.

12. Ibid., p. 198.

13. See especially William Allen, *An Admonition to the Nobility and People of England and Ireland*, pp. VIII–XXIX.

14. Ibid., p. IIII.

15. Allen, *True, Sincere, and Modest Defence*, pp. 99, 97. For a more thorough discussion of Allen's views on papal power, see T. H. Clancy, *Papist Pamphleteers*, pp. 49–55.

16. William Allen, *The Copy of a Letter . . . Concerning the Yielding up of the City of Daventrie*, pp. 6, 7–9.

17. Ibid., p. 13.

18. Ibid., pp. 14–18.

19. Ibid., pp. 22, 23.

20. For an example, see Thomas Bluet, *Important Considerations, which Ought to Move all True and Sound*

*Catholics . . . to Acknowledge . . . that the Proceedings of Her Majesty . . . Have Been Both Mild and Merciful*, pp. 24–25.

21. L. Hicks, "Robert Parsons S. J. and the *Book of Succession*," pp. 126–28. Hicks's evidence on the authorship of the book seems more convincing than most of his arguments on other points.

22. Ibid., p. 109.

23. Many of Doleman's arguments are lifted from William Rainold's tract in support of the French Holy League, *De Justa Reipublicae in Reges Impios et Haereticos . . . Authoritate*, although he integrates the material in a new way. See Clancy, *Papist Pamphleteers*, pp. 60–63.

24. R. Doleman [pseud. Robert Parsons and possibly others], *A Conference About the Next Succession to the Crown of England*, pt. 1, pp. 123–25. (All subsequent references to this work are to pt. 1.)

25. Ibid., pp. 3–7.

26. Ibid., pp. 7–8.

27. Ibid., p. 9.

28. Ibid., pp. 15–19 (on the advantages of monarchy); pp. 125–29 (on the advantages of the hereditary principle).

29. Ibid., pp. 21, 22.

30. Ibid., pp. 23–25. The fact that Doleman overrates the importance of some of the bodies he mentions does not affect the point.

31. Ibid., pp. 66–67.

32. Ibid., pp. 71–72.

33. Ibid., pp. 77–78.

34. Ibid., p. 82.

35. Ibid., p. 73.

36. Ibid., pp. 174–75.

37. Ibid., p. 175.

38. Ibid., pp. 82–84.

39. Ibid., pp. 119, 120.

40. Ibid., p. 114.

41. Ibid., pp. 197–200. This pas-

sage also seems to be typical of a major weakness in Doleman's system. He says that the commonwealth's decisions on the succession must be accepted by private men, but neither here nor elsewhere does he make clear who in the commonwealth has the right to depose a prince and how the deposition may legitimately be carried out.

42. Ibid., p. 200.
43. Ibid., p. 202.
44. Ibid., pp. 203–4.
45. Ibid., pp. 206, 207.
46. Ibid., p. 205.
47. Ibid., pp. 211–12.
48. Ibid., pp. 213, 214.
49. Robert Parsons, *A Brief Apology or Defence of the Catholic Ecclesiastical Hierarchy*, pp. 187b–88. Peter Holmes has recently discovered a Latin translation of the *Conference*, apparently intended for papal officials, that includes a chapter not included in the English original. The extra chapter defends the right of the papacy to decide the question of the English succession. See Peter John Holmes, "The Political Thought of the Elizabethan Catholics," pp. 232–45.
50. Parsons, *Conference*, p. 216.
51. Ibid., pp. 217, 218.
52. Robert Parsons, *The Jesuit's Memorial for the Intended Reformation of England*. For the dating of the work, see J. J. Scarisbrick "Robert Persons's Plans for the 'True' Reformation of England," pp. 19–20.
53. Scarisbrick, "Robert Persons's Plans," pp. 33–40.
54. Parsons, *Jesuit's Memorial*, pp. 1–6.
55. Ibid., pp. 13–16.
56. Ibid., pp. 20, 21.
57. Ibid., pp. 21–22.
58. Ibid., p. 203.
59. Ibid., p. 205.

60. Ibid., pp. 29–30.
61. Ibid., p. 207.
62. Ibid.
63. The council's appointment is discussed in ibid., pp. 70–71. The main discussion of its role is pp. 70–101.
64. Ibid., pp. 71–75, 89–90.
65. Ibid., pp. 32–33.
66. Ibid., p. 34.
67. Ibid., p. 32.
68. Ibid., pp. 36–43.
69. Ibid., pp. 36, 40.
70. Ibid., pp. 43, 44.
71. Ibid., p. 22.
72. Ibid., pp. 191–93.
73. Ibid., p. 114.
74. Ibid., for example, pp. 116–19, 131–33.
75. Ibid., pp. 195–202.
76. Ibid., pp. 119–35.
77. Ibid., p. 145.
78. Ibid., pp. 131–32.
79. Ibid., p. 132.
80. Ibid., p. 49.
81. Ibid., pp. 50–51.
82. Ibid., pp. 53–55.
83. Ibid., pp. 56–57, 63–64.
84. Ibid., pp. 57, 64.
85. Ibid., p. 105.
86. Ibid., pp. 102–4.
87. Ibid., p. 104.
88. Ibid., pp. 68–72.
89. Ibid., pp. 220–21.
90. Ibid., for example, pp. 30, 74, 131–33, 176–77, 215–16.
91. Ibid., p. 30.
92. Ibid., pp. 3–5.

*Chapter 3*

1. John Bossy, "The Character of Elizabethan Catholicism." Peter John Holmes, "The Political Thought of the Elizabethan Catholics," pp. 112 ff., seems to modify this view somewhat but not to affect the main point.
2. Bossy, "Character of Eliza-

bethan Catholicism," pp. 41, 39.
3. Text of the oath (1606) in
J. P. Kenyon, ed., *The Stuart
Constitution*, pp. 458–59. The oath's
most objectionable feature was that
the oath-taker was required not
merely to repudiate the doctrine
"that princes which be excommunicated or deprived by the pope may
be deposed or murdered by their
subjects," but to call it "impious and
heretical"—thereby effectively allowing a Protestant temporal ruler to
define heresy. On Catholics and the
oath, see also Hugh Aveling,
*Northern Catholics*, pp. 247–48, and
John Bossy, "The English Catholic
Community 1603–1625," pp. 93–95.
4. A. O. Meyer, *England and the
Catholic Church under Queen Elizabeth*,
pp. 33–58.
5. Ibid., pp. 68–69.
6. F. X. Walker, "The Implementation of the Elizabethan Statutes
against Recusants, 1581–1603," pp.
275 ff.
7. See, for example, Roger B.
Manning, "Catholics and Local Office Holding in Elizabethan Sussex,"
pp. 47–61.
8. Walker, "Elizabethan Statutes
against Recusants."
9. Walker, "Elizabethan Statutes
against Recusants," is perhaps the
most thorough description of the
enforcement machinery of the
recusancy laws. Aveling, *Northern
Catholics*, pp. 13–20, and Roger B.
Manning, *Religion and Society in
Elizabethan Sussex*, pp. 129–51,
describe the structure and problems
of the enforcement machinery in
their areas. Elliot Rose, *Cases of
Conscience*, contains interesting material on legal problems of Catholics.
10. See Manning, "Catholics and
Local Office Holding," and Aveling,
*Northern Catholics*, pp. 115–18.

11. For example, see J. T. Cliffe,
*The Yorkshire Gentry from the Reforma-
tion to the Civil War*, pp. 210–30,
especially 228–30; Vincent Burke,
"The Economic Consequences of
Recusancy in Elizabethan Worcestershire," pp. 71–77; and Mary E.
Finch, *The Wealth of Five Northamptonshire Families, 1540–1640*, pp. 66–99.
12. J. H. Pollen and William
MacMahon, eds., *The Venerable Philip
Howard, Earl of Arundel*, pp. 103–4.
13. *The Life of St. Philip Howard*,
pp. 5–7.
14. His biographer dates his
Catholic convictions from his wit-
nessing the disputation of Campion
and his companions with some
Protestant ministers in 1581; ibid.,
pp. 8–9.
15. Pollen and MacMahon, *Philip
Howard*, pp. 52, 110.
16. Ibid., especially pp. 46–48.
17. Ibid., pp. 104–6.
18. Ibid., pp. 102–3.
19. Ibid., p. 114.
20. Ibid., p. 110 ("Ce jeune
seigneur conte d'Arundel a prins
quelque nouveau mescontentement,
ou de se voir icy bien peu respecté,
ou pour estre en son coeur de la
Religion Catholique").
21. Ibid., p. 147.
22. Ibid., p. 268; *Life of Howard*,
pp. 39–40.
23. Pollen and MacMahon, *Philip
Howard*, pp. 209, 215–16.
24. *Dictionary of National Biography*,
s.v. "Browne, Anthony"; *Cokayne's
Complete Peerage*, 9:94–100.
25. See J. E. Neale, *Elizabeth I and
Her Parliaments*, 1:75. For Montague's
other activities in Elizabeth's first
two parliaments, see pp. 45, 73, 80,
and 120.
26. Roger B. Manning, "Anthony
Browne, 1st Viscount Montague,"
p. 107.

27. Ibid., p. 109.

28. "Richard Leigh," *The Copy of a Letter Written Out of England to Don Bernardin de Mendoza*, pp. 24–25. Burghley's authorship is proved in Conyers Read, "William Cecil and Elizabethan Public Relations," pp. 45 ff.

29. Manning, "Anthony Browne," p. 107.

30. Richard Smith, *The Life of Lady Magdalen Viscountess Montague*, pp. 19–20. Smith, who was chaplain to Montague's widow, ascribes his occasional conformity to the counsel of a timid chaplain and describes his constant refusal to attend heretical services after a new chaplain had told him it was forbidden.

31. Ibid., p. 43.

32. Manning, *Elizabethan Sussex*, pp. 158–63.

33. Timothy J. McCann, "The Parliamentary Speech of Viscount Montague against the Act of Supremacy, 1559," pp. 54, 53.

34. Ibid., pp. 55, 56.

35. Ibid., p. 55.

36. Ibid., p. 52.

37. John Strype, *Annals of the Reformation*, vol. 1, pt. 1, pp. 442–43.

38. Ibid., pp. 442, 445.

39. Ibid., p. 443.

40. Many of his papers are printed in the Historical Manuscripts Commission, *Report on Manuscripts in Various Collections*, 3:1–154. A good deal of information on Tresham may be found in Godfrey Anstruther, *Vaux of Harrowden*. For his finances and family history, see Finch, *Five Northamptonshire Families*, pp. 66–99.

41. CRS, *Miscellanea 2*, p. 27.

42. This tendency may have been partly in response to the financial burdens imposed on recusants.

43. Historical Manuscripts Commission, *Various Collections*, 3:97.

44. Ibid., p. 23.

45. For example, ibid., pp. 26–27, 32–33, 115–16.

46. Ibid., pp. 28–29. This letter (dated 27 May 1583) is rather puzzling, in that it speaks as if the countess to whom it is addressed had been Bedford's wife during his exile under Queen Mary and as if she were the mother of his children. According to the *Dictionary of National Biography*, Bedford's first wife, the mother of all his children, died in 1562, and the countess to whom Lady Tresham was writing did not become his wife until 1566.

47. Ibid., pp. 116–17, 128–31. There is no indication of the purpose for which this memorandum was drawn up.

48. Ibid., p. 27.

49. Ibid., p. 56.

50. Ibid., pp. 55–56.

51. Ibid., pp. 34–43. The reception of the petition is described in Roger B. Manning, "Richard Shelley of Warminghurst and the English Catholic Petition for Toleration of 1585," pp. 265–74. In the bill's original form the receiving of priests was also made treason. Tresham's petition assumes that this is the question at issue.

52. Historical Manuscripts Commission, Various Collections, 3:39, 125, 39.

53. Ibid., pp. 52, 52, 54.

54. Ibid., pp. 117–23. Tresham's account, of course, is unlikely to have lost anything in the telling.

55. See especially ibid., p. 119.

56. Ibid., p. 121.

57. Ibid.

58. Ibid., p. 122. Cattelyne was vicar of All Saints, Northampton.

59. Ibid., p. 19.

60. Ibid., pp. 39, 38.

61. Ibid., p. 38.

62. Ibid., p. 40.
63. Ibid., p. 41; Tresham's italics.
64. Ibid., p. 40.
65. Ibid., p. 41.
66. Ibid., p. 114. Hill was reprieved from execution and lived, mostly in exile, until 1644.
67. Foley, 3:725.
68. Robert Léchat, *Les réfugiés anglais dans les Pays-Bas espagnols durant le règne d'Élisabeth*, p. 204.
69. For Copley's life before his exile, see the introduction to Sir Thomas Copley, *Letters of Sir Thomas Copley*, pp. xx–xxvii.
70. Ibid., pp. 6, 30.
71. Ibid., p. 11.
72. Ibid., p. 140.
73. Ibid.; occurs often, for example, p. 44.
74. Ibid., for example, p. 28.
75. Ibid., p. 67.
76. Ibid., pp. 116–17.
77. Ibid., p. 3.
78. Ibid., p. 158.
79. Ibid., p. 129.
80. Ibid., pp. 32–33.
81. Ibid., p. 155.
82. Ibid., p. 150.
83. Ibid., p. 135.
84. Ibid., pp. xxiii–xxiv.
85. Biographical information about Wright may be obtained in T. E. Stroud, "Father Thomas Wright."
86. Ibid., pp. 192–93.
87. *An licitum sit Catholicis in Anglia arma sumere, et aliis modis, reginam et regnum defendere contra Hispanos*; English version in Strype, *Annals*, vol. 3, pt. 2, pp. 583–97.
88. Ibid., pp. 584–85.
89. Ibid., p. 584.
90. Ibid., pp. 585–86.
91. Ibid., p. 591.
92. Ibid., p. 594.
93. Ibid.
94. Ibid., p. 595.
95. Ibid., p. 587.
96. Ibid., pp. 589, 590.
97. Wright does admit one case when subjects may obey the pope against their ruler—when the subjects of a king "by a unanimous consent" (i.e., by the whole community or the "chief heads") have informed the pope that their souls would be endangered by continued obedience (ibid., p. 590). Since the pope must await the initiative of the subjects, this is not a major exception to the pope's effective elimination from politics, although it does imply a limitation of the ruler's powers by the people.
98. Ibid., p. 586.
99. Ibid., pp. 586–87.
100. Ibid., p. 587.
101. Ibid., p. 588.
102. Ibid., pp. 588–89.
103. Ibid., p. 591.
104. Ibid., pp. 591–92.
105. Ibid., p. 590.
106. Ibid., p. 592.
107. Ibid.
108. Ibid., pp. 592–93.
109. Paul L. Hughes and James F. Larkin, eds., *Tudor Royal Proclamations*, 3:86–93.
110. For this and the subsequent history of Southwell's work, see Robert Southwell, *An Humble Supplication to Her Majesty*, ed. R. C. Bald, Introduction, pp. xii–xvii.
111. Southwell, *Humble Supplication* (ERL 123), pp. 31–45.
112. T. G. Law, ed., *The Archpriest Controversy*, 2:95–99.
113. For example, Southwell, *Humble Supplication*, pp. 52 ff.
114. Ibid., p. 6.
115. Ibid., pp. 53–56.
116. Ibid., pp. 29, 29–30.
117. Ibid., pp. 66, 62.
118. Ibid., p. 67.
119. Ibid., pp. 26–28, 22–23.
120. Ibid., pp. 8–9.

121. Ibid., pp. 67–70.
122. Ibid., pp. 70–72.
123. Ibid., p. 72.
124. Ibid., pp. 26–27.
125. Ibid., p. 26.
126. Ibid., p. 73.
127. Ibid., pp. 60–61.

Chapter 4
1. Bernard Basset, *The English Jesuits from Campion to Martindale*, pp. 13–26.
2. Ibid., pp. 29–30; CRS, *Miscellanea 2*, p. 78.
3. Basset, *English Jesuits*, pp. 32–33.
4. Philip Hughes, *Rome and the Counter-Reformation in England*, pp. 180–81.
5. Some documents relevant to the Campion-Parsons mission are in L. Hicks, ed., *Letter and Memorials of Father Robert Parsons S.J.*, pp. 28–123, and in CRS, *Miscellanea 2*, pp. 186–201.
6. J. H. Pollen, *The English Catholics in the Reign of Queen Elizabeth*, p. 370.
7. T. H. Clancy, *Papist Pamphleteers*, pp. 126–27.
8. John E. Parish, "Robert Parsons and the English Counter-Reformation," pp. 39–40.
9. Peter Guilday, *The English Catholic Refugees on the Continent, 1558–1795*, pp. 107 ff.
10. Foley, vol. 7, pt. 1, pp. lxvi–lxviii. The first list names only two Jesuits as being in prison, but Robert Southwell had also been imprisoned since June of 1592.
11. John Bossy, *The English Catholic Community 1570–1850*, pp. 204–7.
12. John Gerard, *Autobiography of an Elizabethan*, p. 29.
13. Godfrey Anstruther, *Vaux of Harrowden*, pp. 111 ff. The Earl of Arundel was attracted to the

Catholic Church by the imprisoned Edmund Campion's disputation with Protestants, advised by Jasper Heywood, and reconciled to the church by William Weston. His wife sheltered Robert Southwell for years while her husband was in prison and as late as 1621 provided funds to purchase a house at Ghent for the society's use. Basset, *English Jesuits*, pp. 98, 102–3, 161.
14. Gerard, *Autobiography*, p. 29. Gerard claims (p. 30) that the chaplain later became friendly to the Jesuits upon seeing that his own status as a priest increased with the increased piety and devotion shown by the household under the Jesuit regime.
15. CRS, *Miscellanea 2*, pp. 177–78.
16. Basset, *English Jesuits*, pp. 99–100. Heywood's action was not supported by his fellow Jesuits; Campion and Parsons had compromised on the issue in 1580. However, Heywood's actions were later attacked as an example of Jesuit arrogance and an attempt to introduce new laws by fiat. One of the great handicaps under which the Jesuits labored was the tendency to hold the whole society responsible for the vagaries of individual members.
17. William Allen, *Letters and Memorials*, pp. 356–58.

Chapter 5
1. See the list of prisoners in T. G. Law, *Jesuits and Seculars in the Reign of Queen Elizabeth*, pp. 135–37.
2. See ibid., p. 23, n. 1, and Godfrey Anstruther, *The Seminary Priests*, pp. 201–2.
3. William Weston, *Autobiography of an Elizabethan*, pp. 161–64. Weston, writing many years after the events he describes, says the period of strict

confinement lasted about six years after his arrival. In fact, it could have lasted only about four years, since Weston arrived in January 1588 and he placed the end of strict confinement shortly before the death of the prisoner Thomas Metham, who died in March 1592 (Anstruther, *Seminary Priests*, p. 229). Weston (p. 168) places his death in 1594.

4. Ibid., pp. 167–68, and John Strype, *Annals of the Reformation*, 4:273–75.

5. *Calendar of State Papers, Domestic, 1598–1601*, pp. 319–20.

6. Strype, *Annals*, 4:273.

7. Weston, *Autobiography*, p. 176, n. 16.

8. Richard Holtby, "Father Richard Holtby on Persecution in the North," p. 140.

9. Hugh Aveling, "The Catholic Recusants of the West Riding of Yorkshire 1558–1790," p. 229.

10. Westminster, vol. 5, no. 32.

11. Law, *Jesuits and Seculars*, p. 135.

12. See *Dictionary of National Biography*, s.v. "Weston, William" (which, however, contains some errors). For his activities as an exorcist, see Weston, *Autobiography*, pp. 24–27.

13. Samuel Harsnet, *A Declaration of Egregious Popish Impostures*, published in London in 1603.

14. Robert Parsons, *A Brief Apology or Defence of the Catholic Ecclesiastical Hierarchy*, p. 64.

15. Weston, *Autobiography*, app. D, pp. 245–46.

16. Ibid., p. 248.

17. John E. Parish, "Robert Parsons and the English Counter-Reformation," pp. 7–8.

18. For example, see Henry Garnet, in P. Renold, ed., *The Wisbech Stirs*, pp. 62–63.

19. Ibid., p. 332, n. 1.

20. Law, *Jesuits and Seculars*, p. 135. For Bagshaw's biography in general, see Anstruther, *Seminary Priests*, pp. 13–17.

21. Law, *Jesuits and Seculars*, p. xlvii.

22. *Douai Diaries*, p. 330. "Bonum habet ingenium et satis aptum ad studia, sed valde est iracundus et difficilis atque inquietus."

23. Renold, *Wisbech Stirs*, p. 329.

24. Foley, 4:45–46.

25. Renold, *Wisbech Stirs*, pp. 59–60 (Garnet to Acquaviva, 12 July 1595); Christopher Bagshaw, *A True Relation of the Faction Begun at Wisbeach*, printed in Law, *Jesuits and Seculars*, p. 19.

26. Renold, *Wisbech Stirs*, p. 4. Rules and covering letter, pp. 1–11.

27. Ibid., p. 10.

28. Ibid., pp. 4, 124.

29. Ibid., p. 4. It is, incidentally, clear from a May 1595 letter of Bagshaw's (ibid., pp. 14–18) that he was aware of the contents of the rules and the covering letter to Garnet.

30. Parsons, *Brief Apology*, pp. 71–72.

31. Renold, *Wisbech Stirs*, p. 59. Garnet's information from inside Wisbech presumably came from Weston.

32. I do not believe that anyone on the anti-Weston side ever mentions this interview—which, to put it mildly, is not conclusive evidence that it did not take place.

33. Renold, *Wisbech Stirs*, p. 60.

34. Ibid., pp. 10–11.

35. Ibid., p. 4.

36. Ibid., p. 315.

37. Garnet to Acquaviva, in ibid., p. 59.

38. Some of the letters are in ibid., pp. 22–46 and 67–83.

39. Ibid., pp. 14–18. Renold assumes that the letter was written to one person, but the fact that Bagshaw addresses his correspondent as "your worships" would seem to indicate that it was written to more than one person.

40. Ibid., p. 15.

41. Ibid., pp. 17, 14–15.

42. Ibid., p. 14.

43. Ibid., pp. 15–16.

44. Ibid., pp. 16–17. Renold (p. 20, n. 9) correctly points out that Bagshaw himself earlier in the letter admitted that Weston had no such thing as "merum dominium." The language of the letter from the eighteen priests to Garnet does, however, lend some plausibility to his attack.

45. To some degree, Weston's authority and that of the rules rested on consent, since no one was subject to the rules who had not agreed to them voluntarily. But the significance of this can be overrated. Under the circumstances, submission to the rules could hardly be anything but voluntary, and the pro-Weston party's implicit and explicit condemnations of their opponents certainly implied that everyone should submit to the rules, even if in fact they did not.

46. These differences between Weston and Bagshaw in some ways reflect differences between "modern" (frequently Jesuit) and traditional views of church practice and structure in the Counter-Reformation church as a whole. See H. O. Evennett, *The Spirit of the Counter-Reformation*, pp. 74–83, and John Bossy's postscript in the same volume, pp. 126–32.

47. Renold, *Wisbech Stirs*, p. 59.

48. Ibid., p. 61.

49. Ibid.

50. Westminster, vol. 5, no. 12.

51. Renold, *Wisbech Stirs*, p. 61.

52. Weston, *Autobiography*, pp. 192–93.

53. Westminster, vol. 5, no. 5. Bagshaw gives a somewhat different account of the episode in *True Relation*, pp. 20–24. If Bagshaw's chronology is correct (which it often is not), the incident must have taken place before June 1595.

54. Hugh Aveling, *Northern Catholics*, pp. 158–59.

55. For an example, see Westminster, vol. 5, no. 32.

56. Renold, *Wisbech Stirs*, pp. 112–14.

57. Ibid., pp. 170–71. The letters to Weston and his followers have apparently not survived.

58. Ibid., pp. 124–28.

59. Ibid., p. 138.

60. Ibid., pp. 136, 138.

61. Ibid., pp. 147, 141–44.

62. Westminster, vol. 5, no. 87.

63. Renold, *Wisbech Stirs*, pp. 147, 158–59.

64. Ibid., p. 102.

65. J. H. Pollen, *The Institution of the Archpriest Blackwell*, p. 19; Renold, *Wisbech Stirs*, pp. 178–82.

66. Renold, *Wisbech Stirs*, p. 182.

67. Bagshaw's letter has apparently not survived; Mush's reply is in ibid., pp. 189–94.

68. Ibid., p. 193.

69. See ibid., pp. 172–73, and Mush's letter, probably to Henry Garnet, in Stonyhurst Anglia A, 1, 79, in which Mush gives a long account of his views on the Roman college stirs and urges that the Jesuits should retain control of the college. The letter is dated in March 1594 (i.e., 1595 if the new year were taken to start on 1 January), but from Mush's references to the situation both at Wisbech and in Rome, the

letter must have been written in early 1596.

70. Robert Léchat, *Les réfugiés anglais dans les Pays-Bas espagnols durant le règne d'Elisabeth*, pp. 174–97.

71. Renold, *Wisbech Stirs*, p. 202, 315.

72. The *Brief Apology*, and *A Manifestation of the Great Folly and Bad Spirit, of Certain in England which Call Themselves Secular Priests*.

73. Parsons, *Brief Apology*, pp. 63b, 64.

74. Ibid., p. 65b. It may be worth noting that Parsons's lists of failings can be divided into two categories: personal dissipation (the last three) and quarreling that threatens community unity (the first four).

75. Parsons, *Manifestation*, p. 4b.

76. Ibid., pp. 4b, 5, 5b.

77. See Bagshaw, *True Relation*, pp. 48–49, 37.

78. Ibid., p. 21.

79. Renold, *Wisbech Stirs*, pp. 250–56. Fisher, it must be said, should not be considered a very reliable witness.

80. Bagshaw, *True Relation*, pp. 22–23.

81. Stonyhurst Anglia A, 2, 65.

82. Bagshaw, *True Relation*, pp. 35, 30.

83. Ibid., pp. 12–13.

84. Ibid., p. 15.

85. Ibid., p. 16.

86. Ibid., pp. 16–19. Bagshaw, who is highly unreliable on details, dates Lewis's death about a year earlier than it actually took place.

87. Ibid., p. 19.

88. Renold, *Wisbech Stirs*, p. 107.

89. Bagshaw, *True Relation*, pp. 25–26.

90. Ibid., pp. 61, 58.

91. Ibid., p. 51.

92. Ibid., p. 14.

*Chapter 6*

1. Parsons's account of these events is in L. Hicks, ed., *Letters and Memorials of Father Robert Parsons S.J.*, pp. 8–28. Many relevant documents are in CRS, *Miscellanea 2*, pp. 65–160. It should be mentioned that one possible reason for the frequent obstreperousness of Roman college students was that they were older, more experienced, and perhaps more impatient of what they considered schoolboy discipline than most sixteenth-century students. The average age of those who took the college oath at its first administration in 1579 was twenty-four. See CRS, *Miscellanea 2*, pp. 131–35.

2. Hicks, *Letters of Parsons*, p. 25.

3. Humphrey Ely, et al. *Certain Brief Notes upon a Brief Apology*, pp. 73–78.

4. The students' complaints are summarized in Sega's report, printed in A. O. Meyer, *England and the Catholic Church under Queen Elizabeth*, pp. 502–7.

5. Foley, 6:507–8. Sega's report (in Meyer, *England and the Catholic Church*, pp. 497–99) lists seventy students at the college in 1585.

6. For Lewis's biography, see Godfrey Anstruther, *The Seminary Priests*, pp. 209–10.

7. See Anthony Kenny, "The Inglorious Revolution 1594–1597," *The Venerabile* 16, no. 4 (May 1954): 244–47. The discussion here has relied heavily on Kenny's account for the narrative of the Roman stirs. It is serialized in this and the next three numbers of *The Venerabile*.

8. Ibid., pp. 246–47.

9. The beginnings of the intrigue are described (in a rather highly colored fashion) by Robert Chambers, a student who soon went over

to the side of the Jesuits, in Stonyhurst Anglia A, 2, 45. The manuscript is entitled "Brevis narratio
eorum . . . qua gesta sunt in Collegio
Anglicano, tempore tumultuum."
The petition to Lewis is printed in
Tierney-Dodd, 3:lxxiii–lxxv.

10. Stonyhurst Anglia A, 2, 45.

11. A connection between the
allegedly lax discipline at Douai and
the Roman disturbances was drawn
by Thomas Worthington and William
Percy in a long letter to Cardinal
Caietan in 1596; see *Douai Diaries*,
pp. 370–71. Worthington, however,
was anxious to discredit Richard Barret, president of Douai, and his evidence therefore may be self-serving.

12. According to Henry Garnet
(P. Renold, ed., *The Wisbech Stirs*, pp.
169–70), when John Mush visited
Rome in 1593 he was temporarily
disgruntled with the Jesuits in
England and spread tales of their
alleged unfriendliness to secular
priests.

13. Ely, *Certain Brief Notes*, p. 77;
Westminster, vol. 5, no. 112.

14. Kenny, in *The Venerabile*, vol.
16, no. 4, pp. 252–54, 258.

15. Ibid., pp. 257–58.

16. Ibid., vol. 17, no. 1, pp. 14–16.

17. Meyer, *England and the Catholic
Church*, pp. 276–77, 270, 489–91.
See also Sega's report of 1585, in
which he definitely sees the
missionary priests as preparing the
ground for a possible rebellion
against Elizabeth (ibid., p. 497).

18. The report is printed in Foley,
6:1–66. One problem in dealing with
Sega's report is that his account of
student complaints is a summary of
the individual depositions of each
student, and it is rarely possible to
tell how many students were behind
a particular complaint or demand.

19. Ibid., pp. 20, 23.

20. Ibid., pp. 19–20, 23, 24.

21. Ibid., pp. 26–28.

22. Ibid., pp. 38–49.

23. Ibid., p. 3.

24. Ibid., pp. 4 and 8.

25. Kenny, *The Venerabile*, vol. 17,
no. 1, pp. 12–13, demonstrates that
one of Sega's prime scapegoats,
Owen Lewis, was innocent of
virtually all of the accusations
against him.

26. Foley, 6:18.

27. Sega refers to Elizabeth by this
name at ibid., pp. 4, 7, 10, 16,
and 18.

28. Ibid., p. 7.

29. Ibid., pp. 54–57.

30. Ibid., pp. 51–59.

31. Ibid., pp. 58, 66.

32. Ibid., p. 58.

33. Ibid., pp. 60–61, 63–64.

34. Ibid., p. 58.

35. Ibid., p. 52.

36. Ibid., pp. 52–54.

37. Ibid., p. 51.

38. Ibid.

39. Kenny, *The Venerabile*, vol. 17,
no. 2, pp. 79–84.

40. Stonyhurst Anglia A, 2, 45.

41. In a letter to Joseph Cresswell
in Madrid, dated 28 July 1596;
Westminster, vol. 5, no. 63. See also
in this connection Agazzari's letter to
Parsons, 27 Aug. 1596, no. 66 in the
same volume.

42. PRO 31/9/111 (Roman Transcripts), pp. 251 ff., 260–74.

43. Ibid., pp. 267–68, 271–72.

44. Kenny, *The Venerabile*, vol. 17,
no. 2, p. 77, n. 1.

45. The letter is summarized by
Sega, in Foley, 6:52.

46. Peter Guilday, *The English
Catholic Refugees on the Continent,
1558–1795*, pp. 106–20; *Douai Diaries*,
pp. 368–77.

47. P. Renold, ed., *Letters of
William Allen and Richard Barret*,

pp. 251, 254.

48. Westminister, vol. 6, nos. 15 and 23.

49. Robert Léchat, *Les réfugiés anglais dans les Pays-Bas espagnols durant le règne d'Elisabeth*, pp. 176–91.

50. Tierney-Dodd, 3:lxxix–xc.

51. For Garnet's views, see Renold, *Wisbech Stirs*, pp. 172–73. See also Barret's letters to Agazzari, in January 1597, in Renold, *Letters of Allen and Barret*, pp. 259–70, in which the connection between Barret's efforts in the Spanish Netherlands and Agazzari's at Rome is demonstrated. Clement VIII also saw the connection between the different geographical areas of English exile activity; when Barret came to talk to him about the English college at Rome in September of 1596 the pope questioned him about the accusations of tyranny leveled at Holt; Renold, *Letters of Allen and Barret*, p. 250.

52. Renold, *Letters of Allen and Barret*, p. 250.

53. Tierney-Dodd, 3:lxxxv.

54. Kenny, *The Venerabile*, vol. 17, no. 2, p. 83.

55. For example, see Westminster, vol. 5, nos. 49 and 71, and vol. 6, no. 15. There is a good deal of information on Gifford in Léchat, *Les réfugiés anglais*, and in John Bossy, "Elizabethan Catholicism," especially the chapter entitled "Propaganda and Ideology" and pp. 158–59.

56. Stonyhurst Anglia A, 2, 17.

57. Renold, *Wisbech Stirs*, p. 248. The quotation is from Fisher's confession to the Roman authorities in March 1598. Fisher's statements in this confession may be exaggerated by a desire to please the authorities, but I think that the basic chronology and, in the early part of the document, Fisher's account of his

motives, are probably substantially correct.

58. Ibid., pp. 249–59. Even at this late date, not all of the later Appellant leaders in England were as willing as Bagshaw to throw themselves wholeheartedly into the anti-Jesuit campaign. John Mush, Richard Dudley, and other priests in the North of England opposed Bagshaw's plans to bring charges against the Jesuits, "partly because it was difficult to support them with legal proofs, and partly lest it might appear that the associations or fellowships which they were at that time seeking to promote among the clergy were inspired, not by zeal for religion, but by jealousy of the Fathers." Ibid., p. 250.

59. T. G. Law, *Jesuits and Seculars in the Reign of Queen Elizabeth*, pp. 111–23.

60. Renold, *Wisbech Stirs*, pp. 261–62.

61. Ibid., pp. 214–15; Renold, *Letters of Allen and Barret*, p. 271.

62. Kenny, *The Venerabile*, vol. 17, no. 3, pp. 136–37, 143.

63. T. G. Law, ed., *The Archpriest Controversy*, 1:28.

64. Kenny, *The Venerabile*, vol. 17, no. 3, p. 143.

65. Tierney-Dodd, 3:lxxviii–lxxx; Law, *Archpriest Controversy*, 1:30–31.

66. Tierney-Dodd, 3:lxxx–lxxxi.

67. Kenny, *The Venerabile*, vol. 17, no. 2, pp. 92–93.

*Chapter 7*

1. Copies of the rules of the association are in Stonyhurst Anglia A, 2, 32, and Westminster, vol. 6, no. 77. The rules were drawn up after Robert Fisher's arrival in England in the summer of 1596 ("Memorandum by Bagshaw," in T. G. Law, ed., *The Archpriest*

*Controversy*, 1:205) and before 13
December of the same year, when
Bagshaw sent a copy of the rules to
Alban Dolman (P. Renold, ed., *The
Wisbech Stirs*, pp. 207–8).

2. Renold, *Wisbech Stirs*, pp.
208–9.

3. Law, *Archpriest Controversy*,
1:205.

4. J. H. Pollen, *The Institution of
the Archpriest Blackwell*, p. 31.

5. See the copy of the rules in
Westminster, vol. 6, no. 77, esp.
under heading "de Residentiis et
Locis." The hostile critique is in
Westminster, vol. 6, no. 78.

6. John Bossy, *The English Catholic
Community 1570–1850*, pp. 204–7.

7. Fisher's confession in Renold,
*Wisbech Stirs*, pp. 250–51.

8. William Clarke, *A Reply unto a
Certain Libel, Lately Set Forth by Father
Parsons*, pp. 8b–9.

9. Law, *Archpriest Controversy*, 1:2.

10. See particularly Robert Parsons, *A Brief Apology or Defence of the
Catholic Ecclesiastical Hierarchy*, pp. 7,
89b–92.

11. John Mush, *Declaratio Motuum*,
p. 21; Humphrey Ely, *Certain Brief
Notes upon a Brief Apology*, pp.
100–101.

12. In spite of Law, *Archpriest
Controversy*, 1:2, n.C, where he
claims that "the unexpected institution of a superior in the character of
an archpriest . . . necessarily put an
end to the scheme." Bagshaw, in
October 1598, does not list the
archpriest's appointment as a cause
of the association's failure, and he
would certainly have done so had
there been any connection. See
Bagshaw's memorandum in Law,
*Archpriest Controversy*, 1:205.

13. Tierney-Dodd, 3:cxvii–cxix.

14. In Cardinal Caietan's letter ap-
pointing Blackwell, Tierney-Dodd,
3:cxx.

15. The letter is printed, with a
hostile running commentary, in
Robert Charnock, *An Answer to a
Fraudulent Letter*.

16. Westminster, vol. 6, no. 71:
"nulla maior potest esse vitiositas
quam optimum esse inimicum."

17. The most coherent Appellant
statement of the limitations on the
office of cardinal protector is in Ely,
*Certain Brief Notes*, pp. 116–54.

18. "Adversos Factiosos in Eccle-
sia," printed in Christopher Bagshaw,
*Relatio Compendiosa Turbarum quas
Jesuitae Angli . . .* , pp. 37–49.

19. Pollen, *Archpriest Blackwell*,
p. 49.

20. The university's statement is
in Tierney-Dodd, 3:cxxx–cxxxi.

21. Printed in Tierney-Dodd, 3:
cxxxiii–cxliv.

22. Tierney-Dodd, 3:clxix–cliv.

23. The *Brief Apology*.

24. An excellent study of French
policy toward the English Catholics
at this time is John Bossy, "Henri IV,
the Appellants and the Jesuits."

25. Anthony Copley, *An Answer to
a Letter of a Jesuited Gentleman* and
*Another Letter of Mr. A. C. to his
Disjesuited Kinsman*; Charles Paget,
"An Answer Made by me Charles
Paget" in Ely, *Certain Brief Notes*;
Henry Constable, *A Discovery of a
Counterfeit Conference*. For Bagshaw's
stay with Constable, John Bossy,
"Elizabethan Catholicism." The ref-
erence is somewhere between pp.
158 and 165.

26. Law, *Archpriest Controversy*,
2:177–78. For similar sentiments
expressed by Gifford in 1586, see
William Allen, *Letters and Memorials*,
p. 262.

27. See John Bennet, *The Hope of
Peace*, pp. 1–4, and Copley, *Answer*,
pp. 3–5.

28. The brief is printed in Tierney-
Dodd, 3:clxxxi–clxxxiii.

29. For example, see Law, *Arch-priest Controversy*, 2:6, 112, where the pope refers to the idea of gaining liberty of conscience in England as a "chimera."

30. Paul L. Hughes and James F. Larkin, eds., *Tudor Royal Proclamations*, 3:254.

31. Tierney-Dodd, 3:clxxxvii–cxci.

32. Ibid., 3:cxci.

*Chapter 8*

1. For a list of the major works of the archpriest controversy, see T. G. Law, *Jesuits and Seculars in the Reign of Queen Elizabeth*, pp. cxxviii–cxlix.

2. Robert Parsons, *A Brief Apology or Defence of the Catholic Ecclesiastical Hierarchy*, p. 10b, 11, 204–4b.

3. See especially Parsons, *An Appendix to the Apology* , passim.

4. Luke 10:16. For examples, see *Manifestation*, p. 29b, *Brief Apology*, p. 204b, and *Appendix*, p. 5b. Parsons, of course, quotes the Vulgate.

5. Parsons, *Appendix*, p. 10.

6. Ibid., pp. 11–11b.

7. Parsons, *Brief Apology*, p. 16b. The passage that Parsons attacks is in the *Copies of Certain Discourses* in the "Preface to the Reader," second to the last page. The preface has no page numbers.

8. Parsons, *Brief Apology*, p. 17. Parsons later (1607) did say that the pope would be deposed by the church for heresy or apostasy. See T. H. Clancy, *Papist Pamphleteers*, p. 94.

9. The gaps were pointed out by Humphrey Ely, *Certain Brief Notes upon a Brief Apology*, pp. 174–76.

10. Parsons, *Appendix*, p. 20.

11. Parsons, *Brief Apology*, pp. 108–108b.

12. Ibid., pp. 113–113b.

13. Ibid., pp. 119–20.

14. Ibid., p. 169b.

15. John Bennet, *The Hope of Peace*, p. 16.

16. *Copies of Certain Discourses*, p. 7.

17. The most extensive discussions of this point are by Anthony Champney in *Copies of Certain Discourses*, pp. 19–29, and by Humphrey Ely, *Certain Brief Notes*, pp. 116–54.

18. For an example of this line of argument, see John Colleton, *A Just Defence of the Slandered Priests*, pp. 13–22.

19. For example, ibid., pp. 256–57.

20. *Copies of Certain Discourses*, p. 29. See also p. 145, and Colleton, *Just Defence*, pp. 251–52.

21. For example, see Anthony Copley, *An Answer to a Letter of a Jesuited Gentleman*, pp. 14–15, and Christopher Bagshaw, *A Sparing Discovery of Our English Jesuits*, pp. 1–2.

22. Bagshaw, *Sparing Discovery*, p. 70.

23. *Copies of Certain Discourses*, pp. 3–4.

24. William Bishop, in *Copies of Certain Discourses*, pp. 149, 151.

25. Champney, in ibid., p. 29.

26. Ibid., p. 14.

27. Colleton, *Just Defence*, pp. 34–35, 49.

28. Ely, *Certain Brief Notes*, pp. 132–33, 133–34.

29. *Copies of Certain Discourses*, Preface, fifth page.

30. Robert Charnock, *A Reply to a Notorious Libel*, p. 62.

31. John Mush, *A Dialogue Betwixt a Secular Priest and a Lay Gentleman*, p. 29.

32. Ibid., pp. 31, 34.

33. Ibid., p. 28.

34. Ibid., p. 29.

35. Ibid., p. 30.
36. Ibid., p. 31.
37. Ibid., p. 39.
38. Colleton, *Just Defence*, p. 251.
39. The Jesuit Richard Holtby, in a letter that was not published but that apparently received wide circulation, also strongly asserted the pope's right to appoint superiors without the consent of the superiors' subordinates. T. G. Law, ed., *The Archpriest Controversy*, 1:194–95.
40. Ely, *Certain Brief Notes*, pp. 253–54.
41. Ibid., pp. 291–92.
42. It might be alleged here that many of the laws that Ely sees as guiding the pope's normal action were made by former popes (see ibid., pp. 133–34). But this does not affect the case very much. The papacy that makes a difference to Parsons is an active, flexible institution; binding a pope to the decisions and procedures of his predecessors is merely another way of tying him to settled forms of law—although it is perhaps a way comparatively easy to accept for those intellectually committed to some version of papal infallibility.
43. See, for example, Law, *Archpriest Controversy*, 2:103, 118.
44. Ibid., 2:118–22.
45. Ibid., 2:119.
46. The critique of the Appellants' plan is in ibid., 2:122–27.
47. The Appellants attempted to rebut this critique; see ibid., 2:127–46. But their rebuttal is largely an attack on the archpriest system rather than a defense of their own and is generally lame in its replies to the objections alleged.

Chapter 9
1. This view seems particularly pronounced in Elizabeth's proclama-

tions after about 1580 and is the central point of the best-known piece of anti-missionary propaganda, Lord Burghley's *The Execution of Justice in England* (1583).
2. Proclamation of 5 Nov. 1602, in Paul L. Hughes and James F. Larkin, eds., *Tudor Royal Proclamations*, 3:250.
3. T. G. Law, ed., *The Archpriest Controversy*, 2:147–52.
4. Robert Parsons, *A Manifestation of the Great Folly and Bad Spirit, of Certain in England which Call Themselves Secular Priests*, pp. 16, 16b.
5. Ibid., pp. 15b–16.
6. Ibid., pp. 17, 17b.
7. Ibid., p. 12b.
8. Ibid., pp. 77b–78.
9. Ibid., pp. 30b–31.
10. Ibid., pp. 34b–35.
11. Ibid., pp. 77b–78.
12. For example, see Law, *Archpriest Controversy*, 2:103–7.
13. Ibid., 2:17, 32–34, 47–48.
14. Parsons, *Manifestation*, pp. 27–27b, 28.
15. Foley, 3:724. In the next sentence Tichborne, himself a Jesuit, says that the Jesuits were the "dogs" of the comparison.
16. See chap. 1, n. 1, p. 209.
17. Parsons, *A Brief Apology, or Defence of the Catholic Ecclesiastical Hierarchy*, the "Epistle to His Holiness," third page (pages in the "Epistle" are unnumbered).
18. Ibid., p. 2.
19. Foley, 3:724–25.
20. Ibid., p. 725.
21. Ibid. Tichborne's language becomes even more confusing than usual in this passage, but the meaning attributed to this remark seems most likely.
22. T. H. Clancy discusses the Allen-Parsons party's views on toleration in *Papist Pamphleteers*, pp. 125–58; pp. 142–58 are particu-

larly relevant here. However, the attempts of the Allen-Parsons party to "justify toleration theoretically" (p. 126) may not be as significant as Clancy seems to think. Attempts to claim the right of liberty of conscience for Catholics seem mainly a stick with which to beat the Protestants; when talking to fellow Catholics, Parsons is unenthusiastic about toleration (see, in addition to the examples mentioned, the quotation in Clancy at the bottom of p. 150). Parsons's occasional attempts to justify toleration of heretics seem essentially pragmatic—as in the *Memorial for the Reformation of England* (mentioned by Clancy and on pp. 27–36 above) where Parsons urges a temporary toleration of heretics in order to make their eventual conversion to Catholicism more secure.

23. Parsons, *Brief Apology*, pp. 181b–82.

24. Ibid., pp. 187b–88.

25. Ibid., pp. 188b–89.

26. Parsons, *Manifestation*, pp. 39–50.

27. Law, *Archpriest Controversy*, 2:6–7, 32–34, 47–48.

28. Ibid., 2:6, 48.

29. Ibid., 2:48; "vultis enim esse inter spinas et non pungi."

30. Ibid., 2:6.

31. It should be mentioned, however, that one of the papacy's political objectives worked strongly in the Appellants' favor. Clement VIII was attempting to reduce what he regarded as excessive Spanish influence in Rome and in Europe and was trying to use France as a counterweight to Spain. The Appellants' hostility to Spain and the patronage of their cause by France did them a great deal of good. See Ludwig von Pastor, *History of the*

*Popes*, 23:195–265, and John Bossy, "Henri IV, the Appellants and the Jesuits," pp. 84–85.

32. John Mush, *Declaratio Motuum*, and Christopher Bagshaw, *Relatio Compendiosa Turbarum quas Jesuitae Angli....*

33. For example, see John Bennet, *The Hope of Peace*, pp. 1–4, and Anthony Copley, *An Answer to a Letter of a Jesuited Gentleman*, pp. 3–5.

34. According to the pro-Jesuit priest John Bavant, shortly after the pope confirmed Blackwell in office in the spring of 1599 his opponents were telling some laymen that Blackwell's appointment had been procured by enemies of the state and that those who had immediately accepted his authority should be treated with caution. Stonyhurst Anglia A, 2, 53.

35. Law, *Archpriest Controversy*, 2:63–64.

36. Ibid., 2:183, 194–95.

37. Lambeth, miscellaneous mss., vol. 2006, fols. 173–74 (Fairhurst Papers).

38. Westminster, vol. 7, no. 41.

39. Lambeth, miscellaneous mss., vol. 2014, fols. 125–26 (Fairhurst Papers).

40. Printed in Tierney-Dodd, 3: clxxxviii–cxci.

41. Thomas Bluet, *Important Considerations, which Ought to Move all True and Sound Catholics . . . to Acknowledge . . . that the Proceedings of Her Majesty . . . Have Been Both Mild and Merciful*. The introduction is by Watson; the passage quoted is on the thirteenth page. The introduction has no page numbers.

42. Robert Charnock, *A Reply to a Notorious Libel*, pp. 136, 137.

43. Ibid., pp. 112, 112–13, 114–15.

44. *Copies of Certain Discourses*, p. 6.

45. Mush, *Declaratio Motuum*, p. 82.

46. Ibid., pp. 8, 24, 82–83.

47. Law, *Archpriest Controversy*, 2:47.

48. Bluet, *Important Considerations*, pp. 6–8.

49. Robert Charnock, *An Answer to a Fraudulent Letter*. There are no page numbers; the passage quoted is on the fifteenth page, excluding the preface.

50. Law, *Archpriest Controversy*, 2:71–73, 213–14.

51. Christopher Bagshaw, *A Sparing Discovery of Our English Jesuits*, p. 7.

52. For examples, see Copley, *Answer*, especially pp. 50 ff.; William Clarke, *A Reply unto a Certain Libel, Lately Set Forth by Father Parsons*, pp. 28b–29, and Watson's introductory epistle to Bluet, *Important Considerations*. The reader may have noted the similarity of these arguments to those of Thomas Wright (pp. 61–67).

53. Bluet, *Important Considerations*, p. 29.

54. Clarke, *Reply*, p. 31.

55. Ibid., pp. 31b–32.

56. Ibid., p. 32b.

57. Bagshaw, *Sparing Discovery*, pp. 55–56, 56.

58. Copley, *Answer*, p. 46.

59. Ibid., pp. 47, 48.

60. Bluet, *Important Considerations*. p. 5.

61. Ibid., p. 21.

62. Clarke, *Reply*, p. 71b.

63. Bagshaw, *Sparing Discovery*, p. 56.

64. "An Answer Made by me Charles Paget . . ." in Humphrey Ely, *Certain Brief Notes upon a Brief Apology*, p. 11 of the piece by Paget; the book contains several pieces, with new pagination starting for each one.

Paget's is the second after the general preface.

65. See J. J. Scarisbrick, "Robert Persons's Plans for the 'True' Reformation of England," p. 33.

66. Bagshaw, *Sparing Discovery*, p. 14.

67. The most violent denunciations along these lines are by William Watson; see especially *A Decacordon of Quodlibetical Questions*, pp. 27–29.

68. Copley, *Answer*, p. 34.

69. Ibid., p. 40.

70. Clarke, *Reply*, p. 28b.

71. Ibid., p.41b.

72. For example, Charnock, *A Reply*, pp. 144–45.

73. Ibid.

74. Bluet, *Important Considerations*, p. 24.

75. Copley, *Answer*, pp. 39–40.

76. Clarke, *Reply*, pp. 36b–42b.

77. Ibid., pp. 40–40b.

78. Ibid., p. 38b.

79. Ibid., pp. 37b–38.

80. Ibid., p. 42.

81. Ibid., pp. 36b, 37.

82. Ibid., p. 37.

83. Ibid. See also p. 41.

84. Ibid., p. 37b.

85. Ibid. The reader may be reminded of the sentiments of Viscount Montague (pp. 46–49).

86. See ibid., pp. 37b–38, on the rights of temporal rulers to deal with religious malcontents who cause disorders in state and church.

87. Ibid., esp. pp.37 and 41.

88. Ibid., p. 39b.

89. Ibid., pp. 40b–42.

90. Lambeth, miscellaneous mss., vol. 2006, fol. 280 (Fairhurst Papers). There are many other friendly (not to say obsequious) letters from various Appellants to Bancroft. The fact that the government dropped the Appellants the moment they lost their

apparent political usefulness indicates that the friendliness (whether genuine or not) was not returned. Bancroft's attitude is probably summed up accurately in a remark attributed to him by Anthony Rivers, S.J. (*vere*, Anthony Hoskins), Parsons's correspondent in London. "He termed both sides knaves, but the Appellants good instruments to serve the state." Foley, 1:42.

91. John Mush, *A Dialogue Betwixt a Secular Priest and a Lay Gentleman*, p. 39.

92. Ibid., pp. 40–43, 61–67.

93. Ibid., p. 56.

94. Ibid., pp. 49, 50.

95. Ibid., p. 50.

96. Ibid., p. 53.

97. Suggestions that they had something to gain by helping Catholics win freedom of conscience were made to politicians other than the queen. Humphrey Ely, in a letter of August 1602, probably to Sir Robert Cecil, describes how his correspondent would have the loyal support of Catholics, both before and after the queen's death, if he would help bring about some toleration for Catholics. See Law, *Archpriest Controversy*, 2:195–200, especially 198–99.

98. Ibid., p. 196.

99. Ely, *Certain Brief Notes*, general preface, p. 5b.

100. Ibid., p. 18.

101. Bluet, *Important Considerations*, p. 21.

102. Mush, *Dialogue*, p. 34.

103. Clarke, *Reply*, p. 76.

Chapter 10

1. William Clarke, *A Reply unto a Certain Libel, Lately Set Forth by Father Parsons*, pp. 59b–60.

2. See pp. 98–101.

3. Clarke, *Reply*, p. 62b.

4. Christopher Bagshaw, *A Sparing Discovery of Our English Jesuits*, p. 7.

5. Ibid.

6. See pp. 100–101.

7. Clarke, *Reply*, p. 4b; *Copies of Certain Discourses*, pp. 156–57.

8. John Mush, *A Dialogue Betwixt a Secular Priest and a Lay Gentleman*, pp. 109–28, discusses this and other aspects of Jesuit rule at the seminaries.

9. For one among many examples, see ibid., pp. 113–14.

10. Bagshaw, *Sparing Discovery*, pp. 15–27.

11. For example, see John Bennet, *The Hope of Peace*, p. 2.

12. Bagshaw, *Sparing Discovery*, pp. 40–41, 46–47, 49.

13. For example, see ibid., p. 38.

14. Ibid., p. 36. Watson's version is in *A Decacordon of Quodlibetical Questions*, pp. 99–101.

15. Other Appellant comments along these lines may be found in Clarke, *Reply*, p. 53, and Anthony Copley, *An Answer to a Letter of a Jesuited Gentleman*, pp. 78–79.

16. For the "modernist" nature of the society and the worries that its innovations caused among European Catholics, see H. O. Evennett, *The Spirit of the Counter-Reformation*, pp. 74–83.

17. It should be mentioned that not all prominent Jesuits were politically involved; Henry Garnet seems to have avoided political questions as far as possible.

18. Thomas Bluet, *Important Considerations, which Ought to Move all True and Sound Catholics . . . to Acknowledge . . . that the Proceedings of Her Majesty . . . Have Been Both Mild and Merciful*, pp. 24–25.

19. For Cresswell, see A. J. Loomie, *The Spanish Elizabethans*, pp. 182–229. An ironic touch of

Henry Tichborne's letter to Thomas Darbyshire is his rejoicing in the influence of Parsons, Holt, and Cresswell at the courts of Rome, Brussels, and Madrid, respectively. Foley, 3:723.

20. Peter Guilday, *The English Catholic Refugees on the Continent, 1558–1795*, pp. 106–20.

21. See Mush, *Dialogue*, pp. 109–28.

22. Foley, 7:lxvii–lxviii.

23. See p. 111.

24. John Gerard, *Autobiography of an Elizabethan*; for example, pp. 22, 24, 25–29.

25. Foley, 6:20. The story was from a hostile source.

26. This has been touched on already, especially in chap. 6. In addition, see Robert Parsons, *A Brief Apology or Defence of the Catholic Ecclesiastical Hierarchy*, chap. 3, where he defends the Jesuits from Appellant attacks and describes their services to the mission at considerable length. For the organization of the Jesuit-run missionary network, see John Bossy, *The English Catholic Community 1570–1850*, pp. 204–7.

27. Foley, 1:305.

28. Gerard, *Autobiography*, pp. xxiv, 113, 40–41.

29. William Weston, *Autobiography of an Elizabethan*, p. 11.

30. Gerard, *Autobiography*, pp. 88, 146.

31. T. G. Law, ed., *The Archpriest Controversy*, 1:79.

32. P. Renold, ed., *The Wisbech Stirs*, p. 202.

33. Ibid., pp. 311–12.

34. Robert Parsons, *A Manifestation of the Great Folly and Bad Spirit, of Certain in England which Call Themselves Secular Priests*, p. 89.

35. *Douai Diaries*, p. 386.

36. Anthony Kenny, "The Inglorious Revolution, 1594–1597," *The Venerabile*, vol. 17, no. 2, p. 85.

37. Christopher Bagshaw, *A True Relation*, in T. G. Law, *Jesuits and Seculars in the Reign of Queen Elizabeth*, pp. 98–99.

38. The allies of the Jesuits are themselves frequently called "Jesuits" or "Jesuited." Thomas Bluet, for example, refers to the Spanish diplomat Bernardino de Mendoza in these terms. *Important Considerations*, pp. 22–23.

39. Gerard, *Autobiography*, p. 37, records how his missionary work around his family's home in Derbyshire was less successful than his efforts elsewhere.

40. John Bossy, "The Character of Elizabethan Catholicism," makes several of these points. See especially pp. 51–52.

41. This leaves out the support that the priest may have derived from personal relationships with people within England, which undoubtedly was often very great. It was, however, a chance personal thing that can have had only a limited effect on the basic social situation.

42. Bossy, "Character of Elizabethan Catholicism," p. 51.

43. Bernard Basset, *The English Jesuits from Campion to Martindale*, pp. 454–56.

44. Bossy, "Henri IV, the Appellants and the Jesuits," pp. 85–86.

Chapter 11

1. *New Catholic Encyclopedia*, 1:773.

2. Westminster, vol. 7, no. 85.

3. J. H. Pollen, *The Institution of the Archpriest Blackwell*, p. 68.

4. P. Renold, ed., *The Wisbech Stirs*, p. 182.

5. Paul L. Hughes and James F.

Larkin, eds., *Tudor Royal Proclamations*, 3:250–55.
6. Tierney-Dodd, 3:clxxxviii–cxci.
7. See chap. 3, no. 3, p. 213.
8. John Bossy, "The English Catholic Community 1603–1625," pp. 94–95. Much of the argument of this paragraph is derived from Bossy's article, pp. 93–95, where he seems to implicitly repudiate his earlier statement that the Appellants saw themselves as bound by "a personal obligation to the queen which would take precedence over all others." "The Character of Elizabethan Catholicism," p. 53.
9. Perhaps the most egregious example of this view is W. K. Jordan's *The Development of Religious Toleration in England from the Beginning of the English Reformation to the Death of Queen Elizabeth*, pp. 82–99, 372–420.
10. John Bossy, "Elizabethan Catholicism: The Link with France," p. 345.
11. Michael Walzer, *The Revolution of the Saints*.
12. See Nicholas Tyacke, "Puritanism, Arminianism, and Counter-Revolution," p. 120.
13. Of the twenty-two men appointed by Elizabeth in 1559–62 to fill bishoprics left empty by those who had held them under Mary, fourteen had been in exile during Mary's reign. Information derived from Sir F. Maurice Powicke and E. B. Fryde, eds., *Handbook of British Chronology*, and from *Dictionary of National Biography*.
14. For Whitgift's Calvinist theology, see John Whitgift, *Works*, 3:611–13.
15. J. J. Scarisbrick, "Robert Persons's Plans for the 'True' Reformation of England," p. 41.
16. Stonyhurst, Anglia A, 3, 36.

17. The intellectual and institutional withdrawal of the émigrés in France from political radicalism is described in John Bossy, "Elizabethan Catholicism: The Link with France," pp. 148–214. See also Bossy, "Character of Elizabethan Catholicism," pp. 54–57, and T. H. Clancy, *Papist Pamphleteers*, pp. 195–97.
18. A. O. Meyer, *England and the Catholic Church under Queen Elizabeth*, pp. 59–73.
19. Christopher Haigh, *Reformation and Resistance in Tudor Lancashire*, pp. 267–68.
20. See Bossy, "Character of Elizabethan Catholicism," especially pp. 44–50.
21. For the seventeenth-century struggles, see Philip Hughes, *Rome and the Counter-Reformation in England*, pp. 312–78, and Bossy, *The English Catholic Community 1570–1850*, pp. 49–77.
For some interesting ideas on "missionary" vs. "hierarchical" conceptions in Catholicism as a whole, see Bossy's postscript to H. O. Evennett, *The Spirit of the Counter-Reformation*, pp. 133–42.

*Appendix*
1. For two extreme examples from opposing viewpoints, see P. Renold's article, "Archpriest Controversy," *New Catholic Encyclopedia*, 1:773, and W. K. Jordan, *The Development of Religious Toleration in England from the Beginning of the English Reformation to the Death of Queen Elizabeth*, especially pp. 82–99, and 372–420. Both works contain numerous factual errors in addition to their faults of approach.
2. J. H. Pollen, *The English Catholics in the Reign of Queen Elizabeth*; Philip Hughes, *Rome and the Counter-Reformation in England*.

3. He does, however, violate impartiality on occasion. For example, his explanation of Blackwell's delay in making public the pope's brief of August 1601, omits the fact that Blackwell was waiting for Parsons to publish his attack on the Appellants—a publication that would have been prohibited under the brief. J. H. Pollen, *The Institution of the Archpriest Blackwell*, pp. 65–66.

4. A. O. Meyer, *England and the Catholic Church under Queen Elizabeth*, pp. 66–73.

5. John Bossy's introduction to Meyer, *England and the Catholic Church*, (1967 ed.), p. xxiv.

6. Bossy's introduction, ibid., pp. xxvii–xxviii; xxx–xxxi. See also John Bossy, *The English Catholic Community 1570–1850*, pp. 35–37.

7. T. H. Clancy, *Papist Pamphleteers*.

8. Among many, one may mention Hugh (J. H. C.) Aveling, *Northern Catholics* and *Catholic Recusancy in the City of York*; Christopher Haigh,

*Reformation and Resistance in Tudor Lancashire*; Roger B. Manning, *Religion and Society in Elizabethan Sussex*; and F. X. Walker, "The Implementation of the Elizabethan Statutes against Recusants, 1581–1603." Elliot Rose, *Cases of Conscience*, is an interesting work of both intellectual and social history.

9. John Bossy, "The Character of Elizabethan Catholicism," especially pp. 44–50; and *English Catholic Community*, pp. 14–20.

10. Bossy, "Character of Elizabethan Catholicism," *passim*.

11. Bossy, *English Catholic Community*, p. 49.

12. See for example John Bennet, *The Hope of Peace*, pp. 1–4, and Anthony Copley, *An Answer to a Letter of a Jesuited Gentleman*, pp. 3–5.

13. Bossy, "Character of Elizabethan Catholicism," p. 53.

14. Bossy, *English Catholic Community*, pp. 35–41, especially 37–39.

15. Ibid., pp. 41–42.

# Bibliography

*Unpublished Sources*
London
   Lambeth Palace Library. Fairhurst
   Papers (miscellaneous mss., vols.
   2006, 2007, 2014).
   Public Record Office. Roman
   Transcripts, vol. 111.
   Westminster Diocesan Archives.
   Vols. 5–7, B24, B48.
Stonyhurst College, Lancashire
   Stonyhurst College Archives. An-
   glia A, vols. 1–3 and 6. The
   xeroxed copies of these documents
   in the Jesuit Library on Mount
   Street in London were the source
   actually used.

*Published Original Sources*
Allen, William. *An Admonition to the
   Nobility and People of England and
   Ireland.* 1588, ERL 74.
———. *An Apology and True Declara-
   tion of . . . the Two English Colleges.*
   1581, ERL 68.
———. *The Copy of a Letter . . .
   Concerning the Yielding up of the City
   of Daventrie.* 1587, ERL 51.
———. *Letters and Memorials.* Edited
   by T. F. Knox. London, 1882.
———. *A True, Sincere, and Modest*

*Defence of English Catholics.* 1584,
   ERL 68.
Bagshaw, Christopher. *Relatio Com-
   pendiosa Turbarum quas Jesuitae
   Angli. . . .* 1601, ERL 71.
———. *A Sparing Discovery of Our
   English Jesuits.* 1601, ERL 39.
———. *A True Relation of the Faction
   Begun at Wisbeach.* 1601. Printed in
   T. G. Law, *Jesuits and Seculars.*
Bennet, John. *The Hope of Peace.* 1601,
   ERL 82.
Bluet, Thomas. *Important Considera-
   tions, which Ought to Move all True
   and Sound Catholics . . . to
   Acknowledge . . . that the Proceedings
   of Her Majesty . . . Have Been Both
   Mild and Merciful.* 1601, ERL 31.
*Calendar of State Papers, Domestic,
   1598–1601.* London, 1869.
Charnock, Robert. *An Answer to a
   Fraudulent Letter.* 1602, ERL 112.
———. *A Reply to a Notorious Libel.*
   1603, ERL 90.
Clarke, William. *A Reply unto a
   Certain Libel, Lately Set Forth by
   Father Parsons.* 1603, ERL 115.
Colleton, John. *A Just Defence of the
   Slandered Priests.* 1602.
Constable, Henry. *A Discovery of a*

*Counterfeit Conference*. 1600, ERL 6.

*Copies of Certain Discourses*. 1601, ERL 84.

Copley, Anthony. *Another Letter of Mr. A. C. to his Disjesuited Kinsman*. 1602, ERL 100.

———. *An Answer to a Letter of a Jesuited Gentleman*. 1601, ERL 31.

Copley, Sir Thomas. *Letters of Sir Thomas Copley*. Edited by Richard Copley Christie. London, 1897.

*The Copy of a Letter, Written by a Master of Art [sic] of Cambridge. . . .* 1584, ERL 192. Commonly known as *Leicester's Commonwealth*.

———. Doleman, R. (pseud. for Robert Parsons and others). *A Conference About the Next Succession to the Crown of England*. 1594, ERL 104.

Elton, G. R., ed. *The Tudor Constitution*. Cambridge: Cambridge University Press, 1972.

Ely, Humphrey, et al. *Certain Brief Notes upon a Brief Apology*. 1602, ERL 171.

Foley, H. J., ed. *Records of the English Province of the Society of Jesus*. 8 vols. London, 1875–83.

Gerard, John. *Autobiography of an Elizabethan*. Translated by Philip Caraman. London and New York: Longmans, Green, 1951.

Harsnet, Samuel. *A Declaration of Popish Impostures*. London, 1603.

Hicks, L., ed. *Letters and Memorials of Father Robert Parsons S.J.* Leeds: CRS, 1942.

Historical Manuscripts Commission. *Report on Manuscripts in Various Collections*. 8 vols. London, 1904.

Holtby, Richard. "Father Richard Holtby on Persecution in the North." In *The Troubles of Our Catholic Forefathers*, edited by John Morris. 3rd Ser. London, 1877.

Hughes, Paul L., and Larkin, James F., eds. *Tudor Royal Proclamations*. 3 vols. New Haven and London: Yale University Press, 1969.

Kenyon, J. P., ed. *The Stuart Constitution*. Cambridge: Cambridge University Press, 1966.

Kingdon, Robert M., ed. *The Execution of Justice in England, by William Cecil, and A True, Sincere, and Modest Defence of English Catholics, by William Allen*. Ithaca: published for the Folger Shakespeare Library by Cornell University Press, 1965.

Knox, T. F., ed. *The First and Second Diaries of the English College, Douay, and an Appendix of Unpublished Documents*. London, 1878.

Law, T. G., ed. *The Archpriest Controversy: Documents Relating to the Dissensions of the Roman Catholic Clergy, 1597–1602*. London, vol. 1, 1896; vol. 2, 1898.

"Leigh, Richard" (*vere* William Cecil, Lord Burghley). *The Copy of a Letter Written Out of England to Don Bernadin de Mendoza*. 1588.

*The Life of St. Philip Howard*. London and Chichester: Phillimore, 1971.

McCann, Timothy J. "The Parliamentary Speech of Viscount Montague Against the Act of Supremacy, 1559." *Sussex Archaeological Collections* 108 (1970): 50–57.

Catholic Record Society (CRS), *Miscellanea 2*. London: CRS, 1906.

Mush, John. *Declaratio Motuum*. 1601, ERL 39.

———. *A Dialogue Betwixt a Secular Priest and a Lay Gentleman*. 1601, ERL 39.

Parsons, Robert (See also under Doleman, R.). *An Appendix to the Apology*. 1602, ERL 272.

———. *A Brief Apology or Defence of the Catholic Ecclesiastical Hierarchy*. 1602, ERL 273.

———. *The Jesuit's Memorial for the*

*Intended Reformation of England.* Edited, annotated, and entitled by Edward Gee. London, 1690.

——. *A Manifestation of the Great Folly and Bad Spirit, of Certain in England which Call Themselves Secular Priests.* 1602, ERL 169.

——. *A Temperate Ward-word, to the Turbulent and Seditious Watch-word of Sir Francis Hastings.* 1599, ERL 31.

Pollen, J. H., and MacMahon, William, eds. *The Venerable Philip Howard, Earl of Arundel.* London: CRS, 1919.

Renold, P., ed. *Letters of William Allen and Richard Barret.* Oxford: CRS, 1967.

——., ed. *The Wisbech Stirs.* London: CRS, 1958.

Smith, Richard. *The Life of Lady Magdalen Viscountess Montague.* Translated by Cuthbert Fursdon, edited by A. C. Southern. London: Sands, 1954.

Southwell, Robert. *An Humble Supplication to Her Majesty.* 1595 (*vere* 1600), ERL 123.

——. *An Humble Supplication to Her Majesty.* Edited by R. C. Bald. Cambridge University Press, 1953. Only the introduction was used.

Strype, John. *Annals of the Reformation.* 4 vols. Oxford, 1824.

Tierney, Brian, ed. *The Crisis of Church and State 1050–1300.* Englewood Cliffs, N.J.: Prentice-Hall, 1964.

Tierney, Mark Aloysius, ed. *Dodd's Church History of England from the Commencement of the Sixteenth Century to the Revolution in 1688. With Notes, Additions, and a Continuation by the Rev. M. A. Tierney.* 5 vols. London, 1839–43.

Watson, William. *A Decacordon of Quodlibetical Questions.* 1602, ERL 197.

Weston, William. *Autobiography of an Elizabethan.* Translated by Philip Caraman. London and New York: Longmans, Green, 1955.

Whitgift, John. *Works.* Vol. 3. Edited by John Ayre. Cambridge, 1853.

Wright, Thomas. "An licitum sit Catholicis in Anglia arma sumere, et aliis modis reginam et regnum defendere contra Hispanos." In Strype, *Annals of the Reformation.* Vol. 3, pt. 2, pp. 583–97.

*Secondary Sources*

Anstruther, Godfrey. *The Seminary Priests: A Dictionary of the Secular Clergy of England and Wales, 1558–1850.* Vol. 1. Ware and Durham: St. Edmund's College and Ushaw College, 1968.

——. *Vaux of Harrowden.* Newport: R. H. Johns, 1953.

Aveling, Hugh. *Catholic Recusancy in the City of York.* n.p.: CRS, 1970.

——. "The Catholic Recusants of the West Riding of Yorkshire 1558–1790." *Proceedings of the Leeds Philosophical and Literary Society, Literary and Historical Section,* 10 (Sept. 1963): 191–306.

——. *Northern Catholics: The Catholic Recusants of the North Riding of Yorkshire 1558–1790.* London: Chapman, 1966.

Basset, Bernard. *The English Jesuits from Campion to Martindale.* New York: Burns and Oates, 1968.

Bossy, John. "The Character of Elizabethan Catholicism." *Past and Present* 21 (1962): 39–59.

——. "Elizabethan Catholicism: The Link with France." Ph.D. dissertation, University of Cambridge, 1961.

——. *The English Catholic Community 1570–1850.* New York: Oxford University Press, 1976.

——. "The English Catholic Com-

munity 1603–1625." In *The Reign
of James VI and I*. Edited by
Alan G. R. Smith. London:
Macmillan, 1973.
———. "Henri IV, the Appellants
and the Jesuits." *Recusant History* 8
(1965): 80–122.
Burke, Vincent. "The Economic
Consequences of Recusancy in
Elizabethan Worcestershire." *Re-
cusant History* 14 (1977): 71–77.
Clancy, T. H. "Notes on Persons's
'Memorial for the Reformation of
England' (1596)." *Recusant History*
5 (1959): 17–34.
———. *Papist Pamphleteers: The Allen-
Persons Party and the Political
Thought of the Counter-Reformation
in England, 1572–1615*. Chicago:
Loyola University Press, 1964.
Cliffe, J. T. *The Yorkshire Gentry from
the Reformation to the Civil War*.
London: Athlone Press, 1969.
*Cokayne's Complete Peerage*. 13 vols.
by G. E. Cokayne. Edited by H. A.
Doubleday and Lord Howard de
Walden, London: The St. Catherine
Press, 1936.
Dickens, A. G. "The First Stages of
Romanist Recusancy in Yorkshire,
1560–1590." *Yorkshire Archaeological
Journal* 35 (1943): 157–81.
*Dictionary of National Biography*.
Edited by Sir Leslie Stephen and
Sir Sidney Lee. 22 vols. London:
Oxford University Press, since
1917.
Evennett, H. O. *The Spirit of the
Counter-Reformation*. Edited with
postscript by John Bossy. Cam-
bridge: Cambridge University
Press, 1968.
Finch, Mary E. *The Wealth of Five
Northamptonshire Families, 1540–
1640*. Oxford: printed for the
Northamptonshire Record Society
by C. Batey at the University
Press, 1956.

Guilday, Peter. *The English Catholic
Refugees on the Continent, 1558–
1795*. London and New York:
Longmans, Green, 1914.
Haigh, Christopher. *Reformation and
Resistance in Tudor Lancashire*.
Cambridge: Cambridge University
Press, 1975.
Hicks, L. "Robert Parsons S.J. and
the *Book of Succession*." *Recusant
History* 4 (1957): 104–37.
Holmes, Peter John. "The Political
Thought of the Elizabethan Catho-
lics." Ph.D. dissertation, Univer-
sity of Cambridge, 1975.
Hughes, Philip. *Rome and the Counter-
Reformation in England*. n.p.: Burns
and Oates, 1942.
Jordan, W. K. *The Development of
Religious Toleration in England from
the Beginning of the English
Reformation to the Death of Queen
Elizabeth*. Gloucester, Mass.:
P. Smith, 1965.
Kenny, Anthony. "The Inglorious
Revolution, 1594–1597." *The Ven-
erabile*, vol. 16, no. 4 (May 1954)
and three subsequent issues.
Law, T. G. *Jesuits and Seculars in the
Reign of Queen Elizabeth*. London,
1889. See also under "Bagshaw"
in original sources section of
bibliography.
Léchat, Robert. *Les réfugiés anglais
dans les Pays-Bas espagnols durant
le règne d'Élisabeth*. Louvain:
Université de Louvain, 1914.
Loomie, A. J. *The Spanish Elizabethans*.
New York: Fordham University
Press, 1963.
Manning, Roger B. "Anthony
Browne, 1st Viscount Montague:
The Influence in County Politics of
an Elizabethan Catholic Noble-
man." *Sussex Archaeological Collec-
tions* 106 (1968): 103–12.
———. "Catholics and Local Office
Holding in Elizabethan Sussex."

*Bulletin of the Institute of Historical Research* 35 (1962): 47–61.
——. *Religion and Society in Elizabethan Sussex*. Leicester: Leicester University Press, 1969.
——. "Richard Shelley of Warminghurst and the English Catholic Petition for Toleration of 1585." *Recusant History* 6 (1962): 265–74.
Mattingly, Garrett. "William Allen and Catholic Propaganda in England." In *Aspects de la propagande religieuse*, vol. 28 Travaux d'humanisme et Renaissance. 163 vols. to date. Geneva: E. Droz, 1957.
Meyer, A. O. *England and the Catholic Church under Queen Elizabeth*. Translated by J. R. McKee. London: K. Paul, Trench, Trubner & Co., 1916. Reprint with introduction by John Bossy. New York: Barnes & Noble, 1967.
Neale, J. E. *Elizabeth I and Her Parliaments*. 2 vols. London: J. Cape, 1953.
*New Catholic Encyclopedia*. 16 vols. Washington, D.C.: Catholic University of America, 1967.
Parish, John E. "Robert Parsons and the English Counter-Reformation." *Rice University Studies* 52 (1966).
Pollen, J. H. *The English Catholics in the Reign of Queen Elizabeth*. London and New York: Longmans, Green, 1920.
——. *The Institution of the Archpriest Blackwell*. London: Longmans, Green, 1916.
Powicke, Sir F. Maurice, and Fryde, E. B. *Handbook of British Chronology*. London: Offices of the Royal Historical Society, 1961.
Read, Conyers. "William Cecil and Elizabethan Public Relations." In *Elizabethan Government and Society:*

*Essays Presented to Sir John Neale.* Edited by S. T. Bindoff et al. London: Athlone Press, 1961.
Rose, Elliot. *Cases of Conscience: Alternatives Open to Recusants and Puritans under Elizabeth I and James I*. Cambridge: Cambridge University Press, 1975.
Rowse, A. L. *Tudor Cornwall*. London: J. Cape, 1941.
Scarisbrick, J. J. "Robert Persons's Plans for the 'True' Reformation of England." In *Historical Perspectives: Studies in English Thought and Society in Honour of J. H. Plumb*. Edited by Neil McKendrick. London: Europa, 1974.
Stroud, T. E. "Father Thomas Wright: A Test Case for Toleration." *Biographical Studies* 1 (1951): 189–219.
Tyacke, Nicholas. "Puritanism, Arminianism, and Counter-Revolution." In *The Origins of the English Civil War*. Edited by Conrad Russell. New York: Barnes & Noble, 1973.
Ullman, Walter, *Medieval Papalism*. London: Methuen, 1949.
Von Pastor, Ludwig. *History of the Popes*. Vol. 22. London: K. Paul, Trench, Trubner & Co., 1933.
Walker, F. X. "The Implementation of the Elizabethan Statutes against Recusants, 1581–1603." Ph.D. dissertation, University of London, 1961.
Walzer, Michael. *The Revolution of the Saints: A Study in the Origins of Radical Politics*. Cambridge, Mass.: Harvard University Press, 1965.

# Index